GREAT RELIGIOUS STORIES

EDITED BY

S. E. FROST, Jr., B.D., PH.D.

EDITOR OF
*The Sacred Writings
of the World's Great Religions*
AND
The World's Great Sermons

GARDEN CITY PUBLISHING CO., INC.

GARDEN CITY, NEW YORK

1945

PREFACE

RELIGIOUS stories appeal to man's whole being and reach into his mind, his heart, and his soul. This is abundantly evident in the 100 stories which constitute this book. Theirs is a spiritual truth that plumbs the depths of the human heart and answers man's most persistent longings. They speak of the dreams and deeds of great souls. They show men and women caught up by eternal ideals, and giving all that they have and are to realization of these ideals.

Throughout the book the human and the divine are blended, as they must always be where the divine stirs the human to dream and hope and work. These are stories of God's working within man to the end that His kingdom shall come upon the earth and He shall reign eternally.

Beginning with the story of Creation, the first part of the book moves through the Old Testament, touching the high points of Israel's growth toward the vision of her finest prophets. The deeply stirring events of the New Testament form the second part, centering about the life of Jesus and the Apostles. The third part of the book relates the struggles, martyrdom, and achievements of the saints, Church Fathers, and later religious leaders, from early Christianity to the present day.

Through these stories of inspiring religious events and experiences shine the beacon lights of great souls along the highway of faith.

S. E. F., JR.

DISCARD

CONTENTS

PART ONE

STORIES FROM THE OLD TESTAMENT

PART TWO

STORIES FROM THE NEW TESTAMENT

PART THREE

STORIES OF SAINTS AND RELIGIOUS LEADERS

FIRST CENTURY STORIES

SECOND CENTURY STORIES

THIRD CENTURY STORIES

PART ONE

STORIES FROM THE OLD TESTAMENT

Creation

IN THE beginning God was, and he created the heavens and the earth. But the earth was "waste and void, and darkness was upon the face of the deep." So the Spirit of God moved over this dark and formless mass, and God said, "Let there be light!" And there was light.

God saw that the light was good, and he divided the light from the darkness. The light he called "day" and the darkness, "night." This was the first day of creation.

On the second day God created the firmament and divided the waters. He said, "Let there be a firmament in the midst of the waters, and let it divide the waters from the waters." This was done as God commanded. And the firmament was called "Heaven," and it separated the waters under the firmament from the waters above the firmament. This was the second day of creation.

Then God said, "Let the waters under the heavens be gathered unto one place, and let the dry land appear." When this was done he called the dry land "earth" and the waters which were gathered he called "seas." And God saw that this was good. Then he said, "Let the earth put forth grass, herbs yielding seed, and fruit-trees bearing fruit after their kind, wherein is the seed thereof, upon the earth." And this was done so that the earth became green and bright with the colors of many flowers and blooming trees in season. This was the third day of creation.

Then God said, "Let there be lights in the firmament of heaven to divide the day from the night; and let them be for signs, and for seasons, and for days and years; and let them be for lights in the firmament of heaven to give light unto the earth." And it was so. God made two great lights. The greater, the sun, ruled the day; the lesser, the moon, ruled the night. And he made the stars also. And God put all these in the heavens to give light to all men. This was the fourth day of creation.

On the fifth day God said, "Let the waters swarm with swarms of living creatures, and let birds fly above the earth in the open firmament of heaven." And so were created the great sea-monsters, and every living creature that moves either in the water or through the air. And God was pleased and he blessed them all, saying, "Be fruitful, and multiply, and fill the waters in the seas, and let birds multiply on the earth." And this was the fifth day of creation.

As the sixth day dawned God said, "Let the earth bring forth living creatures after their kind, cattle, and creeping things, and beasts of the earth after their kind." And it was so. And God created on this day the beasts of the earth after their kind, and the cattle after their kind, and everything that creepeth upon the ground after its kind.

But God's work was not completed. So, as the sixth day drew toward twilight, God said, "Let us make man in our image, after our likeness; and let them have dominion over the fish of the sea, and over the birds of the heavens, and over the cattle, and over all the earth, and over every creeping thing that creepeth upon the earth.

"And God created man in his own image, in the image of God created he him; male and female created he them. And God blessed them, and God said unto them, 'Be fruitful, and multiply, and replenish the earth, and subdue it; and have dominion over the fish of the sea, and over the birds of the heavens, and over every living thing that moveth upon the earth.'

"And God said, 'Behold, I have given you every herb yielding seed, which is upon the face of all the earth, and every tree, in which is the fruit of a tree yielding seed; to you it shall be for food; and to every beast of the earth, and to every bird of the heavens, and to everything that creepeth upon the earth, wherein there is life, I have given every green herb for food.'"

And God was pleased as darkness covered the sixth day of creation.

On the seventh day God saw his work completed and he rested from all his work which he had made. "And God blessed the seventh day, and hallowed it, because that in it he rested from all his work which God had created and made."

Adam and Eve

GOD made man in his own image. He formed man "of the dust of the ground, and breathed into his nostrils the breath of life; and man became a living soul."

And God planted a beautiful garden "eastward, in Eden," where he could place this masterpiece of his workmanship. Out of the ground God caused to grow every tree and every herb that was pleasing to the sight and good for food, even "the tree of life also in the midst of the garden, and the tree of the knowledge of good and evil." And the garden was watered by a river which flowed out of the garden and into four heads.

In this garden God placed man "to dress it and keep it." And God gave Adam, for this was the name of the first man, a solemn command, "Of every tree of the garden thou mayest freely eat; but of the tree of the knowledge of good and evil, thou shalt not eat of it, for in the day that thou eatest thereof thou shalt surely die."

But Adam was alone in the garden, and God knew that it

"is not good that man should be alone." So he resolved to make a companion, a helpmeet for him. He first caused a deep sleep to fall upon Adam, and while he slept God "took one of his ribs, and closed up the flesh instead thereof; and the rib, which Jehovah God had taken from the man, made he a woman, and brought her unto the man." And Adam and Eve, for this was the name given to the woman whom God had made from the rib of Adam, lived together in the Garden of Eden in innocence and without shame, for neither sin nor the sense of sin had entered into the garden.

Now, when God had created all the beasts, he created the serpent, a beast more subtle than all the rest. And the serpent came to Eve and taunted her, saying, "Yea, hath God said, 'Ye shall not eat of every tree of the garden?'"

And Eve answered the serpent, "Of the fruit of the trees of the garden we may eat; but of the fruit of the tree which is in the midst of the garden, God hath said, 'Ye shall not eat of it, neither shall ye touch it, lest ye die.'"

But the serpent was crafty, and he tempted Eve by telling her, "Ye shall not surely die; for God doth know that in the day you eat thereof, then your eyes shall be opened, and ye shall be as God, knowing good and evil."

The serpent had sown distrust in the garden, mankind's distrust of his Creator. When Eve was convinced that the fruit of the tree was good for food and that by eating it she would become wise, "she took the fruit thereof, and did eat; and she gave also unto her husband with her, and he did eat." Then innocence left them, their eyes were opened, and they knew that they were naked and were ashamed. So "they sewed fig-leaves together, and made themselves aprons."

In the cool of the evening God came to walk in the garden which he had planted and talk with the man and the woman. But Adam and Eve did not come to meet him as before. They hid from God's presence, fearful of the sin they had committed.

And God called to Adam, saying, "Where art thou?"

And Adam answered, "I heard thy voice in the garden, and I was afraid, because I was naked, and I hid myself."

Then God asked Adam, "Who told thee that thou wast naked? Hast thou eaten of the tree whereof I commanded thee that thou shouldst not eat?"

Adam answered, "The woman whom thou gavest to be with me, she gave me of the tree, and I did eat."

When God turned to Eve, she said, "The serpent beguiled me, and I did eat."

God was very angry and hurt, because man, his master-piece, had disobeyed him. He was angry with the serpent and cursed it, saying, "Because thou hast done this, cursed art thou above all cattle, and above every beast of the field; upon thy belly shalt thou go, and dust shalt thou eat all the days of thy life; and I will put enmity between thee and the woman, and between thy seed and her seed; he shall bruise thy head, and thou shalt bruise his heel."

And God was angry with Adam because he had listened to the tempting of Eve, and he said, "Cursed is the ground for thy sake; in toil shalt thou eat of it all the days of thy life; thorns also and thistles shall it bring forth to thee; and thou shalt eat the herb of the field. In the sweat of thy face shalt thou eat bread, till thou return unto the ground; for out of it wast thou taken; for dust thou art, and unto dust shalt thou return."

Then God made for Adam and for Eve coats of skins and clothed them and sent them forth from the garden "to till the ground from whence Adam was taken." And at the entrance to the garden God placed the Cherubims "and a flaming sword which turned every way, to keep the way of the tree of life."

☆

Cain and Abel

Two sons were born to Adam and Eve after they had been driven from the Garden of Eden.

The first-born was named Cain. He grew to be a tiller of the soil—a strong, rough fellow of the land. His brother was Abel, a sensitive youth who devoted himself to keeping his father's sheep.

Now, as often happens, these brothers did not understand each other. They were too different. The things that appealed to Cain seemed crude to Abel. And what Abel liked seemed weak and unworthy to Cain.

At the time of sacrifice both boys brought the fruits of their labors to be offered up to God. Cain, the farmer, brought an offering from the land and placed it upon the altar. Abel brought the firstlings of his flock, fat young animals, and sacrificed them to God.

Abel had brought the best, and God was pleased. But Cain had tried to cheat God. The best he had kept back, and had offered to God only the second best. And God had respect for Abel's offering "but unto Cain and to his offering he had not respect."

This made Cain very angry. His countenance became dark with hatred toward his brother so that God spoke to him and said, "Why art thou wroth? And why is thy countenance fallen? If thou doest well, shall it not be lifted up? And if thou doest not well, sin coucheth at the door; and unto thee shall be its desire; but do thou rule over it."

Cain knew that he had not done well and that God's action was just. But his anger increased until it burned at white heat in his breast,—until the very presence of Abel was hateful to him.

One day, when both boys were in the field and no other person was near, Cain let his anger get the better of him and in the heat of passion killed his brother. To cover up this evil deed, Cain hid his brother's body and went about his work hoping that he would not be accused.

But he reckoned not with God. For God came to Cain asking, "Where is Abel thy brother?"

Cain's answer showed the kind of man he was. "I know not," he lied. Then he added, "Am I my brother's keeper?"

Then God answered, "What hast thou done? The voice of thy brother's blood crieth unto me from the ground."

Then God pronounced a curse upon Cain, saying, "And now cursed art thou from the ground, which hath opened its mouth to receive thy brother's blood from thy hand. When thou tillest the ground, it shall not henceforth yield unto thee its strength. A fugitive and a wanderer shalt thou be in the earth."

God's curse awakened Cain to the awfulness of his crime and he cried out, "My punishment is greater than I can bear. Behold, thou hast driven me out this day from the face of the ground; and from thy face shall I be hid; and I shall be a fugitive and a wanderer in the earth; and it will come to pass that whosoever findeth me will slay me."

But such easy death was not for Cain. He must live and suffer for his crime. To this end God said, "Therefore whosoever slayeth Cain, vengeance shall be taken on him sevenfold." And God made a sign for Cain, a mark bold upon his forehead, so that all might see and, seeing, would not smite him, but let him live in the ever-consciousness of his guilt.

Noah and the Great Flood

GOD created man good and pure, but sin came when the serpent tempted Eve and she yielded. And sin grew as men became many and women began to bear children. God saw all this,—how wickedness spread and how even the thoughts and the imaginations of the thoughts of man's heart were evil continually,—and God was angry so that he repented "that he had made man on the earth, and it grieved him at his heart."

In his anger and grief God determined to destroy man and all living creatures. "I will destroy man whom I have created from the face of the ground;" God said, "both man, and beast, and creeping things, and birds of the heavens; for it repenteth me that I have made them."

But there was one man among all the earth's population who found favor in God's sight. He was a righteous man and perfect in his generation. His name was Noah. To Noah God said, "The end of all flesh is come before me; for the earth is filled with violence through them; and, behold, I will destroy them with the earth."

Then God commanded Noah to make an ark of gopher wood 300 cubits in length, 50 cubits wide, and 30 cubits high,—an ark three stories high and covered inside and out with pitch.

"And I," God said, "do bring the flood of waters upon the earth, to destroy all flesh, wherein is the breath of life, from under heaven; everything that is in the earth shall die. But I will establish my covenant with thee; and thou shalt come into the ark, thou, and thy sons, and thy wife, and thy sons' wives with thee. And of every living thing of all flesh, two of every sort shalt thou bring into the ark, to keep them alive with thee; they shall be male and female. Of the birds after their kind, and of the cattle after their kind, of every creeping thing of the ground after its kind, two of every sort shall come unto thee, to keep them alive. And take thou unto thee of all food that is eaten, and gather it to thee; and it shall be for food for thee, and for them."

And Noah did as God had commanded. He built the ark, supplied it with food, and collected birds and beasts and creeping things, two of each, male and female, to keep alive until the flood was over.

When all preparations had been made and Noah and his wife, their three sons and their wives, and two of each animal, bird, and creeping thing on the earth had entered the ark, it began to rain. For forty days and forty nights the rain continued and gradually all the earth was covered with water even to the tops of the mountains. The ark rose and floated on the water. In it was preserved all the life that was left on the earth. Every other living thing was destroyed by the flood which covered the earth for a hundred and fifty days.

On the fortieth day, when the rain ceased, Noah opened a window in the ark and sent out a raven which flew about above the waters. Then he sent a dove to see if the waters had receded at all. But the dove could find no place to alight, so she returned to the ark. A few days later Noah released the dove again and this time she returned in the evening carrying an olive-leaf in her mouth. "So Noah knew that the waters were abated." Seven days later Noah released the dove again and this time she did not return but found a dry resting place away from the ark.

As the waters gradually receded, the ark came to rest on top of Mount Ararat. There it remained as the waters all about continued to dry up and more and more land appeared. As soon as the earth was dry, God said to Noah, "Go forth from the ark, thou, and thy wife, and thy sons, and thy sons' wives with thee. Bring forth with thee every living thing that is with thee of all flesh, both birds, and cattle, and every creeping thing that creepeth upon the earth; that they may breed abundantly in the earth, and be fruitful, and multiply upon the earth."

And Noah obeyed God and went forth from the ark, all his family and all the living creatures that had weathered the storm in the ark. And Noah erected an altar unto God and made a burnt offering in thanksgiving for his safety. And

God smelled the sweet savor and said in his heart, "I will not again curse the ground any more for man's sake, for that the imagination of man's heart is evil from his youth; neither will I again smite any more everything living, as I have done. While the earth remaineth, seedtime and harvest, and cold and heat, and summer and winter, and day and night shall not cease."

Then God made a covenant with Noah, a promise that never again would he destroy living things on the earth. And, as a sign of this covenant God placed a great and beautiful bow of all colors in the sky above the earth. Then God said, "I do set my bow in the cloud, and it shall be for a token of a covenant between me and the earth. And it shall come to pass, when I bring a cloud over the earth, that the bow shall be seen in the cloud, and I will remember my covenant, which is between me and you and every living creature of all flesh; and the waters shall no more become a flood to destroy all flesh."

☆

The Tower of Babel

THE children of Noah, and their children, and their children's children were many so that people were moving everywhere throughout the world, building cities and homes, and making new things to satisfy their wants.

And the whole world spoke one language, the language of their fathers and their fathers' fathers. Even though they scattered far and wide and did not see each other again, they kept the same language and spoke as one.

A large group of the children of Noah moved eastward until they found a level expanse of land, a plain, reaching far in all directions, fertile and inviting. Their leaders were impressed by the location and decided to settle there and build a city.

So the people gathered clay and slime to make bricks. Some gathered stones from nearby places. And all began to build houses and a mighty wall around the city. Each one worked diligently and soon the city began to rise out of the plain and the builders were happy and proud.

When the city was nearly completed, some of the leaders conceived a great plan. "Come," they said, "let us build in the center of our city a tower that shall reach even to heaven so that we may climb up to the home of God and, perhaps, learn of his secrets."

This idea fascinated many of the people, but some were not enthusiastic. They feared that God would be displeased at man's attempt to invade the privacy of his home and cautioned the people, saying, "Let us be content with our city and our homes. It is better that we take unto ourselves a name and be united lest we be scattered throughout the world. We are men, and not gods."

But their caution did not prevail and the people set about enthusiastically to make bricks and build a tower which would reach even unto heaven beyond the stars. They labored in the heat of the sun and in the cool of the evening, such was their enthusiasm, and such was the fascination of the prospect of reaching heaven. No one was allowed to be idle, though it is true that few could be found who wanted to shirk the great work that was being done. Such is the power of an idea and an aspiration over men.

But God saw what the men and women of the city were doing, and he was not pleased, for the God of Israel was a jealous god and was quick to anger when man became too ambitious. So he thought in his heart, "Behold, they are one people, and they have all one language; and this is what they begin to do; and now nothing will be withholden from them, which they purpose to do."

As his displeasure grew, God said, "Come, let us go down,

and there confound their language, that they may not understand one another's speech."

So God went down to the city and moved among the people, though they knew him not. And he confounded their tongues so that every man spoke a different language and none could understand his neighbor. So great was the confusion that men began to quarrel and fight and soon they left off building their city and the tower and were scattered abroad from thence upon the face of all the earth.

"Therefore was the name of it called Babel; because God did there confound the language of all the earth; and from thence did God scatter them abroad upon the face of all the earth."

Lot's Wife Is Turned to Salt

WHEN Abraham, following Jehovah's instructions, left his home in Ur of the Chaldees, he took Lot, his brother's child, and his family and possessions. In spite of famine and wars with tribes through whose territories they passed, both Abraham and Lot were able to accumulate great wealth in cattle, silver, and gold.

So vast were the possessions of these two men that the land between Beth-el and Ai, where they journeyed after a sojourn in Egypt, was not able to support them. Further, strife had developed between the herdsmen of Abraham and those of Lot.

Abraham saw that he and his nephew could not long continue dwelling together and suggested to Lot, "Let there be no strife, I pray thee, between me and thee, and between my herdsmen and thy herdsmen, for we are brethren. Is not the whole land before thee? Separate thyself, I pray thee, from me. If thou wilt take the left hand, then I will go to the right; or if thou wilt take the right hand, then I will go to the left."

This suggestion appealed to Lot, especially since he was to be permitted first choice. He saw that the plain of Jordan was well watered and offered every prospect for wealth and prosperity. So he chose the east, and he and his people settled in the cities of the plain while Abraham and his people dwelt in the land of Canaan. Lot and his wife moved into the large and prosperous city of Sodom.

But they had not dwelt there long before war broke out between the king of Sodom, Bera, along with Birsha, king of the neighboring city of Gomorrah, and other kings in the area. After a long time of severe fighting, the kings of Sodom and Gomorrah were beaten and killed and the victors raided their cities, taking, among other things, Lot and all his possessions.

Messengers came to Abraham with news of his nephew's fate, and he immediately organized an army and set out against the captors. Driving them as far as Damascus, Abraham rescued Lot and all his possessions and restored them to the land of their choice.

The new king of Sodom went out to meet Abraham and his victorious armies and offered to bestow upon him great gifts and a tenth of all the booty captured from the enemy. But Abraham would take nothing, and turned it all over to those who had fought with him.

Freed from the threat of enemy kings, Sodom and Gomorrah turned to their old wicked ways. Sin was rampant in the cities so that Jehovah became angry and said, "Because the cry of Sodom and Gomorrah is great, and because their sin is very grievous, I will go down now, and see whether they have done altogether according to the cry of it, which is come unto me; and if not, I will know."

Abraham knew that Jehovah was angry and planned to destroy the wicked cities, but Lot and his people were there and Abraham begged God to spare them. "Wilt thou consume the righteous with the wicked?" he asked Jehovah. "Peradventure there are fifty righteous within the city, wilt thou consume and not spare the place for the fifty righteous that are therein?"

Jehovah heard Abraham's plea and consented to spare Sodom if fifty righteous people could be found living there. But Abraham could not find the fifty people. And he went back to Jehovah and received the promise that the city would be spared if forty-five righteous people could be found. Time and again Abraham searched the city without success and time and again he returned to Jehovah, each time lowering the number. From forty-five he went to forty, then to thirty, then twenty, and finally to ten. But not even ten righteous people could be found in the city so that the negotiations between Abraham and Jehovah were broken off and "Abraham returned unto his place."

Then Jehovah sent two angels to warn Lot to flee from the city with his family before destruction should come upon it. But, when Lot brought the warning to his sons-in-law, they mocked him and even would restrain him from leaving the city. But Jehovah rescued him from his enemies and brought him and his wife and his two unmarried daughters outside the city. Then Jehovah said, "Escape for thy life. Look not behind thee, neither stay thou in all the plain. Escape to the mountain, lest thou be consumed."

But Lot feared the mountain and the people who dwelt there, and begged for permission to flee to Zoar. Jehovah listened, and granted his request.

Then, when Lot and his family were outside the city, and at a safe distance "Jehovah rained upon Sodom and Gomorrah brimstone and fire from Jehovah out of heaven. And he overthrew those cities, and all the plain, and all the inhabitants of the cities, and that which grew upon the ground."

The destruction was marvelous to see, and Lot's wife forgot the warning of Jehovah, "look not behind thee," and turned to see the fire and smoke, "and she became a pillar of salt."

Although Lot moved on to Zoar and dwelt there for a time, he was eventually forced to flee into the mountains where he lived in a cave with his two daughters and, so far as is known, died there.

Abraham and Isaac

ISAAC was the son of Abraham's old age, conceived of Sarah, his favorite wife, and Abraham loved him dearly.

However, before Isaac was born to Abraham, when he was growing old and found himself with no child by Sarah, Abraham had taken unto himself another wife, one who had served as Sarah's handmaiden, an Egyptian, named Hagar. And she bore him a son whom he named Ishmael.

Now, since Hagar had given Abraham a son, she came to despise the barren Sarah. When she could stand it no longer, Sarah went to Abraham and said, "My wrong be upon thee. I gave my handmaid into thy bosom, and when she saw that she had conceived, I was despised in her eyes. Jehovah judge between me and thee."

But Abraham loved Sarah and said to her, "Behold, thy maid is in thy hand. Do to her that which is good in thine eyes."

Sarah dealt harshly with Hagar and when Isaac was born, in Abraham's hundredth year, his father was overjoyed. On the day that Isaac was weaned, Abraham made a great feast and all were happy except Ishmael, who knew that this child threatened his inheritance. When Sarah saw him at the feast mocking, she was very angry and said to her husband, "Cast out this handmaid and her son, for the son of this handmaid shall not be heir with my son, even with Isaac."

Abraham realized the unfairness of this, and did not want to obey Sarah. But, in a dream he was told that both Isaac and Ishmael would head generations of families to his honor and that he should do as Sarah had ordered.

"And Abraham rose up early in the morning, and took bread and a bottle of water, and gave it unto Hagar, putting it on her shoulder, and gave her the child, and sent her away. And she departed and wandered in the wilderness of Beersheba."

With Hagar and her son out of the way, Isaac grew into young manhood and into the love of both his parents. Each day the love of Abraham for his son deepened until it enveloped his whole heart.

Then God decided to prove Abraham. He came to him and said, "Abraham, take now thy son, thine only son, whom thou lovest, even Isaac, and get thee into the land of Moriah, and offer him there for a burnt-offering upon one of the mountains which I will tell thee of."

Abraham knew one answer, and one only. Early in the morning he arose, saddled his ass, and taking Isaac and two of the young men of his household, began the rough climb up the mountainside to the place where God had directed him.

After climbing for three days, Abraham "lifted up his eyes and saw the place afar off." Then he said to the young men, "Abide ye here with the ass, and I and the lad will go yonder, and we will worship, and come again to you."

Abraham's heart was heavy as he walked slowly toward the spot that was to be the place of his supreme sacrifice. Isaac carried the wood for the altar, and his father "took in his hand the fire and the knife."

It is natural that Isaac was mystified. Abraham had told him nothing and, as a well-trained son, he asked no questions but followed where his father bade. But, when the two had set out alone, he could contain himself no longer and asked, "My father, behold, the fire and the wood, but where is the lamb for a burnt-offering?"

Abraham must have been tempted to deny God and turn back at this simple question from his beloved son. His heart was near to breaking. But his faith was greater than his fear and he answered, "God will provide himself the lamb for a burnt-offering, my son." And they went on together.

When they came to the place which God had appointed, Abraham built an altar and laid the wood on it. Then he began to bind Isaac. Each turn of the cord was as a dagger piercing his heart. His hand trembled and he wanted to cry out against a God who would demand so great a sacrifice from a father. Isaac's eyes were filled with wonder. Was he to be the sacrifice? But, no, his father loved him too deeply. Yet, Isaac knew that his father loved God more, and would not deny any command he made.

Abraham's hand was more steady now. Isaac lay across the altar, his young face looking up toward the heavens and his clear blue eyes watching his father with confidence and trust. "God will provide himself the lamb for the burnt-offering," kept echoing in his mind. "God will provide . . . God will provide."

Abraham raised the knife and pointed it at the heart of his son. His hand trembled a little and his eyes were almost blinded with the tears he would not let flow out. He was about to strike the fatal blow when he heard a voice calling, "Abraham! Abraham!"

He turned and saw an angel of Jehovah standing there. "Here am I," he answered.

"Lay not thy hand upon the lad, neither do thou anything unto him, for now I know that thou fearest God, seeing thou hast not withheld thy son, thine only son, from me."

And Abraham looked toward the thicket where there was a noise as if something there were trying to escape from a trap, and beheld "behind him a ram caught in the thicket by his horns." Abraham took the ram and offered him up as a burnt-offering in the place of his son.

And God was pleased with Abraham and promised that he would bless him and his seed and through his seed would bless all people and all nations forever.

Isaac and Rebekah

ABRAHAM was old and knew that the time must come soon when he would be gathered to his fathers. During his long life he had served Jehovah well and Jehovah had prospered him greatly. His cattle roamed contentedly among the hills; his gold and precious jewels were piled high in strong chests; his lands stretched as far as the eye could see; and his servants honored and respected him. As he approached the sunset of life, Abraham had everything to make him happy.

But there was a longing in his soul. Wealth and power were his, but in a foreign country, for he dwelt among the Canaanites far from his own people. Often he thought of home and the brothers he had left to pioneer in a strange land, and the old man's heart was heavy.

It was now time that his beloved son, Isaac, take a wife; but not a wife from among the Canaanites. True, there were many acceptable women among these people. Abraham knew this, and he also knew that Jehovah had promised that his seed would make a mighty nation. He could not think of this nation as a mixture of Hebrew and Canaanite, but as pure Hebrew stretching down through the ages.

So he called to his side his most faithful servant and said, "Put, I pray thee, thy hand under my thigh, and I will make thee swear by Jehovah, the God of Heaven and the God of the earth, that thou wilt not take a wife for my son of the daughters of the Canaanites, among whom I dwell; but thou shalt go unto my country, and to my kindred, and take a wife for my son Isaac." And the servant swore as Abraham asked.

Loading ten camels with gold and silver and precious jewels, the servant set out for Mesopotamia, to the city of Nahor, where many of Abraham's relatives lived. As the caravan approached the city, the servant devised a plan for picking a wife for his master's son. Stopping at a well on the edge of town to which the young women were accustomed to come in the evening for water, he stood and prayed, "O Jehovah, the God of my master Abraham, let it come to pass that the damsel to whom I shall say, 'Let down thy pitcher, I pray thee, that I may drink,' and she shall say, 'Drink, and I will give thy camels drink also,' let the same be she that thou hast appointed for thy servant Isaac."

Scarcely had he finished speaking when Rebekah, the daughter of Abraham's brother, appeared, carrying a pitcher upon her shoulder. Rebekah was a virgin, and fair to behold, and the servant of Abraham asked her for water as he had planned. Not only did she give him drink, but she filled the trough time and again until all his camels had drunk their fill.

It had come to pass as he planned, and the servant felt assured that Rebekah was the one for whom he had come. In token of his mission, he gave her a golden earring and two bracelets for her hands. When he asked if he might spend the night at her house, she replied, "We have both straw and provender enough, and room to lodge in." Then Rebekah ran to her house and told her brother Laban what had happened.

At once Laban ran out to invite the stranger to enter his house and partake of his food. After the meal, the servant of Abraham told his mission and how he had picked Rebekah from among all the women at the well as a possible wife for Isaac. He concluded his recital by saying: "And I bowed my head, and worshipped Jehovah, and blessed Jehovah, the

God of my master Abraham, who had led me in the right way to take my master's brother's daughter for his son. And now if ye will deal kindly and truly with my master, tell me. And if not, tell me, that I may turn to the right hand, or to the left."

Both Laban and Bethuel, Rebekah's mother, were happy that Abraham's servant should have chosen Rebekah and promised that he could take her. Then the servant gave them all jewels and raiment, gifts from his master, and they enjoyed a festive meal in celebration of the betrothal.

The next morning Rebekah and her damsels joined the caravan of Abraham's servant and began the long journey back to Canaan.

Isaac dwelt in the land of the South, in Beer-lahai-roi. In the evening, as was his custom, he went out into the fields to meditate. "And he lifted up his eyes, and saw, and, behold, there were camels coming. And Rebekah lifted up her eyes, and when she saw Isaac, she alighted from the camel. And she said unto the servant, 'What man is this that walketh in the field to meet us?' And the servant said, 'It is my master.' And she took her veil and covered herself.

"And the servant told Isaac all the things that he had done. And Isaac brought her into his mother Sarah's tent, and took Rebekah, and she became his wife. And he loved her. And Isaac was comforted after his mother's death."

Jacob and Esau

WHEN Isaac, Abraham's favorite son, lifted up his eyes and saw Rebekah coming toward him, he loved her and she became his wife. But Rebekah was barren and Isaac was greatly distressed. In his misery he turned to Jehovah who heard his prayer and Rebekah conceived and two babes "struggled together within her."

And Rebekah went unto Jehovah and asked, "If it be so, wherefore do I live?"

Jehovah answered her: "Two nations are in thy womb, and two peoples shall be separated from thy bowels: and the one people shall be stronger than the other people; and the elder shall serve the younger."

When her days were fulfilled, two sons were born to Rebekah. The first "came forth ruddy all over like a hairy garment, and they called his name Esau. And after that came forth his brother, and his hand had hold on Esau's heel; and his name was called Jacob."

As the boys grew to manhood, the characteristics which were manifest at birth drew them farther and farther apart. Esau was a skilled hunter, one who loved the fields and the open countryside. Jacob preferred quiet and peace and the life of the city. One brother was of the woods and its ways, while the other had the softness and serenity which comes from the security of human companionship.

Isaac, their father, loved Esau, a boy who had all the manly qualities which other men honor. But Rebekah loved the quiet and tender Jacob. Neither could fully understand the other. To Isaac, Jacob was not quite a man as men should be, while Esau was most fully a man. To Rebekah, Esau was wild, while Jacob was a comfort to her soul and a companion to a mother who had no daughters to love.

And the boys were not companionable, as brothers should be. Rather, they despised each other for their differences. Then, too, Jacob was envious of his brother. Had not they both been born at the same time? What if Esau saw the light of the world first, did not Jacob come forth holding his heel? Why should this mere accident of birth cut him off from his father's inheritance and blessing? Thoughts like these rankled in Jacob's bosom.

One day Esau came in tired and hungry from the field and

found his brother boiling pottage. He was faint, and said to Jacob, "Feed me, I pray thee, with the red pottage, for I am faint."

Jacob saw an opportunity to avenge himself upon his brother, and he said, "Sell me first thy birthright."

Now, the birthright meant little to Esau, and he was over-hungry, so he answered, "I am about to die, and what profit shall the birthright do me?"

When Esau had taken an oath that his brother could have the birthright, he received bread and pottage of lentils, "and did eat and drink, and rose up, and went his way."

Years passed, and Isaac grew old. His eyes failed so that he was nearly blind. Knowing that his time on earth was short, he called to his side his favorite son and said, "Behold now, I am old and I know not the day of my death. Now therefore take, I pray thee, thy weapons, thy quiver and thy bow, and go out to the field, and take me some venison. And make me savory meat, such as I love, and bring it to me, that I may eat, that my soul may bless thee before I die."

Rebekah was also jealous that her favorite among the boys should be second and lose the birthright. So, when she heard Isaac preparing to bless Esau and give him the family inheritance, she called Jacob to her side and said, "Behold, I heard thy father speak unto Esau thy brother, saying, 'Bring me venison, and make me savory meat, that I may eat, and bless thee before Jehovah before my death.' Now therefore, my son, obey my voice according to that which I command thee. Go now to the flock, and fetch me from thence two good kids of the goats. I will make them savory meat for thy father, such as he loveth. Thou shalt bring it to thy father, that he may eat, so that he may bless thee before his death."

Now, Jacob wanted the blessing of his father, and he was not above lying or cheating to get it, but he was afraid that his mother's scheme would not work. He said, "Esau my brother is a hairy man, and I am a smooth man. My father peradventure will feel me, and I shall seem to him as a deceiver. I shall bring a curse upon me, and not a blessing."

Rebekah had already thought of this and had foreseen how to fool the old man even here. "Upon me be thy curse, my son," she said, "only obey my voice, and go fetch me them." And Jacob obeyed.

When he had brought the young kids, Rebekah prepared savory food for her husband in the manner he liked, making the meat of kids smell and taste like venison. Then she dressed Jacob in the clothing of his brother, garments smelling of the woods, and put the skins of the slaughtered kids on his hands and upon the smooth parts of his neck. Then he took the food prepared by his mother and went in to his father.

When Jacob entered his father's quarters, Isaac asked, "Who art thou, my son?" And the young man responded, "I am Esau, thy first-born. I have done according as thou badest me. Arise, I pray thee, sit and eat of my venison, that thy soul may bless me."

Isaac felt that there was something wrong and asked, "How is it that thou hast found it so quickly, my son?"

"Because Jehovah thy God sent me good speed."

Still doubting, Isaac said, "Come near, I pray thee, that I may feel thee, my son, whether thou be my very son Esau or not." And Jacob came near so that his father could feel him. The hands of the old man moved slowly over the boy's hands, his neck, and head. Then he said, "The voice is Jacob's voice, but the hands are the hands of Esau."

After a moment Isaac asked Jacob again, "Are thou my very son Esau?"

"I am," he lied.

The old man took the venison and did eat. Then Jacob brought him wine, and he drank until he was contented. When he was satisfied, he said, "Come near now, and kiss me, my son."

When Jacob had bowed himself before his father and had received his father's kiss, the old man smelt of his raiment and blessed him, saying: "See, the smell of my son is the smell of a field which Jehovah hath blessed: and God give thee of the dew of heaven, and of the fatness of the earth, and plenty of grain and new wine: let people serve thee, and nations bow down to thee: be lord over thy brethren, and let thy mother's son bow down to thee: cursed be every one that curseth thee, and blessed be every one that blesseth thee."

Then Jacob arose and departed from his father's presence. But scarcely had he gone when Esau returned from the hunt with venison for Isaac. He prepared it as his father liked, and carried it in to the old man. When Isaac realized what Jacob had done, he said, "Thy brother came with guile, and hath taken away thy birthright."

Then the older son begged, "Hast thou not reserved a blessing for me?" and he wept bitterly.

And the father said: "Behold, of the fatness of the earth shall be thy dwelling, and of the dew of heaven from above; and by thy sword shalt thou live, and thou shalt serve thy brother; and it shall come to pass, when thou shalt break loose, that thou shalt shake his yoke from off thy neck."

This made Esau hate Jacob so that he swore in his heart, "The days of mourning for my father are at hand, then will I slay my brother Jacob." Rebekah heard of this oath and warned Jacob to flee to her brother, Laban, and wait there until Esau's anger died down. And he went, and abode with his uncle and among his uncle's people for a time.

Rachel and Leah

JACOB had tricked his father and his brother by stealing the birthright and blessing due the elder of the two boys. The wrath of his brother, Esau, burned hot and he breathed dire threats of murder. Isaac, old and blinded, was confused and deeply hurt, for he loved Esau far more than he did Jacob.

Rebekah, who had been at the bottom of the deception and who had planned it well, knew that her favorite son, Jacob, was in danger. How could she save him? She pondered until a brilliant idea struck her.

Abraham had sent all the way from Canaan to his brother's lands in far away Mesopotamia for a wife for his son Isaac. Now Jacob was ready to marry and all about him were the women of the Canaanites. Surely Isaac would not want his son to take one of them for a wife. He, too, as his father before him, would want his son to marry from among his own people.

When Rebekah suggested this to Isaac, he agreed immediately and, calling Jacob to his side, said, "Thou shalt not take a wife of the daughters of Canaan. Arise, go to Padan-aram, to the house of Beth-el, thy mother's father, and take thee a wife from the daughters of Laban, thy mother's brother."

This was Jacob's release from the danger that threatened him. He could go far from his brother's wrath, but he was not running away,—he would go with his father's blessing. Truly Rebekah was a clever woman.

Jacob went as his father had instructed, and came to "the land of the children of the East," where he found a well and herdsmen tending their flocks. When he inquired of these, "Know ye Laban, the son of Nahor?" they not only answered in the affirmative but also pointed to a girl leading some sheep toward the well and said, "Behold, Rachel his daughter cometh with the sheep."

Jacob was overjoyed at this meeting, "and Jacob kissed Rachel, and lifted up his voice, and wept. And Jacob told Rachel that he was her father's brother, and that he was Rebekah's son; and she ran and told her father."

Laban was happy to greet his sister's child and brought him to his abode and treated him lavishly. And Jacob remained with Laban for a month. At the end of the month

Laban said to him, "Because thou art my brother, shouldest thou therefore serve me for nought?"

Now Laban had two daughters. Leah, the elder, had eyes that showed a soft tenderness, while Rachel, the younger, "was beautiful and well-favored." Jacob loved Rachel. So, he laid before Laban a plan: "I will serve thee seven years for Rachel, thy younger daughter." This pleased Laban, and the bargain was made.

When the seven years were passed, Jacob came to Laban and asked for his reward, saying: "Give me my wife, for my days are fulfilled, that I may go in unto her." Laban agreed, and made a great feast to celebrate the occasion. But, when the evening was late and the feast had reached its height, Laban covered his daughter Leah with a veil and brought her to Jacob who took her and went in unto her.

When the morning came and Jacob realized that he had taken Leah and not Rachel, he was angry and went immediately to Laban, saying, "What is this thou hast done unto me? Did not I serve with thee for Rachel? Wherefore hast thou beguiled me?"

But Laban had an excuse. "It is not so done in our place," he said, "to give the younger before the first-born. Fulfill the week of this one, and we will give thee the other also for the service which thou shalt serve with me yet seven other years."

Jacob knew that Laban was right, and that he had been unwise not to realize the custom of the land. So, Jacob served Laban another seven years and received Rachel as his wife.

Years later, it was Rachel who bore Jacob the son who was to bless his memory and save his people from the ravages of famine. His name was Joseph.

☆

Joseph and His Brothers

JACOB had many sons. Leah, his first wife, bore him Reuben, Simeon, Levi, Judah, Issachar, and Zebulun. Rachel, the wife of his choice and for whom he was forced to serve Laban an extra seven years, bore him Joseph and Benjamin. Two sons were born of him to Zilpha, Leah's handmaiden, Gad and Asher; and Dan and Napthali were his sons by Bilhah, Rachel's handmaiden.

Of these twelve, Jacob loved Joseph most "because he was the son of his old age," and he made him a coat of many colors. The brothers knew this and hated Joseph "and could not speak peaceably unto him."

Joseph was a dreamer. Sensitive, shy, and quiet, he was nevertheless certain of himself and walked among his brothers with an air of superiority which did not endear him to them.

One day he came among them with the announcement that he had dreamed a dream. "We were binding sheaves in the field," he said, "and, lo, my sheaf arose, and also stood upright, and, behold, your sheaves came round about and made obeisance to my sheaf." Words like these angered his brothers. "Shalt thou indeed reign over us?" they asked, "or shalt thou indeed have dominion over us?" And they hated him all the more.

At another time he had a dream which he told to his brothers and his father. "Behold, I have dreamed yet a dream," he said, "and, behold, the sun and the moon and eleven stars made obeisance to me." His brothers hated him yet more for this, but his father rebuked him, saying, "What is this dream that thou hast dreamed? Shall I and thy mother and thy brethren indeed come to bow down ourselves to thee to the earth?"

The anger of the brothers toward Joseph grew until they began to plan ways of ridding themselves of him and his dreams. Then, when the brothers were feeding their flocks in Shechem, Jacob sent Joseph to "see whether it is well with thy brethren, and well with their flocks." Meantime, they had moved their flocks to Dothan where Joseph eventually found them.

"And they saw him afar off, and before he came near unto them they conspired against him to slay him." As he approached they said to each other, "Behold, this dreamer cometh. Come now therefore and let us slay him, and cast him into one of the pits, and we will say, 'An evil beast hath devoured him,' and we will see what will become of his dreams."

Reuben heard the plot and was not willing that his young brother should be so treated. "Let us not take his life," said he. "Shed no blood. Cast him into this pit that is in the wilderness, but lay no hand upon him." In this way Reuben hoped to save his brother and return him to his father later.

The plan of Reuben pleased the other brothers. They hated Joseph, but few relished the idea of killing him. Thus, when Joseph came into the camp of his brothers, they stripped his coat, the coat of many colors, from his back and cast him into a dry pit nearby. Then they sat down to eat.

As evening came on and Joseph languished in the pit, a caravan of Ishmaelites, traveling from Gilead to Egypt on a trading expedition, was seen approaching from a distance. This gave Joseph's brother Judah an idea. "What profit is it if we slay our brother and conceal his blood?" he asked. "Come and let us sell him to the Ishmaelites, and let not our hand be upon him, for he is our brother and our flesh."

The brothers discussed this proposal and, finally, decided that this was a good way to get rid of Joseph without having his blood upon them. This decision was made by all except Reuben, who was not then at the camp.

So, when the merchants came to their camp, the brothers

of Joseph drew him up from the pit and sold him for twenty pieces of silver.

Reuben was torn with grief when he returned and found that Joseph was not in the pit. He felt a responsibility for the lad, he being the oldest of the sons of Jacob. To have his brother disappear in this manner worried him greatly. But the others explained what they had done and convinced Reuben of the wisdom of their act.

Then the group hatched a plot to fool their father, Jacob. They took Joseph's coat, the coat of many colors given to him by his father, and dipped it in the blood of a freshly killed goat to make it look as though it were saturated with the blood of Joseph. Then they took it to Jacob, saying, "This have we found. Know now whether it be thy son's coat or not?"

Jacob knew and cried out in grief, "It is my son's coat. An evil beast hath devoured him. Joseph is without doubt rent in pieces." Then Jacob tore his garments and put sackcloth upon his loins and mourned for his son many days.

Meantime the Ishmaelite merchants took Joseph to Egypt, where they sold him to Potiphar, captain of the guards of Pharaoh's palace.

Joseph in Egypt

As a slave of Potiphar, captain of Pharaoh's guards, Joseph began to exhibit exceptional ability, so that everything he undertook prospered. It was not long before Potiphar recognized the talent of this young man and placed him in a most responsible position. He was made overseer in Potiphar's house and all the details of the place were left in his hands. Indeed, so great was Joseph's responsibility that, after a time, his master "knew not aught that was with him, save the bread which he did eat."

This high position of responsibility gave Joseph the free run of Potiphar's house and access to all his wealth. But Joseph was honest and trustworthy and cared for his master's possessions as if they were his own.

In time, Potiphar's wife began to notice that Joseph was "comely and well-favored," and she cast her eyes upon him and said, "Lie with me." But Joseph refused, saying, "Behold, my master knoweth not what is with me in the house, and he hath put all that he hath into my hand. He is not greater in this house than I. Neither hath he kept back anything from me but thee, because thou art his wife. How then can I do this great wickedness, and sin against God?"

This did not satisfy Potiphar's wife and she sought almost daily to lure him to her couch. But he harkened not unto her. Then, one morning when he went into Potiphar's house to do his work and there were no other men in the house, Potiphar's wife caught him by his garment and cried, "Lie with me!" But Joseph fled, leaving his garment in her hands.

When Potiphar returned from his work, she showed him the garment of Joseph and said, "The Hebrew servant, whom thou hast brought unto us, came in unto me to mock me. As I lifted up my voice and cried, he left his garment by me, and fled out." This angered Potiphar greatly, and he had Joseph thrown into prison.

Here again Joseph showed his ability and very soon the keeper of the prison "committed to Joseph's hand all the prisoners that were in the prison. Whatsoever they did there, he was the doer of it. The keeper of the prison looked not to anything that was under his hand, because Joseph was with him. That which he did, Joseph made it to prosper."

In time the king of Egypt became offended with his butler and his baker and had both thrown into prison. These men were placed in the ward with Joseph, so that the three soon became well acquainted.

While in prison, both the butler and the baker had dreams which worried them very much. When they told Joseph, he offered to interpret the dreams for them. The butler had dreamed that he saw a vine with three branches. As the vine grew, it bore grapes which the butler took and pressed into the king's cup and gave it to the king to drink. The baker dreamed that he held three baskets of bread on his head and the topmost basket was filled with baked foods for Pharaoh, but birds came and ate all the food from the top basket.

Joseph explained to the butler that in three days he would be returned to his place as the king's butler, but to the baker he explained that in three days he would be taken from the prison and hanged. Now, on the third day was the king's birthday, and it was done as Joseph had prophesied.

After Joseph had lain in prison for two years, Pharaoh had two dreams which troubled him much. In the first he saw seven fat kine come up from the reed-grass along the river and graze in the fields. After them came seven lean kine which did eat of the fat ones until they were no more. In the second dream he saw seven ears of grain come up on one stalk, rank and good. But seven thin and blasted ears sprang up on the same stalk and swallowed up the seven fat ears. When Pharaoh awoke, he was much troubled and sent for his chief magicians to interpret his dream. But no one could give him the meaning.

Then the king's butler remembered Joseph and how he had interpreted accurately both his dream and the dream of the baker. He told the king and Joseph was brought into the royal presence at once. After the king's dreams had been told to him, he explained that Egypt was going to enjoy seven years of great prosperity and abundant harvests. Then, he told Pharaoh, there would be seven years of great famine such as the land had never known before.

After he had interpreted the king's dreams, Joseph advised him to find a discreet and wise man whom he could put over all the land to conserve the harvests of the prosperous years so that the people would have food during the lean years. This seemed wise to Pharaoh and he appointed Joseph as overseer.

"God hath showed thee all this," he said to Joseph. "There is none so discreet and wise as thou. Thou shalt be over my house and according unto thy word shall all my people be ruled. Only in the throne will I be greater than thou." Then Pharaoh took off his signet ring from his hand and put it upon Joseph's hand, arrayed him in vestments of fine linen, and put a gold chain about his neck. Joseph rode in the chariot next behind the king and all the people bowed down to him as they were wont to do to the king.

Joseph, then about thirty years old, went out over all the land of Egypt to plan for the coming of the famine. Each city and village made preparations to store grain and food for its use. So great was the store of food laid up in the land during the seven years of prosperity that no one could number it. Everywhere were great piles of grain and food and other things necessary, and all the people were happy.

Then came the famine as Joseph had predicted. For seven years Egypt and all the lands nearby suffered. Crops were blasted and nothing grew from the soil. But the people of Egypt had enough and to spare because Joseph had planned well.

Jacob, abiding in the land of Canaan, heard that there was grain in Egypt and sent ten of his sons to buy enough for his people, keeping the youngest, Benjamin, at home lest harm befall him. When the brothers arrived and made their request before Joseph, he recognized them at once but they did not know that the great administrator was their brother.

Joseph abused them and accused them of being spies and ordered them to leave one of their number in Egypt until they should return home and bring their youngest brother to him. Simeon was chosen, bound, and left as a hostage when the others set out for home, their grain bags bulging with food for their people.

On the way the brothers were surprised to find that the money for which they had purchased the grain was in the sacks. This frightened them and, when they arrived home and told their father, they were certain that no good could come from what had happened. Then, as the famine became more severe and the grain which had been brought from Egypt was exhausted, Jacob was forced, in spite of his fears, to send Benjamin with his brothers for more grain.

Back in Egypt they found things more confusing than before. First, they were treated with some courtesy and Joseph asked about their father and seemed to show interest in their welfare. But, after their sacks had been filled with grain and they had set out for home, they were arrested and taken back to the palace, accused of stealing from Joseph.

When their sacks were opened, Joseph's silver cup was found in Benjamin's sack. Then the brothers were sorely afraid. They knew that if Benjamin did not return with them, Jacob would be wild with grief and might destroy them and their families. In fear, they begged Joseph to have mercy. Judah acted as spokesman for the group, telling Joseph how much Jacob loved Benjamin and pleading with him to return the boy for his father's sake.

This was more than Joseph could stand, and he broke down in grief. Then he made himself known to his brothers and forgave them. At first the brothers were startled beyond words and could hardly believe that they were not living a horrible dream. Then they were convinced and happy, especially when Joseph begged them to return home and bring his father to Egypt where he and his people could have grain and food as long as the famine continued.

The brothers returned to Canaan and told their father all that had happened. In great joy at knowing that his favorite son was not dead as he had believed these many years, Jacob gathered his possessions and brought them into Egypt. "And Israel dwelt in the land of Egypt, in the land of Goshen. And they gat them possessions therein, and were fruitful and multiplied exceedingly."

The Childhood of Moses

JOSEPH came to Egypt by accident. His brothers, because of their intense dislike for him, sold him to traders who resold him to Potiphar, a high official in Pharaoh's army. Joseph's family, his brothers and father, came to Egypt during the great famine which devastated the land for seven years. Although Jacob, Joseph, and eventually all the brothers died in Egypt, they and their children were fruitful and increased abundantly, and multiplied, and waxed exceedingly mighty until "the land was filled with them."

When a new Pharaoh came to the Egyptian throne, one who had not known Joseph, he noted that the children of Israel were great in number,—greater and mightier than the Egyptians. This made him afraid that the Hebrews might rise up against the Egyptians in time of war.

To guard against this, Pharaoh ordered that the Hebrews be "set over with taskmasters to afflict them with their burdens." Indeed, these Hebrews were made slaves and forced to work at building houses and cities and other hard and menial tasks. But, the more these people were persecuted, the more they multiplied and spread.

Now the Pharaoh was indeed worried and he ordered all midwives to destroy at birth every male child they attended, but allow the girls to live. The midwives feared God and did not obey the order of the Pharaoh. When he noted that male children of the Hebrews were not being killed, he called the midwives to him and asked for an explanation.

Their excuse was that Hebrew wives were "lively" and delivered their children before the midwife could arrive.

Seeing that this did not work, the Pharaoh sent out a royal order demanding that every son born to a Hebrew woman was to be cast into the river and destroyed. Grave penalties were announced for anyone who disobeyed this order.

Now, a son was born to a woman of the house of Levi, a goodly child and well formed. Hoping to escape the condemnation of the Pharaoh, the mother hid her child for three months and would tell no one of it. When she could no longer keep it hidden, "she took for him an ark of bulrushes and daubed it with slime and with pitch. She put the child therein, and laid it in the flags by the river's brink." She also placed the child's sister nearby to watch and see what happened to the child.

It was not long before the daughter of Pharaoh came down to the river to bathe. Her maidens, walking along the bank of the river, discovered the child in his little ark and brought him to their royal mistress, who had compassion on the child and desired to keep him as her own.

At this point the sister of the child came from her hiding place and asked, "Shall I go and call thee a nurse of the Hebrew women, that she may nurse the child for thee?"

When Pharaoh's daughter gave her consent, the child went and informed the babe's mother of what had happened. She came immediately to the river's brink where Pharaoh's daughter said to her, "Take this child away, and nurse it for me, and I will give thee thy wages."

The woman took her child and nursed it. The boy grew and waxed strong and well-featured until it was time to return him to Pharaoh's daughter. She received him gladly, making him truly her son and christening him Moses "because I drew him out of the water."

☆

Moses and the Plagues of Egypt

MOSES, born of a Hebrew mother and reared as the son of the daughter of Pharaoh, felt deeply the sufferings of his people in Egypt. He saw them forced to gather their own straw for making bricks and heard their bitter cries when, unable to find enough straw, they were beaten for not producing the required number of bricks. This child of luxury and position whose later training was planned to make him think and act like any other member of Pharaoh's household, never forgot the lessons taught him by his mother during the years that she was his nurse.

When he, as a young man, saw an Egyptian beating one of his own people, he killed the Egyptian and buried him in the sands. But, on the next day, when he saw two Hebrews fighting and attempted to stop them, he was startled by the reply of one of the antagonists: "Who made thee a prince and a judge over us? Thinkest thou to kill me, as thou killest the Egyptian?"

Thus, Moses found himself in a strange position. He yearned to help his own people, to relieve them of their burdens and was willing even to commit murder to rescue one from unjust oppression. But, he had been reared in Pharaoh's house, and his own people did not trust him. They thought he wanted to rule over them. They saw in him a traitor who was to be feared.

Believing that his crime was generally known, Moses fled to the mountains, to the land of Midian. Here he married a daughter of Jethro, a Midian priest, and remained for several years hidden from both Pharaoh and his people.

One day, when he was tending the flocks of his father-in-law in the mountains, he saw flames leaping from out a bush nearby, but the bush was not burned. Coming closer to see this strange phenomenon, God spoke to him from the bush saying, "I have seen the afflictions of my people in Egypt and have come to rescue them from Pharaoh." Then God added to Moses, "I will send thee unto Pharaoh, that thou mayest bring forth my people, the children of Israel, out of Egypt."

But Moses hesitated and held back. "Who am I," he asked, "to do this great thing? Who shall I tell them sent me? How can I convince them of my earnestness?" Moses remembered how his people had misunderstood and doubted him, and he feared that they would yet believe him a spy from Pharaoh, a traitor to his people, or one wishing to rule over them.

God answered his objections by promising to be with him at all times. Then he taught Moses how to convince the people of his powers. He bade Moses to cast down the rod in his hand, and it became a snake. Then Moses picked the snake up and, lo, it was a rod again. Moses put his hand into his bosom and drew it out white with leprosy. Then he put his hand back in his bosom and drew it out, and it was clean. God also showed him how to turn water into blood and back into water again.

When Moses protested that he was not eloquent and could not make convincing speeches, God appointed his brother, Aaron, to accompany him as his spokesman. Thus these two men, Moses and Aaron, set out upon the long, hard task of delivering their people from the bondage into which they had gradually fallen since the days of Joseph.

They made their first appeal to Pharaoh, asking that the Hebrews be permitted to journey three days into the wilderness to make a sacrifice to Jehovah. Pharaoh refused the request and, because he felt that Moses and Aaron were inciting these slaves and causing them to become lazy, made their burdens greater and their taskmasters more cruel.

This turn of events caused many Hebrews to hate Moses and Aaron, saying, "Before you came among us, we had straw for the bricks and our burdens were not so heavy.

Now, they have taken even the straw from us and they force us to work harder. You will be our death." Such accusations troubled Moses and his brother so that they appealed to Jehovah for help and assurance.

Jehovah answered by pledging his power eventually to rescue his people from the Egyptians. He made elaborate promises and then instructed Moses and Aaron in a number of acts which were to convince Pharaoh that he should release the Hebrews.

At first Moses and Aaron appeared before Pharaoh and pitted their strength against the wise men and magicians of the court. Moses threw down his rod, and it became a serpent. All the magicians and sorcerers did the same, and their rods also turned to serpents. But the serpent that was Moses' rod devoured all the other serpents.

This merely hardened Pharaoh's heart against the Hebrews so that Moses undertook a second miracle. He waved his rod over the waters and they were turned to blood. All the fish in these waters died and the people were loathe to drink any water in the land. But, since the court magicians showed that they too could turn water into blood, this did not convince Pharaoh that he should free the Hebrews.

Moses, then, caused a plague of frogs to infest the land. Vast hoards of frogs came from all the waters and covered the country so that there was no place outside or inside the Egyptian homes where there were not many frogs. In despair, Pharaoh called Moses to his court and promised to release the Hebrews if he would remove the frogs. But, when Moses had caused all the frogs to die and Pharaoh saw "that there was respite," he hardened his heart and refused to honor his promise.

This was followed by a plague of lice and then by swarms of flies. Then all the cattle of the Egyptians died. Then came a plague of boils followed by hail storms over all the land. Then the land was covered with locusts which ate everything that was grown. Then thick darkness covered the entire land so that no one could see even in front of him. But Pharaoh refused to free the Hebrews.

As a last resort, Jehovah smote the first-born in every Egyptian home and the Angel of Death spread its wings over the land and only the homes of the Hebrews were free from death. So great was the cry throughout Egypt that Pharaoh relented and sent the Hebrews out of the land to wander in the wilderness for many years.

Moses Receives the Ten Commandments

FOR THREE MONTHS the Children of Israel wandered in the wilderness beyond the Red Sea. They had escaped from the bondage of Egypt and been saved from the armies of Pharaoh, but they were not happy. When starvation faced them in the wilderness, they accused Moses, their leader, and preferred slavery in Egypt to death in the wilderness.

Each time that this army of Hebrews seemed on the brink of disaster, Moses had been able to save them through the intervention of Jehovah. When, as they approached the Red Sea, they looked back to see Pharaoh's armies bearing down upon them, Moses had parted the waters so that they marched across on dry ground. Then, as the Egyptians rushed into the space between the walls of water, the sea was joined again so that this mighty army was drowned. When the Hebrews were thirsty and found a well of bitter water, Moses had cast a tree into the well and the water became sweet. Again, when there was no more food for this vast multitude, Jehovah rained manna from heaven and sent flocks of quail for them to kill and eat. At another time, when the people were thirsty and could find no water in the wilderness, Moses smote a rock and water in abundance gushed from it to slake the thirst of his people. When the Hebrews were attacked by Amalek in Rephidim, Moses held his hand in the air, giving victory to his people just as the sun was setting.

During all this time, the Hebrews had seen the miracles of Jehovah and the work of Moses, but they murmured against him often. But, in the third month of the exile, Jehovah called to Moses and he journeyed with his people to the foot of Mount Sinai. When all the people were assembled, a thick cloud covered the mountain and violent thunder and lightning shook its mighty peak.

"And Moses brought forth the people out of the camp to meet God." Then Jehovah came down in fire upon the top of the mountain and called Moses to come up and talk with him. There, alone with Jehovah in the clouds and smoke that enveloped the mountain, Moses received ten commandments from God by which to govern his people.

"And God spake all these words, saying, 'I am Jehovah thy God, who brought thee out of the land of Egypt, out of the house of bondage.

" 'Thou shalt have no other gods before me.

" 'Thou shalt not make unto thee a graven image, nor any likeness of anything that is in heaven above, or that is in the earth beneath, or that is in the water under the earth. Thou shalt not bow down thyself unto them, nor serve them. For I Jehovah thy God am a jealous God, visiting the iniquity of the fathers upon the children, upon the third and upon the fourth generation of them that hate me, and showing loving kindness unto thousands of them that love me and keep my commandments.

" 'Thou shalt not take the name of Jehovah thy God in vain, for Jehovah will not hold him guiltless that taketh his name in vain.

" 'Remember the sabbath day to keep it holy. Six days shalt thou labor, and do all thy work. But the seventh day is a sabbath unto Jehovah thy God. In it thou shalt not do any work, thou, nor thy son, nor thy daughter, thy man-servant, nor thy maid-servant, nor thy cattle, nor the stranger that is within thy gates. For in six days Jehovah made heaven and earth, the sea, and all that in them is, and rested the seventh day. Wherefore Jehovah blessed the sabbath day, and hallowed it.

" 'Honor thy father and thy mother, that thy days may be long in the land which Jehovah thy God giveth thee.

" 'Thou shalt not kill.

" 'Thou shalt not commit adultery.

" 'Thou shalt not steal.

" 'Thou shalt not bear false witness against thy neighbor.

" 'Thou shalt not covet thy neighbor's house; thou shalt not covet thy neighbor's wife, nor his man-servant, nor his maid-servant, nor his ox, nor his ass, nor anything that is thy neighbor's.' "

For forty days Moses remained in the mountain with Jehovah. When the people saw that he was away for so long a time, they feared that he was lost and would not return to them again. So, they built a golden calf and worshipped it.

Then Moses came down from the mountain bearing the commandments on two tables of stone. When he saw what had taken place and how the people had turned from Jehovah to worship a calf of gold, he was exceedingly angry and cast the tables of the commandments upon the ground and they broke in fragments. Then he destroyed the golden calf and forced the people to choose between Jehovah and other gods.

This choice having been made, Moses returned to Jehovah to plead for forgiveness for his people. Jehovah received his plea and forgave the people and gave Moses new tables of commandments to keep forever among the people.

☆

Samson and Delilah

MANOAH, a man of Zorah, was overjoyed when an angel of Jehovah told him that his wife, barren for many years, would bear him a child. He offered a sacrifice to Jehovah and followed carefully all the directions about the child given him by the angel. When the child came, they called him Samson and reared him in the fear of Jehovah.

Now, this child of delight grew to bring grief and heartache to his parents. Even when he was a young man, he went among the Philistines, then the rulers of the Hebrews, and found there a woman whom he wanted for his wife. Though his mother and father attempted to dissuade him from marrying out of his people, he would not listen to them, but insisted, "Get her for me, for she pleaseth me well."

When Manoah could not dissuade Samson, he went to the Philistines with his wife and his son to make arrangements for the union. On the way a young lion attacked them, but Samson "rent him as he would have rent a kid. He had nothing in his hand." Then the party went on to talk to the woman.

Upon returning to take her, Samson noted that a swarm of bees had built a hive in the carcass of the lion. He took of the honey and did eat, and gave some to his mother and father.

At the wedding feast Samson made a wager that he could propose a riddle that no one could answer. Immediately the challenge was accepted and his riddle was: "Out of the eater came forth food, and out of the strong came forth sweetness." He gave them seven days to divine the riddle. If they failed in that time, they were to pay the wager.

As time slipped by and the wedding guests were unable to solve the riddle, they sought the aid of Samson's bride. She nagged him and begged that he show his love for her by telling her alone the answer. At last he weakened and entrusted the secret to her. But she told her people and they, of course, won the wager. When they came to give him the answer, Samson realized how he had been betrayed and said, "If ye had not plowed with my heifer, ye had not found out my riddle." Then, in anger, Samson killed a number of the Philistines and left his bride with her father and went to his own father's home.

When his anger cooled, he returned to his wife's house with a kid as a peace offering. But, to his dismay, her father had given her to another, thinking that Samson did not want her. He then tried to give Samson his younger daughter, but Samson would have none of her, and went away angry.

To avenge himself for this wrong, Samson caught three hundred foxes, tied every two tails together, and attached firebrands to the tails of each pair. When this was done, he set fire to the brands and ran the frightened foxes through the grain fields and oliveyards of the Philistines, burning them to the ground. This so angered the Philistines that they burned the woman whom Samson had married and her father, holding them responsible for this great disaster.

But they were not satisfied, and a great army went to Samson and bound him tightly and took him to the Philistines for punishment. Samson submitted to being bound and taken among the men of the Philistines. When he and his guards arrived, he broke his bonds as if they were flax, and, grasping the jawbone of an ass in his mighty hands, slew a thousand Philistines.

Then Samson escaped to Gaza where he was surrounded by Gazites who sought to ambush and slay him. But, as his enemies lay in wait, he stole out at midnight "and laid hold of the doors of the gate of the city and the two posts, and plucked them up, bar and all, and put them upon his shoulders, and carried them up to the top of the mountain that is before Hebron."

In time Samson came to love Delilah, a woman of the valley of Sorek. As soon as this became known to the Philistines, they persuaded her to discover for them the secret of Samson's great strength that they might destroy him. For a time Samson toyed with Delilah, telling her things that were not true and watching her surprise when she realized that she had been fooled. Each time Samson would mention some new way to bind him so that he could not escape. But, when he was bound, he broke the fetters easily and laughed loudly at his tormentors. For Samson was a happy giant, slow of wit and very much a child at heart.

Finally, Samson told Delilah, "There has not come a razor upon my head, for I have been a Nazarite unto God from my mother's womb. If I be shaven, then my strength will go from me, and I shall become weak, and be like any other man." This she believed and, as he slept, she called one who shaved off "the seven locks of his head."

When Samson awoke, he attempted to free himself from the enemies who swarmed upon him to subdue him, but was without strength and was made a prisoner easily. Then the Philistines blinded this giant and made him grind grain in the prison house, bound and disgraced.

After a time of deep humiliation, Samson was taken into the presence of a party of Philistines who had gathered to make a sacrifice to their god Dagon. The blind giant was to serve as the butt of jokes and his torment was for the enjoyment of the guests. When they had tired of this form of sport, they placed Samson between the pillars that held the roof of the house.

Then Samson said to the lad who held him by the hand, "Suffer me that I may feel the pillars whereupon the house resteth, that I may lean upon them." The lad did as he requested, and Samson took hold of both pillars and prayed to Jehovah for strength, "O Lord Jehovah, remember me, I pray thee, and strengthen me, I pray thee, only this once, O God, that I may be avenged at once of the Philistines for my two eyes." His prayer was answered. Straining his every muscle, he pulled the pillars down and the roof of the house fell upon three thousand Philistines and himself, and all were killed. Samson had his vengeance, even in death.

The Story of Ruth

DURING the time of the judges in Judea, a famine ravaged the land so that many families moved to other countries and other peoples where food was more plentiful. One such family was that of Elimelech who took his wife, Naomi, and his two sons and journeyed to the land of the Moabites.

Sorrow followed close upon the heel of these exiles, for Elimelech died soon after the family had settled in Moab, leaving his widow and her two sons. In time the boys each took wives of the Moabite women, Orpha and Ruth, and were happy. But death called the sons while they were yet young men, leaving their widows without children.

The heart of Naomi was heavy, and she yearned to return to her country where "Jehovah had visited his people in giving them bread." Calling her daughters-in-law to her side she said, "Go, return each of you to her mother's house. Jehovah deal kindly with you, as ye have dealt with the dead, and with me. Jehovah grant you that ye may find rest, each of you in the house of her husband."

At first they both protested and begged to be allowed to go to Judea with Naomi, but Naomi persuaded Orpha to return to her parents. Ruth, however, refused to be persuaded and begged Naomi: "Entreat me not to leave thee, and to return from following after thee; for whither thou goest, I will go; and where thou lodgest, I will lodge. Thy people shall be my people, and thy God my God. Where thou diest, will I die, and there will I be buried. Jehovah do so to me, and more also, if aught but death part thee and me."

This plea won Naomi so that she took Ruth back to Judea and to the city of Bethlehem, and it was the beginning of the barley harvest.

Being poor widows, Naomi and Ruth had to go into the fields along with other poor people and pick up the heads of grain dropped by the harvesters. Ruth, by chance, picked the fields of a wealthy kinsman of Naomi, Boaz, and followed the gleaners, gathering what she could find.

Boaz saw her and inquired of her lineage and relations. He also gave instructions that she should be allowed to take a few heads of grain even from the sheaves and that no one was to bother her or interfere in any way with her work. He told Ruth to remain in his fields and not leave for others, and gave her many privileges not accorded to the poor gleaners. When Ruth showed her surprise at this treatment, Boaz told her, "It hath fully been showed me all that thou hast done unto thy mother-in-law since the death of thy husband; and how thou hast left thy father and thy mother, and the land of thy nativity, and art come unto a people that thou knewest not heretofore. Jehovah recompense thy work, and a full reward be given thee of Jehovah, the God of Israel, under whose wings thou art come to take refuge."

When Ruth told Naomi how Boaz gave her many privileges and was kind to her, she was happy and cried, "Blessed be he of Jehovah, who has not left off his kindness to the living and to the dead. The man is nigh of kin unto us, one of our near kinsmen."

Then Naomi gave her daughter-in-law some sage advice. First, she was to remain in the fields of Boaz until the end of both the barley and the wheat harvest. At the time of threshing, she was to wait until Boaz had eaten and drunk and lain down to sleep. Then, she was to uncover his feet and lie at them, "and he will tell thee what thou shalt do."

Ruth followed her mother-in-law's instructions, and "at midnight, the man was afraid and turned himself, and, behold, a woman lay at his feet." When he discovered that it was Ruth, he pledged to perform the duties of a kinsman, if the kinsman who was closer than he refused to do his duty.

On the following day Boaz went to the city gate as was the custom and discussed the matter with the near kinsman. At last they agreed that Boaz should be permitted to redeem Ruth and all her dead husband's possessions, and sealed the agreement. Then Ruth and Boaz were married. Of this union came Obed, the father of Jesse, who was the father of the great king, David.

David against Goliath

IN THE DAYS of Saul, King of Israel, the Philistines came out to do battle and destroy their enemies. So great was their strength that Saul and all the armies of Judah were afraid.

While the armies of the Philistines were posed over against the armies of Saul awaiting battle, there came from among the Philistines a champion named Goliath. This man was a mighty giant, well trained in battle and a master in the use of arms. As he strode from the camp of the Philistines onto the plain between the opposing armies, he was fearful to behold and Israel was greatly afraid.

This champion stood in the open plain and cried to the armies of Israel, "Why are ye come out to set your battle in array? Am not I a Philistine, and ye servants of Saul? Choose you a man for you, and let him come down to me. If he be able to fight with me, and kill me, then will we be your servants. But, if I prevail against him, and kill him, then shall ye be our servants, and serve us."

The armies of Israel heard this challenge and were sore afraid. No one in their ranks could be matched with the mighty challenger of the Philistines. And they hid in their tents and trembled.

Now, there was among the sons of Israel one named David, the son of Jesse. He was the youngest of the eight sons of his father and had been kept at home to tend his father's sheep while his brothers followed Saul to battle with the Philistines.

It was David's custom to carry food and other necessities to his brothers from time to time and to bring back to his father news of the armies of Israel and of his brothers. On one of these trips David saw the giant, Goliath, standing on the plain between the armies and heard him cry forth his challenge. He also saw how the warriors of Israel were afraid and hid in their tents.

David made inquiry and found that Saul was ready to give sumptuous rewards to anyone who would go out and meet this giant in battle. The prize included the daughter of the king and freedom in Israel for his father's house.

David's brothers suspected that he had some plan or would attempt to glorify himself by fighting the giant, and they were angry. "Why art thou come down?" they asked. "With whom hast thou left those few sheep in the wilderness? We know thy pride, and the haughtiness of thy heart, for thou art come down that thou mightest see the battle."

But David answered them, "What have I now done? Is there not a cause?"

When David's words were told to Saul, he sent for the young man and tried to dissuade him from foolhardy battle with a giant more than twice his size. David met all his arguments with assurance that Jehovah, who had always helped him, would be at his side. When it became evident that David would not be discouraged, Saul had him dressed in a coat of mail and had a brass helmet put on his head. But David divested himself of this armor and advanced to meet the giant with nothing but a staff in his hand and five smooth stones in his shepherd's bag, together with a sling.

Goliath strode out to make his daily boast in loud voice to the children of Israel. When he saw that a mere youth carrying a shepherd's staff was advancing to fight with him, he was angry and cried, "Am I a dog, that thou comest to me with staves? Come to me, and I will give thy flesh unto the birds of the heavens, and to the beasts of the field."

When he had finished David cried out so that all the assemblied armies could hear, "Thou comest to me with a sword, and with a spear, and with a javelin; but I come to thee in the name of Jehovah of hosts, the God of the armies of Israel, whom thou hast defied. This day will Jehovah deliver thee into my hand, and I will smite thee, and take thy head from off thee. I will give the dead bodies of the host of the Philistines this day unto the birds of the heavens, and to the wild beasts of the earth, that all the earth may know that there is a God in Israel and that all this assembly may know that Jehovah saveth not with sword and spear, for the battle is Jehovah's, and he will give you into our hand."

Then David drew near to Goliath and the giant ran to destroy him quickly. When Goliath was close enough, David took a stone from his shepherd's bag and put it in his sling and smote Goliath in the forehead. His aim was true and his arm strong. The stone hit Goliath in the center of his forehead and sank deep into his skull so that he fell forward on his face. David rushed upon this fallen champion, drew his own sword, and cut off Goliath's head.

When the Philistines saw that their champion was dead, they fled with the men of Israel in hot pursuit. In the meantime David took the head of Goliath to Jerusalem and put it in a tent with his armor. As a reward for this deed of daring, Saul made David a member of his own household.

David and Jonathan

DAVID, the youngest son of Jesse, had slain Goliath and brought on a complete rout of the Philistine enemies of Israel. He was, for the moment, a hero among his people. Now he stood before King Saul holding in his hand the head of Goliath and receiving high honors from his ruler.

Saul had a son near David's age called Jonathan. He sat near his royal father while the young hero talked with the king. As he watched David, "the soul of Jonathan was knit with the soul of David, and Jonathan loved him as his own soul." His joy knew no bounds when he heard the king order that David should remain in the royal house as a protégé of the throne.

During the days that followed, David and Jonathan saw much of each other and their friendship deepened. In time, the two young men made a solemn covenant of friendship and the royal heir "stripped himself of the robe that was upon him, and gave it to David, and his apparel, even to his sword, and to his bow, and to his girdle."

Saul grew in appreciation of David and gave him added responsibilities and greater authority in his kingdom. He even "set him over the men of war," and his exploits became so famous among the people that everyone liked him and sang his praises.

On one occasion, when David and Saul were returning from an expedition against the Philistines, the women came out to meet them, singing: "Saul hath slain his thousands, and David his ten thousands." Here, for the first time, Saul began to realize that David's popularity might eventually overthrow him and cut off the inheritance of his son.

The more Saul thought of this, the more his anger against David increased and the more he feared David's growing power among the people. The king even tried to kill David, but was not successful. Then he plotted to give his daughter to David as his wife so that she might betray him to the Philistines. But Michal, his daughter, loved David and the plot failed.

In desperation, Saul gave orders to Jonathan and to all his servants to kill David. But Jonathan told David of this plot and advised him to flee into hiding until he should consult with his father and try to change him toward David. "Let not the king sin against his servant, against David," Jonathan argued. "He hath not sinned against thee. His words have been to thee-ward very good. He put his life in his hands, and smote the Philistine, and Jehovah wrought a great victory for all Israel. Thou sawest it and didst rejoice. Wherefore then wilt thou sin against innocent blood, to slay David without a cause?"

This argument convinced Saul and he accepted David back into his good graces, but not for long. In another engagement with the Philistines David was so successful that Saul's envy was kindled against him and he sent spies to slay David. This time Michal, David's wife, saved him by letting him down out of their house through a window so that he could escape. Then she put the teraphin, the sacred image, in bed and covered it with bedclothes. When Saul's messengers came to get David, she told them that he was ill. This excuse did not stop Saul. He ordered that he be brought to him in bed. "And when the messengers came in, behold, the teraphin was in the bed, with the pillow of goats' hair at the head thereof."

Then began a long period when David and those who

followed him were pitted against Saul and his followers, much to David's dislike. During all this time Jonathan was close to his friend, David, and often warned him of Saul's schemes to slay him. Indeed, had it not been for Jonathan, David would have been killed very early in his career.

Meantime David's popularity among the people grew until everywhere men and women were praising him as "king of the land." As the revolt against Saul grew, and as David's popularity increased and his armies waxed strong, Saul became desperate and more frenzied than he had ever been before. He killed a priest of God and did many other things that made his associates doubt his sanity.

In time, Jonathan realized that Saul was no longer fit to rule and that everything pointed to David's becoming the next king. But he loved David and was not jealous, even though it meant that he, the son of the king, would not inherit the throne. Meeting David one day in the woods, he said, "Fear not, for the hand of Saul, my father, shall not find thee. Thou shalt be king over Israel, and I shall be next unto thee. That also my father Saul also knoweth."

Thus the armies of David and those of the king fought back and forth among the hills and on the plains, when both were not fighting the Philistines. After one of these battles, a man came to David from the camp of Saul with news that Saul and Jonathan were dead and their armies routed. Indeed, the man had found Saul standing alone watching the defeat of his armies. When Saul saw that there was no hope, he had asked the man to slay him, and the man had obeyed. The news both hurt and angered David. He wept bitterly and went into deep mourning. He also ordered the man slain for having killed God's anointed one.

Then David, the sweet singer of Israel, composed a lament in memory of Jonathan, his true friend: "Jonathan is slain upon thy high places. I am distressed for thee, my brother Jonathan. Very pleasant hast thou been unto me. Thy love to me was wonderful, passing the love of woman.

How are the mighty fallen, and the weapon of war perished!"

David and Bath-sheba

DAVID became the great king of Israel. He had been anointed by the prophet and proclaimed by the people before whom, on numerous occasions, he had proved his ability as a fighter and a leader. Both God and man had sanctioned his kingship and placed much authority in his hands. But, amidst all his strength, David was weak and an easy prey of temptation.

On a certain evening he was walking on the roof of the king's house when he saw a woman bathing. She was beautiful to look upon and David was so overcome with lust for her that he sent the royal messengers to bring her to his rooms. When she arrived he discovered that she was the wife of Uriah the Hittite, one of David's soldiers.

This did not deter David, for his lust was great. Rather, he lay with her in his rooms. Then she arose and returned to her house. Now, Uriah was away fighting and knew nothing of his wife's unfaithfulness. He was faithful to his king, knowing not that this king had violated his home.

Very soon Bath-sheba, for that was the name of Uriah's wife, sent word to David saying, "I am with child." Sorely distressed, David summoned Uriah to the king's house under the pretext of wishing a report on the progress of the war. When Uriah had given his report David said to him, "Go down to thy house, and wash thy feet."

When Uriah left the king's presence, a "mess of food" was dispatched to his house from the royal larder. But Uriah did not go home. Rather, he slept at the door of the king's house with the servants. When this news reached

David, he called Uriah to him and said, "Art thou not come from a journey? Wherefore didst thou not go down unto thy house?"

"The ark, and Israel, and Judah, abide in booths, and my lord Joab and the servants of my lord are encamped in the open field," Uriah replied. "Shall I then go into my house, to eat and to drink, and to lie with my wife? As thou liveth, and as my soul liveth, I will not do this thing."

David's plan had failed since Uriah refused, in the name of the soldiers' code, to lie with his wife and thereby make David's child appear to be his own. But the king was not beaten. He had another plan which he immediately set about to try. He ordered Uriah to remain in the king's house for two days. During this time, he gave him wine until he was drunk. This also failed, for even under the influence of strong drink, Uriah refused to go home and lie with his wife.

In desperation, David resorted to his last plan. He wrote a message to Joab, Uriah's officer, and sent it by Uriah. The message said, "Set ye Uriah in the forefront of the hottest battle, and retire ye from him, that he may be smitten and die."

Joab did as the king had ordered, and Uriah was killed. When a messenger brought the news to David, he praised Joab for his generalship, but Uriah's wife "made lamentation for her husband." When the period of mourning was past, David summoned her to his house and she became his wife.

David thought that he had covered up his sin skillfully so that no one would know what he had done. Uriah was dead and could not bear witness against him. Now Bath-sheba was his wife, and the child who was to be born would appear to everyone to be the king's. David was pleased with himself and his cleverness.

But David was not so clever as he had believed himself to be. For Nathan, a prophet of Jehovah, came to him and recited a story to which the king listened attentively: "There were two men in one city; the one rich, and the other poor. The rich man had exceeding many flocks and herds, but the poor man had nothing save one little ewe lamb which he had bought and nourished up. It grew up together with him and with his children. It did eat of his own morsel, and drank of his own cup, and lay in his bosom, and was unto him as a daughter. And there came a traveller unto the rich man, and he spared to take of his own flock and of his own herd, to dress for the wayfaring man that was come unto him, but took the poor man's lamb, and dressed it for the man that was come to him."

This story made David very angry and he cried out in his wrath and said, "As Jehovah liveth, the man that hath done this is worthy to die. He shall restore the lamb fourfold because he did this thing, and because he had no pity."

But Nathan, pointing his accusing finger at David, said, "Thou art the man!" He told David how Jehovah had given him the kingship and all manner of power and wealth and many wives, yet he had stolen Uriah's wife and caused Uriah to die. Then Nathan pronounced the curse of Jehovah upon David. He told him that he would be harassed by wars for the remainder of his life, that his wives would be taken by his enemies, and that the child whom Bath-sheba was carrying would die.

When Bath-sheba's child was born it grew healthily for a time but soon became ill and lay near to death. Each day David fasted and prayed for the child's life, but Jehovah would not listen and at last the child died as Nathan had predicted. The punishment of Jehovah had been visited upon the father through the child.

Later Bath-sheba bore David another child, and they called his name Solomon.

☆

King Solomon

DAVID had sworn that, of all his sons, Solomon, who had been born to him by Bath-sheba, should ascend to the throne at his death.

As the old king saw life slipping away, aware of the many rivalries that awaited his death to break out, he called Zadok the priest, Nathan the prophet, and Benaiah the son of Jehoiada and ordered them to anoint Solomon king over Israel and proclaim it to the people. This move was not acceptable to all since there were rival forces in the mighty kingdom claiming the throne, and ominous rumblings were heard on all sides.

When David's days were few in number, he called Solomon to his side and charged him, saying, "I am going the way of all the earth. Be thou strong therefore, and show thyself a man. Keep the charge of Jehovah thy God, to walk in his ways, to keep his statutes, and his commandments, and his ordinances, and his testimonies, according to that which is written in the law of Moses, that thou mayest prosper in all that thou doest."

Soon David died and was buried with his fathers in "the city of David." Solomon was alone. The problems of a great kingdom pressed heavily upon him. Aware of the tasks ahead and of his need for counsel and guidance, he turned to the source of all wisdom and strength, to Jehovah, the God of Israel. In a dream Jehovah appeared to the new king and offered to grant whatever wish he might ask. Confessing his inexperience, the king prayed for a discerning heart. He was rewarded with the gift of wisdom beyond that of others so that his name has become a synonym for the wise one.

Years passed and troubles increased. Gradually Solomon spread the influence of his kingdom throughout the world.

His ships sailed to Ophir and Tarshish where there were spices and gems to be had. From the horse-breeding lands of the north his traders came with the finest of animals to draw their chariots. Gold piled up beyond all dreams in the land and the fame of its wealth spread far and wide.

At one time, the famed Queen of Sheba, hearing of the fabulous wealth of Solomon, made a visit to his palace to satisfy herself that it was not all rumor and falsehood. When she had come and seen for herself, she said, "It was a true report that I heard in mine own land of thine acts and of thy wisdom. Behold, the half was not told me. Thy wisdom and prosperity exceed the fame which I heard. Happy are thy men, happy are these thy servants, that stand continually before thee and that hear thy wisdom."

Solomon was pleased to hear these words and to know that the kingdom of his father David had prospered under his guidance. But he knew that the wisdom was not his alone. God had answered his request and given him wisdom. To do honor to the God of his fathers, he planned to build a beautiful temple in Jerusalem, a center of worship for all the people and a symbol of his faith and that of Israel.

With the help of Hiram, king of Tyre, Solomon gathered an army of skilled workers and brought to Jerusalem fine cedars from Lebanon, stones from the quarries of faraway lands all cut to fit, gold and silver and fine brass from the mines of the world, and precious stones from the far corners of other lands. These were fashioned by the most expert artists that could be found, and the temple rose in all its glory before the eyes of the people.

In return for all this, Solomon gave Hiram and others who helped grain and food produced by the people of his kingdom in great quantities. Thereby he established friendships with rulers and potentates everywhere and there reigned peace instead of war.

When the work was completed and the temple stood in all its glory in Jerusalem, Solomon called together all the priests of the land to dedicate the edifice to the worship of God. The ark, which had accompanied Israel through the wilderness and served as a center of worship these many years, was placed in the center of the temple, and about it were elaborate candlesticks and other sacred emblems and vessels. Then all the people gathered to worship and proclaim the greatness of Solomon who had provided a house for God and a place of worship for the people.

Amidst all the celebrating and singing of praises, rumblings of discontent were growing louder and louder. Rival forces stirred up the people to cry against the rule of Solomon. Many coveted the throne upon the death of the king and began to lay their plans to take it by force. Crafty enemies were poised on the border of the kingdom, waiting for the right time to march in and take what they wanted.

Solomon knew all this and was not happy. His last days were filled with forebodings and he went to his grave with the fear that all he had accomplished might be destroyed in rivalries and unholy alliances. And this was all too true. Rehoboam, his son, ascended to the throne only to face a rebellion led by his brother Jeroboam. Great masses of laborers who had been forced to work on the temple and other buildings of Solomon's reign rose up in rebellion. The forces of the oppressed joined with those of the covetous and chaos surged through the realm.

The glory and splendor of Solomon's reign was soon darkened by the upsurging of forces which he and his father David had brought into being and which they alone had been able to control. They broke the kingdom apart and the decline began which resulted in eventual dismemberment of the nation and the scattering of the Jews throughout the world.

☆

Solomon's Wise Decision

THE WISDOM of Solomon was known far and wide in his kingdom. At the height of his reign, two women who were harlots came before King Solomon ranting and accusing each other, and begging him to decide their case.

One of the women explained the matter to the king thus: "Oh, my lord, I and this woman dwell in one house. I was delivered of a child with her in the house. On the third day after I was delivered this woman was delivered also. We were together. There was no stranger with us in the house, save we two in the house.

"This woman's child died in the night, because she lay upon it. She arose at midnight and took my son from beside me while thine handmaiden slept, and laid it in her bosom, and laid her dead child in my bosom.

"When I arose in the morning to give my child suck, behold, it was dead. But when I had looked at it in the morning, it was not my son, whom I did bear."

When the first woman had finished her story, the other one cried out in great anger, "Nay; but the living is my son and the dead is thy son." And the women began to accuse each other in the king's presence.

When the king had listened to the women for some time and could reach no decision as to whom the living child belonged, he called one of his guards and said, "Fetch me a sword." And when the sword was brought, the king said, "Divide the living child in two, and give half to the one and half to the other."

Then the woman who had first made the accusation said to the king, "Oh, my lord, give her the living child and in no wise slay it."

But the other woman said, "It shall be neither mine nor thine. Divide it."

By this time Solomon knew whose the child was and said to his guards, "Give her the living child, and in no wise slay it. She is the mother thereof." And the mother who was willing to lose her child rather than see it killed by the king's guards rejoiced as she held her son close to her bosom. But the other woman went away cursing the king.

The Story of Elijah

WHEN KING AHAB, under the baneful influence of his Tyrian wife, Jezebel, was threatening to suppress the worship of Jehovah and make Baal-worship the court religion, there appeared before him a rugged Tishbite by the name of Elijah pronouncing the curse of Jehovah upon the land: "As Jehovah, the God of Israel, liveth, before whom I stand, there shall not be dew nor rain these years, but according to my word."

Leaving the king with this prophecy ringing in his ears, Elijah retired to a lonely spot by the brook of Cherith where he would have water to drink during the long dry spell that was to follow. Twice a day, in the morning and in the evening, Jehovah sent ravens with bread and meat to feed the prophet.

When even the brook of Cherith dried up, Jehovah commanded Elijah to move to Zarephath where a widow lived who had been instructed to care for him and keep him hid from the authorities. The woman was willing to hide Elijah, but her store of supplies was so small that she feared she could not feed him. To her surprise, however, the more meal she took from her jar and the more oil she drained from her cruse, the more they remained full. There was food enough for all.

But after Elijah had been a guest in the widow's house for some time, her son was taken sick and died. This made the woman believe that Elijah had brought a curse upon her and her family. To disprove this, Elijah took the son into his chamber and prayed to Jehovah for return of the boy's soul. Jehovah heard his prayer and life came back into the cold body and it revived. When Elijah restored the boy to his mother, she said, "Now I know that thou art a man of God, and that the word of Jehovah is in thy mouth in truth."

After three years Elijah came out of hiding and appeared before Ahab. Meantime famine had spread over the entire land because of the drought and the king had sent out expeditions to search for water, but none could be found. Elijah informed the king that rain would come only after he had staged a contest with the prophets of Baal.

Ahab was willing to do anything for rain since he and his people were near to starvation. So, following Elijah's instructions, he had four hundred and fifty prophets of Baal assembled on Mount Carmel. Here they built an altar to their god while Elijah built an altar to Jehovah. Then each slew a bullock and arranged the meat in proper fashion upon the altars.

Elijah permitted the prophets of Baal to work first before the multitudes of people gathered to see what would happen. All day these prophets called upon their god, but to no effect. Elijah taunted them with, "Cry aloud, for he is a god. Either he is musing, or he is gone aside, or he is on a journey, or peradventure he sleepeth and must be awakened." This angered the prophets of Baal, but there was no response to their cries.

As evening drew nigh, the prophets of Baal were exhausted and could cry no longer. They had cut themselves, according to their custom, until blood gushed from their veins and they were weak and disheartened.

Then Elijah took over. He made the test more difficult by ordering that water be poured over his altar until a deep ditch which he had dug about it was filled and water dripped from all the logs. Then he prayed for Jehovah to demonstrate his powers before all the people. "Then the fire of Jehovah fell and consumed the burnt-offering, and the wood, and the stones, and the dust, and licked up the water that was in the trench."

When the people saw this, they cried, "Jehovah, he is God! Jehovah, he is God!" Then they turned upon the prophets of Baal and slew them all.

Elijah had won over the prophets of Baal, but there was no rain and the people were restless. On top of Mount Carmel, Elijah bowed himself down upon the earth and put his face between his knees. His servant was ordered to "go up now and look toward the sea." But he reported that he could see nothing. Again and again, for seven times he went. At the seventh time he reported a cloud "as small as a man's hand." Elijah knew that here was the answer to his praying. The skies darkened and a storm broke. Rain came at last after three years of drought and famine.

Jezebel was angry. Elijah had caused the destruction of her prophets of Baal, and she took an oath to destroy him. To escape the queen's wrath, Elijah fled into the wilderness and there, under a juniper tree, he sat and bemoaned his fate, being the only prophet of Jehovah left, and persecution following after him. But an angel appeared to him and opened his eyes so that he saw his mission in its true perspective and he heard the voice of Jehovah in "a still small voice," which bade him anoint Elisha, son of Shaphat, in his stead. So, Elijah, finding Elisha "plowing with twelve yoke of oxen before him, and he with the twelfth," passed by him and cast his mantle upon him.

This completed, Jehovah caused a great whirlwind to be created and it spread itself over the prophet and lifted him into heaven in a chariot of fire drawn by horses of fire.

☆

The Story of Judith

NEBUCHADNEZZAR, king of Babylon, was warring with King Arphaxad, ruler of the Medes. Among his hosts he wanted soldiers from all lands and peoples under his control or in any way subject to him. His call was answered by many, but the Hebrews mocked him and turned away his messengers with insults.

This angered the great king exceedingly and he swore vengeance upon those who flaunted his power and authority. To this end he called his chief captain, Holofernes, and sent him forth with orders to destroy the Children of Israel and lay their cities in ruins.

Now, the Hebrews lived in high mountains which they could defend easily against an invading host. Holofernes and his armies came to the borders of the land, but soon realized the impossibility of storming it because of the many hills and narrow passes. Then one among them proposed that the usual ways of war be abandoned and that Holofernes take only the sources of the water supply. Thus, he argued, the people would be reduced to thirst and eventually to death and an easy victory would follow.

This advice seemed good, and the mission was carried out easily. Now the Hebrews in the hills saw their water shut off and knew that it would not be long before they would have to surrender. They took counsel and cried to their God for help. They decided that unless help came in five days they would come down and place themselves in the hands of the enemy.

But Judith, a widow in the land, heard of the decision and was sorely troubled. She knew that Holofernes had sworn vengeance upon her people and that surrender would mean destruction. Thus she begged the leaders to trust God and not tempt him with threats. Then she proposed that they permit her to carry out a plan which she refused to reveal to anyone. In desperation they consented.

That night she washed herself and put on fine robes and many jewels. Then, with her handmaidens, she left the hills for the camp of the enemy. When Holoferne's men saw her coming they marvelled at her beauty and consented immediately to take her to their leader.

To him she explained that the Hebrews were going to surrender and that she had fled to Holofernes to escape the destruction that would follow. He listened with only half an ear, so smitten was he with her beauty. When she had finished, he permitted her to remain with his troops and to go nightly into the nearby hills to pray.

For several nights she and her maidens left the camp and went away to pray, returning before morning and spending the day in a special tent provided by the king's chief captain.

One night Holofernes prepared a banquet and asked Judith to attend. She accepted and entered into the festivities, drinking wine with the guests and displaying her beauty before all until they became intoxicated. When Holofernes had drunk far more than was his custom and lay in a stupor, and the other guests had left, she dismissed the guards on the pretext that she wished to be alone with Holofernes.

When all was quiet and she was the only one left in the tent of Holofernes, who lay drunk on his bed, she took his scimitar, cut off his head and hid it in a basket of food along with the canopy of his bed. Then she and her maidens slipped away, presumably to pray in the hills.

But this time she returned to her people and showed them the head of Holofernes and reported that the time for attack had arrived. As the sun rose in the morning, the Hebrews hung the head of Holofernes on their wall and attacked the enemy. Men were running everywhere in search of their leader. They called to Holofernes in his tent, but got no answer. At first they thought he was alone with Judith and hesitated to disturb him. When the situation became desperate and he still did not answer, they opened the tent only to discover his headless body on the floor and the canopy gone.

Leaderless, the enemy was an easy prey for the Hebrews who routed the hosts and took great stores of booty. Then, back in their land, they turned to celebrating the victory and to praising the courage and clear wit of Judith who had saved them from terrible destruction and defeat.

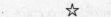

The Story of Esther

XERXES, king of Media and Persia, mighty ruler over one hundred and twenty-seven provinces reaching from India even to Ethiopia, made a feast to which all the people both great and small who were in Shushan, the palace city, were invited. When the eating and drinking had lasted for many days and both the king and the people were hot with wine, Xerxes ordered Vashti, the queen, to appear before the revelers "to show the people and the princes her beauty, for she was fair to look on."

This was an insult to the queen, and she refused to come. Xerxes would not have commanded so had he been free from drink, for in the East women were not to be made a show of before men, unless they were of questionable reputation.

Vashti's refusal angered the king greatly, but there might be more serious consequences of her act. As Memucan, one of the princes of Persia and Media who "saw the king's face and sat first in the kingdom," pointed out to the king, "Vashti the queen hath not done wrong to the king only, but also to all the princes and to all the people that are in the provinces. For this deed of the queen will come abroad unto all women, to make their husbands contemptible in their eyes, when it shall be reported."

Xerxes realized the seriousness of the queen's action and ordered that Vashti be banished from the king's presence and deprived of her royal estate. This was to impress upon all wives in the kingdom the fact that they should at all times give honor and respect to their husbands.

When the king's wrath had cooled, he ordered his servants to go throughout the kingdom and gather all the fair young virgins who could be found so that a queen might be picked from among them.

Now, there lived in Shushan a certain Jew named Mordecai who had as his ward his beautiful cousin, Esther, daughter of his uncle. This young Jewess was brought, along with other virgins of the kingdom, to the palace to be tried by the king. Mordecai instructed her not to make known her people nor her kindred lest this prejudice the king against her.

When Esther was taken before the king, she found favor in his sight and was made queen in place of Vashti.

Mordecai was sitting at the king's gate when he heard of a plot among the king's chamberlains to lay hands on his royal person and destroy him. He told Esther and she, in turn, told the king who, finding the information true, had the plotters hanged and the incident written in "the book of the chronicles."

Among the king's favorites was Haman, a prince of high estate and evil mind. As he moved about he expected everyone to bow down to him. But Mordecai refused to do him this reverence. This angered Haman greatly, especially when he discovered that the man who refused to bow to him was a Jew.

Here was an opportunity, Haman thought, to wreak his vengeance upon Mordecai and upon his people throughout the kingdom. With this in mind, he went to the king with a statement that there were certain people in the realm who did not obey the king's laws or follow his commandments. He asked the king for permission to have these people destroyed. So convincing was his plea that the king gave permission and sent out an order through every province that on the thirteenth day of the twelfth month every Jew should be destroyed, even the women and children. Haman was happy, and he sat and drank with the king.

When Mordecai heard of the king's decree he was deeply disturbed and sent word to Esther that she go immediately to the king and beg him to retract the order. But Esther explained that no one was permitted to go before the king unless he was called. If this law was disobeyed, the person was subject to immediate death unless the king held out his golden sceptre. Esther had not been summoned into the king's presence for thirty days.

These facts were well known to Mordecai, but he pointed out to Esther, "Think not with thyself that thou shalt escape in the king's house more than all the Jews. For if thou altogether holdest thy peace at this time, then will relief and deliverance arise to the Jews from another place, but thou and thy father's house will perish. Who knoweth whether thou art not come to the kingdom for such a time as this?"

This plea won Esther over and she resolved to approach the king even at the risk of her own life. When she had prepared herself and stood in the inner court of the king's palace, she was welcomed by the king who extended to her his golden sceptre and promised to grant whatever request she would make. Then Esther invited the king and Haman to a banquet in her chambers.

During the banquet the king renewed his pledge to grant Esther's wish, but she replied with another invitation to a banquet on the following night. This pleased Haman greatly. Was he not invited to the queen's feast along with the king, and for two nights together? This was a high honor, and he was happy.

But his happiness was marred by the sight of Mordecai at the king's gate. His wife and his friends advised him to have a high gallows built in the court yard and to ask special permission of the king to hang Mordecai the following morning.

The king could not sleep that night and had the book of records of the chronicles read to him. The reader came to the account of Mordecai's warning and the hanging of the conspirators. Xerxes was worried because he had not honored Mordecai for this service. By chance, Haman had come to see the king about the hanging of Mordecai and was summoned into the king's presence at once. The king asked him what "shall be done unto the man the king delighteth to honor"? Haman thought this meant himself, so he did not restrain himself in suggesting things to be done. When he had finished, the king told him to see that all he had suggested was done for Mordecai. This gave Haman no chance to ask for Mordecai's life on the gallows.

At the queen's banquet that night, the king repeated his pledge to grant her request, even to the half of his kingdom. Then Esther asked for her own life and that of her people. When the king realized what Haman had done, he ordered that he be hanged on the gallows prepared for Mordecai and that Mordecai be set over the house of Haman and be given authority to countermand the order for extermination of the Jews.

Mordecai was not satisfied with forestalling the killing of all Jews in the kingdom. He wanted vengeance upon all the enemies of the Jews. With this in mind, he issued an order under the king's seal granting to the Jews the right to "gather themselves together and to stand for their life, to destroy, to slay, and to cause to perish, all the power of the people and province that would assault them, their little ones and women, and to take the spoil of them for a prey" on the day which had been set aside for killing the Jews.

On the appointed day the Jews, with Xerxes' sanction,

fell upon their enemies and all who would do them hurt, and there was great slaughter everywhere throughout the empire. The killing over, the Jews rested on the following day and celebrated it with feasting and rejoicing at their deliverance.

Since Mordecai was now high in the king's favor, he wrote to all the Jews in all the provinces ruled over by Xerxes ordering that they should set apart the fourteenth and the fifteenth days of the twelfth month as an annual period of celebration to commemorate their deliverance from persecution. This they called Purim, the feast of the "pur," or "lot."

The Story of Job

"THERE was a man in the land of Uz whose name was Job, and that man was perfect and upright, and one that feared God and turned away from evil." He had seven sons and vast herds of cattle and sheep and other signs of wealth. Job was so righteous that he even offered special sacrifices for his children lest there be some unconscious sin on their part for which reparation had not been made in full.

When the "sons of God came to present themselves before Jehovah," Satan stood among them. His presence caused God to boast of Job and his goodness. "There is none like him on earth," the Divine said, "a perfect and upright man, one that feareth God and turneth away from evil."

Satan had an answer: "Doth Job fear God for nought? Hast not thou made a hedge about him, and about his house, and about all that he hath, on every side? Thou hast blessed the work of his hands and his substance is increased in the land." Then Satan issued a challenge to God. "Put forth thy hand now, and touch all that he hath, and he will renounce thee to thy face."

God was quick to accept the challenge, for he had a great faith in Job. "Behold," he said, "all that he hath is in thy power, only upon himself put not forth thy hand."

So it came about that Satan began testing Job. As his sons were eating and drinking in the house of his oldest son, messengers came to Job with the news that enemies had stolen his oxen and asses and killed all his servants save one, that fire had destroyed his sheep and his shepherds save one, that the Chaldeans had stolen his camels and slain his servants save one, and that a great wind had destroyed his oldest son's house and all his sons and daughters.

These blows did not shake Job's faith. His answer was simple and straight, "Naked came I out of my mother's womb, and naked shall I return thither. Jehovah gave, and Jehovah hath taken away; blessed be the name of Jehovah."

Again the "sons of God" appeared before Jehovah, and Satan stood among them. This time God taunted Satan with his failure, since Job had endured so much misfortune without sinning. To this Satan replied, "Skin for skin; yea, all that a man hath will he give for his life. Put forth thy hand now and touch his bone and his flesh, and he will renounce thee to thy face."

God accepted this challenge, giving Job over to Satan, demanding only that he spare his life.

This time Satan smote Job with boils from his feet to his head so that he sat among the ashes and scraped himself with a potsherd. So intense was his suffering that his wife urged him to renounce God and die. But Job was strong in his faith and answered his wife, "Shall we receive good at the hand of God, and shall we not receive evil?"

While Job sat on the ash heap and bemoaned his fate, his three friends, Eliphaz the Temanite, Bildad the Shuhite, and Zophar the Naamathite, came to comfort him. They found Job in the depths of gloom, cursing the day he was born and wishing that he were dead.

Eliphaz, a scholar, argued with Job. He tried to show Job that all suffering came from sin and that Job must have transgressed against God to deserve this dire punishment. Since suffering is always the result of sin, he urged Job to turn to God and ask forgiveness. Job listened, but could not agree. He knew that his life had been upright and that he had no sin worthy of the suffering he was enduring.

Eliphaz having failed, Bildad, a man of tradition, turned to Job advancing the idea that history was full of instances where the evil suffered while no one could recount a case of the good suffering. This did not convince Job, and Bildad had to retire.

Zophar, a common-sense man, also appealed to Job. God knows everything, he argued, and has always dealt rightly with all men. Then he urged Job to confess his sin and be cleansed of his unrighteousness.

Job had listened attentively, but was not convinced by the arguments of either the man of cold intellect, the man of tradition, or the man of common sense. Their arguments did not ring true, for Job knew that he was upright and not deserving of this punishment.

When the three friends of Job could offer no solution to this problem of the suffering of the good, a young man called Elihu spoke up with the suggestion that God, being greater than man, is not forced to give a reason for his actions. Whatever God does is right because God is God. Man has no right to judge God's actions.

As Elihu finished speaking, God answered out of a great wind, telling of his might and his mighty works. Man, God said, is here but a moment and he is weak. God created everything and controls all. What is little man that he should even try to understand the ways of God?

Job was chastened and repented his attempt to discover

the ways of God. Then God restored all of Job's possessions and doubled them, and cleansed him of his boils. Job had endured God's testing and had learned the greatness of God. As a reward the remainder of his life was full of blessings and prosperity and he lived a hundred and forty years.

☆

The Story of Jonah

JONAH, son of Amittai, heard the voice of Jehovah saying, "Arise, go to Nineveh, that great city, and cry against it; for their wickedness is come up before me." But Jonah had no desire to preach in Nineveh or in any other place. Hoping to escape from the presence of Jehovah and to free himself of the call to preach, he went down to Joppa where he took ship for Tarshish.

After he had paid the fare and boarded the ship, he climbed down into the innermost parts of the vessel and was soon fast asleep.

"But Jehovah sent out a great wind upon the sea, and there was a mighty tempest on the sea, so that the ship was like to be broken." Fear gripped the mariners, and each man cried unto his god for protection as they tossed into the sea whatever of the cargo might lighten the vessel. But the storm raged and nothing that anyone did lessened the fierceness of the wind and the waves.

Then the shipmaster came to Jonah and said, "What meanest thou, O sleeper? Arise, call upon thy God, if so be it that God will think upon us, that we perish not." Jonah knew that it would do no good for him to call upon Jehovah, and he knew further why the storm had arisen. He was not surprised, then, when the men on the ship cast lots to discover "for whose cause this evil is upon us," to see the lot fall upon him. He confessed that he was fleeing from the presence of Jehovah and that the storm was Jehovah's way of showing his anger.

"What shall we do unto thee, that the sea may be calm unto us?" they asked.

"Take me up, and cast me forth into the sea. So shall the sea be calm unto you. I know that for my sake this great tempest is upon you."

But the mariners did not want to drown Jonah if they could avoid it. So, they rowed hard. But the sea became more violent and threatened to engulf their vessel at any moment. In desperation, they cast Jonah into the sea and saw him swallowed up by the waves. Immediately, the sea ceased its raging and the wind and the waves were calmed.

God was not through with Jonah. He prepared a great fish to swallow Jonah. And Jonah remained in the belly of the fish three days. During this time Jonah prayed to Jehovah pledging himself to obey the voice of God if he should be saved from this most unnatural prison. "And Jehovah spake unto the fish, and it vomited out Jonah upon dry land."

Thoroughly chastened, Jonah went to Nineveh as God had instructed and preached throughout the great city, saying, "Yet forty days, and Nineveh shall be overthrown." His preaching was so successful that all the city, from the least to the greatest, put on sackcloth and sat in ashes repenting of their sins. Jehovah saw the earnestness of the citizens of Nineveh and repented "of the evil which he said he would do unto them, and he did it not."

This angered Jonah greatly. He wanted to see Nineveh destroyed and to enjoy the suffering of the people. Their salvation made him want to die. So, he went outside of the city where he made a booth to protect himself from the sun, and there he sat and begged God to take his life.

While he sat and bemoaned his fate, Jonah saw that God

had prepared a gourd vine to cover his booth and shade him from the heat of the sun, and Jonah was glad. But, on the morrow God prepared a worm which smote the gourd so that the hot east winds of the day caused it to wither and die. Then the sun beat upon Jonah's head and he fainted and was near to death.

Then God said to Jonah, "Doest thou well to be angry for the gourd?"

"I do well to be angry, even unto death."

"Thou hast had regard for the gourd, for which thou hast not labored, neither madest it grow, which came up in the night," God pointed out to Jonah. "Should not I have regard for Nineveh, that great city, wherein are more than sixscore thousand persons that cannot discern between their right hand and their left hand, and also much cattle?"

Nebuchadnezzar's Dream

JOHOIKIM had ruled Judah three years when Jerusalem was besieged and taken by Nebuchadnezzar, the king of Babylon.

As was the custom in war, Nebuchadnezzar took some of the vessels of the house of God and placed them in the treasure-house of his god. He also chose from among the Hebrew youths those best-favored and skilled in knowledge and understanding to be trained for high positions at his court.

Among the young men selected for these favors were Daniel, Shadrach, Meshach, and Abed-nego, devout Jews who preferred a diet of pulse and water to wine and dainties from the larder of the king.

Daniel and his companions had not been long in the

king's service when Nebuchadnezzar dreamed a dream that troubled him much. Not only did the contents of the dream worry Nebuchadnezzar, but the fact that he could not recall what the dream was about worried him more. He knew he had dreamed a bad dream, but what it was and what it meant eluded him.

In his agitation, the king called together all the magicians, the enchanters, and the sorcerers of the realm. When they had assembled, he said to them, "I have dreamed a dream, and my spirit is troubled to know the dream."

"Tell thy servants the dream, and we will show the interpretation," the wise men answered.

This response angered the king, who commanded his wise men, "The thing is gone from me. If ye make not known unto me the dream and the interpretation thereof, ye shall be cut in pieces, and your houses shall be made a dunghill. But if ye show the dream and the interpretation thereof, ye shall receive of me gifts and rewards and great honor. Show me the dream and the interpretation thereof!"

Here was an impossible assignment, and the wise men knew it. "There is not a man upon the earth," they answered, "that can show the king's matter, forasmuch as no king, lord, or ruler, hath asked such a thing of any magician, or enchanter, or Chaldean. It is a rare thing that the king requireth, and there is no other that can show it before the king except the gods whose dwelling is not with flesh."

This made the king very angry so that he issued an order that all the wise men of Babylon should be destroyed. This included Daniel and his companions, for they had become known as possessors of exceptional knowledge and understanding. So Daniel proposed to the king that at a set time he would come before the court and interpret the dream.

Meantime Daniel prayed to his God for a revelation of the king's dream, and his companions prayed also. Then was the secret revealed to Daniel in the night and he praised God for his mercies.

At the appointed time Daniel was brought into the presence of Nebuchadnezzar and stood before the entire court. When the ceremonies had been completed, the king asked Daniel, "Art thou able to make known unto me the dream which I have seen and the interpretation thereof?"

Daniel explained that no one could do that save God. Then he made known to the king and his court that God had revealed the secret to him so that all praise should be given not to him but to God.

The dream, Daniel explained, was a great image with head of gold, breasts and arms of silver, belly and thighs of brass, legs of iron, and its feet of iron and clay mixed. As the image stood before the king in his dream a great stone "cut out without hands" struck the image upon its feet and broke it into fine powder which the wind carried away. Then the stone became a great mountain which filled the whole earth.

Nebuchadnezzar and all the wise men were struck with wonderment that Daniel could recount a dream that even the dreamer could not remember. As Daniel described the figure, the dream came back to the king and he knew that the young man standing before him spoke the truth.

Then Daniel explained the dream. He said that the present kingdom of Nebuchadnezzar was the head of gold. After him would come a kingdom of silver, then one of brass followed by one of iron, each inferior to the present kingdom. At last, he prophesied, the kingdom will be divided and some branches, those of clay, will be destroyed while those of iron will endure. When this condition had continued for a time, God would set up a kingdom that would destroy all other kingdoms and would rule over all the world.

Daniel closed his interpretation with these words of warning: "The great God hath made known to the king what shall come to pass hereafter. The dream is certain, and the interpretation thereof sure."

When Daniel had finished, the king fell on his face and worshipped him, confessing the power of the Hebrew's God and conferring great honors upon Daniel and his companions.

The Fiery Furnace

NEBUCHADNEZZAR, king of Babylon, made a great image of gold and set it up in the Plain of Dura. Here, by royal decree, were assembled all the high dignitaries of the land,— the satraps, deputies, governors, judges, treasurers, counsellors, sheriffs, and all the rulers of the provinces.

Then the king issued a decree: "To you it is commanded, O people, nations, and languages, that at what time ye hear the sound of the cornet, flute, harp, sackbut, psaltery, dulcimer, and all kinds of music, ye fall down and worship the golden image that Nebuchadnezzar the king hath set up. Whoso falleth not down and worshippeth shall the same hour be cast into the midst of a burning fiery furnace."

At the sound of music everyone in the vast assembled multitude fell down and worshipped as the king had ordered, except three young Hebrews whom Nebuchadnezzar had appointed to positions of power because of their friendship with Daniel, the interpreter of the king's dream. Immediately the news that these three youths, Shadrach, Meshach, and Abed-nego, had refused to bow down and worship the golden image was brought to the king by some Chaldeans who were jealous of the power granted the Hebrews.

Nebuchadnezzar was shaken with rage and fury at this news, and ordered the young men brought before him at once. When they stood in his presence, the king repeated his order and warned them of their fate if they refused to obey.

He concluded his warning with a challenge, "Who is that god that shall deliver you out of my hands?"

To this the young men replied, "O Nebuchadnezzar, we have no need to answer thee in this matter. If it be so, our God whom we serve is able to deliver us from the burning fiery furnace, and he will deliver us out of thy hand, O king. But if not, be it known unto thee, O king, that we will not serve thy gods nor worship the golden image which thou hast set up."

Nebuchadnezzar could not brook such defiance, and he was full of fury and the form of his visage was changed. He gave immediate orders that the furnace should be heated seven times hotter than ever before and that the three youths be bound and cast into the midst of the flames. This was done without delay and the three youths were thrown into the fire by picked soldiers of the king's armies. But, so hot was the fire that the soldiers were consumed by the heat and died.

When the king looked into the furnace to see how quickly the bodies of the three youths would be consumed, he was astonished to see not three but four persons walking about in the flames free from all harm. He called his counsellors and said, "Did not we cast three men bound into the midst of the fire?"

"True, O king," they replied.

"Lo, I see four men loose, walking in the midst of the fire, and they have no hurt. The aspect of the fourth is like a son of the gods." With this, Nebuchadnezzar came near to the mouth of the furnace and called the young men to come out.

"Then Shadrach, Meshach, and Abed-nego came forth out of the midst of the fire," and all the assembled multitudes "saw these men, that the fire had no power upon their bodies, or was the hair of their heads singed, neither were their hosen changed, nor had the smell of fire passed on them."

Nebuchadnezzar was convinced of the power of the god whom these youths worshipped and issued a decree: "Every people, nation, and language, which speak anything amiss against the god of Shadrach, Meshach, and Abed-nego, shall be cut in pieces, and their houses shall be made a dunghill; because there is no other god that is able to deliver after this sort."

Then the king promoted the youths to positions of yet greater power in Babylon and showered them with honors and their god with praise.

The Handwriting on the Wall

NEBUCHADNEZZAR was dead, and in his stead his son Belshazzar, a wanton and ribald youth, reigned over the great Babylonian empire.

At one of the king's many feasts for his lords and retainers, when the guests were filled with food and addled with drink, Belshazzar gave orders that the golden and silver vessels which his father had taken from the temple in Jerusalem be brought so that he and his guests might drink wine from them. When the vessels were brought, the revelers amused themselves by drinking toasts to their pagan gods.

Suddenly, as they drank and blinked their bleared eyes, a man's hand appeared above the candlesticks and, with one of its fingers, began to write in livid letters, "MENE, MENE, TEKEL, UPHARSIN," on the plaster of the royal banquet hall. As one by one saw the hand writing, the noise of revelry died away to a low moaning, and then to silence. Fear sobered the king's guests while their host trembled so that the joints of his loins were loosed, and his knees smote one against the other.

After the first wave of fear had spent itself, the king called for the enchanters, soothsayers, and the Chaldeans, and ordered them to interpret the meaning of this strange event. When they hesitated and seemed confused, he promised that to the one who could reveal the mystery of this writing he would give purple robes and a golden chain for his neck, and would make him the third ruler in the land. But even this did not open their understanding, and they stood before the king dumb, unable to read the language or to tell its meaning.

Belshazzar was deeply troubled and afraid when his queen came to the banquet house with a reminder that there abode in the kingdom a soothsayer of superior ability, Daniel. She reminded her lord how he had interpreted the dreams of his father, Nebuchadnezzar, and how he had been made chief of the king's magicians. Desperate and afraid, the king had Daniel brought before him and showed him the writing on the wall. He also made Daniel the same offer that he had made to the other magicians, if he could interpret the words.

Daniel did not want the rewards, but he was able to read the writing clearly. Before he gave his interpretation, he compared Belshazzar to his father, pointing out that Nebuchadnezzar had suffered deeply before he humbled himself before God. "And thou his son," he concluded, "hast not humbled thy heart, though thou knewest all this, but hast lifted up thyself against the Lord of heaven."

Then, looking squarely at the trembling and afraid king, Daniel said, "This is the interpretation of the thing: MENE,—God hath numbered thy kingdom and brought it to an end. TEKEL,—thou art weighed in the balances and art found wanting. PERES,—thy kingdom is divided and given to the Medes and the Persians."

Belshazzar was satisfied, and ordered that Daniel be clothed in purple and that a gold chain be hung about his neck, and he was made the third ruler in the kingdom.

But before dawn Belshazzar was slain and Darius, the Mede, took the kingdom for his own, fulfilling the prophecy written on the plaster above the candlesticks in Belshazzar's banquet hall.

Daniel Delivered from the Lions

ONE of the first things Darius did after he became ruler of the Babylonian empire was to reorganize the government. He placed over the kingdom one hundred and twenty satraps to rule in the provinces. Over these he placed three presidents. One of these presidents was Daniel, the interpreter of dreams and head of the magicians under Nebuchadnezzar.

Being gifted in government and a man of integrity, Daniel outshone all the other presidents so that Darius was thinking of placing him over the whole realm.

When rumors of the king's intentions reached the other presidents and the satraps, they were violently jealous and sought to discover some fault in Daniel which would discredit him in the king's mind. But Daniel's life was above reproach and, search as they might, they could find nothing blameful in him.

Then someone remembered that Daniel was a Jew and did not worship the gods of the empire. Here was a point at which they could strike, and they began immediately to make plans to discredit him.

All the other presidents and the satraps assembled before Darius with what seemed to be a harmless document which they asked him to sign. This was a royal statute proclaiming that for a period of thirty days no one in the empire should ask a petition of any god or man save of the king. Anyone disobeying this interdict should be cast into a den of lions. Darius read it, was pleased, and affixed his signature and seal "according to the law of the Medes and Persians, which altereth not."

Daniel's enemies had their weapon and they posted spies immediately to catch him in their trap. Daniel knew of the interdict but, as was his custom, three times each day he knelt before his opened window facing Jerusalem, praying and giving thanks to God.

The conspirators very soon had their evidence and reported it to Darius. But the king was most unhappy. He valued Daniel highly and did not realize before that this simple royal decree would ensnare his most trusted officer. However, though he wanted very much to save Daniel, he knew that the decree had been sealed and signed and was not alterable even by the king. The presidents and satraps reminded Darius that he could not circumvent his own law and that he had to punish Daniel as the law stated.

There being no way out, Darius ordered that Daniel be cast into the lions' den. But he added to Daniel, "Thy God whom thou serveth, he will deliver thee." Then he had a great rock rolled in front of the den and placed the royal seal upon it so that "nothing might be changed concerning Daniel."

Then the king returned to his royal chamber and passed the night in fasting, for sleep had fled. Early the next morning he went in haste to the den where he cried in a lamentable voice, "Daniel, O Daniel, servant of the living God, is thy God, whom thou servest continually, able to deliver thee from the lions?"

From the depths of the den he heard Daniel speak, "O king, live forever. My God hath sent his angel and hath shut the lions' mouths, and they have not hurt me." This made the king exceedingly glad and he ordered that Daniel be lifted from the den at once.

But the king was angry with the conspirators who had plotted to destroy Daniel. As a punishment he ordered that they be brought, along with their wives and their children, to be cast into the lions' den. Their fate was far different from that of Daniel, for they were devoured by the lions almost before they reached the floor.

When the king's wrath had been appeased by this slaughter, he issued a decree commanding all the people to "tremble and fear before the God of Daniel, for he is the living God."

Judas Maccabeus

ALEXANDER THE MACEDONIAN, son of Philip, who is called "the Great," ruled a multitude of nations and peoples not the least of which were Greece and Palestine. Now, in his youth Alexander had been a pupil of the famed Aristotle and had come to love everything Greek. When he spread his rule over the ancient world, he sought to make this world Greek in thought and in spirit. The Greek language was spoken and read in many lands, Greek ideals became the ideals of men of many nations, and the ways and customs of the Greeks were adopted in the entire empire of Alexander.

Alexander's dream of Hellenizing the world did not die with him, but was further realized by those among whom he divided his kingdom. Antiochus IV, king of Syria, strove to make Greek ideals and customs supreme in Palestine. He was aided materially by the higher classes who organized themselves into a Hellenistic party pledged to Greece and its ways. A son of the king, Antiochus Epiphanes, furthered the work so that a "place of exercise," in the manner of the Greeks, was built close by the temple in Jerusalem and a great number of the Jews forsook the ways of their fathers "and joined themselves to the Gentiles, and sold themselves to the devil."

This led to the formation of a party of opposition, the

Hasidīm, or "the pious," pledged to obey and support the ancient law of their fathers and their tradition. While Joshua, head of the Hellenistic faction, who changed his name to Jason, was assuming by force the high-priesthood and the armies of Antiochus were plundering the temple and killing those who resisted them, members of the Hasidīm were organizing secret groups for revolt.

Gradually Antiochus built up anger among the loyal Jews at his extreme measures. While some, fearful of their lives, obeyed his commands to build pagan altars in their places of worship and to sacrifice to the gods of the empire, the numbers opposed to this interference with the religion of the Hebrews grew stronger. The climax came when a royal edict went out ordering the erection of heathen altars in every township in Palestine and the appointment of officers to deal with all who refused to worship the heathen gods.

At Modin there lived Mattathias, a man descended from Simeon, a priest of the sons of Joarib, and his five sons. These devout Jews, loyal to their tradition, saw the blasphemies that were committed in Judah and in Jerusalem and were sore troubled in their hearts. When Mattathias was ordered to sacrifice in accord with heathen customs, he not only refused but slew the officers in charge, tore down the heathen altar, and thereby gave the signal for open revolt against all Hellenizing attempts by Antiochus.

Fleeing to the mountains with his sons, Mattathias organized the revolt and appointed his son Judas, who is called Maccabeus (the Hammer), captain and military leader of the forces of resistance. Many loyal Jews flocked to the camp of Judas while others formed their own bands of resistance in the wild mountains a distance from Jerusalem.

One of these bands, made up largely of Sabbatarians, Jews who followed the strict laws of the Sabbath to the letter, refused to fight when they were attacked because it was the Sabbath. Thus they were overcome easily and more than a thousand men, women, and children were ruthlessly slaughtered. This led Mattathias and his sons to the decision that they would resist the enemy every day of the week and in every way, if they were attacked.

Then, in 166 B.C. Mattathias died, leaving the military leadership of his people to Judas, charging him with a holy mission. "Be not afraid of the words of a sinful man," he charged, "for his glory shall be dung and worms. Today he shall be lifted up, and tomorrow he shall in no wise be found, because he is returned unto dust, and his thought is perished. And ye, my children, be strong, and show yourselves men in behalf of the law, for therein shall ye obtain glory."

Judas proved himself worthy of all his father's trust and confidence. He exhibited such military genius that one by one the enemies of the Jews were destroyed. "And he gat his people great glory, and put on a breastplate as a giant, and girt his warlike harness about him, and set battle in array, protecting the army with his sword. And he was like a lion in his deeds, and as a lion's whelp roaring for prey. And he pursued the lawless, seeking them out, and he burnt up those that troubled his people. And the lawless shrunk for fear of him, and all the workers of lawlessness were sore troubled, and salvation prospered in his hand. And he angered many kings, and made Jacob glad with his acts, and his memorial is blessed forever. And he went about among the cities of Judah, and destroyed the ungodly out of the land, and turned away wrath from Israel."

He overcame the Syrian general Apollonius, who led an army against him. Then Seron, Lysias, and Gorgias fell before his might and genius. When his enemies moved with great hosts against him, he showed his skill by leading part of the attackers off while he destroyed the others.

When at last the hosts of the enemy seemed destroyed, Judas entered Jerusalem where the sanctuary had been desecrated and the altar profaned. There he found shrubs growing in the courts and the chambers of the priests pulled down. Then the people rent their garments and put ashes on their heads in token of their suffering and disgrace. After consultation it was decided to pull down the defiled altars and build others that could be dedicated afresh.

When the building was completed and the temple was restored with new golden and silver ornaments, and the sacred emblems had been placed all about, there was a great gathering of the people to dedicate this restored temple and its altars to the God of their fathers.

"And Judas and his brethren and the whole congregation of Israel ordained that the days of the dedication of the altar should be kept in their seasons from year to year by the space of eight days, from the five and twentieth day of the month Chislev, with gladness and joy." And today loyal Jews everywhere celebrate this festival with the Feast of Dedication, which is called Chanukah.

But the end was not yet. The Gentiles took counsel as to how they might destroy the temple and put down the rebellion of Judas and his followers. A plan was laid and Lysias attacked the temple mount, throwing back Judas and threatening to defeat him completely. Judas and his hosts were saved only because Lysias was obliged to hasten back to Antioch to keep a rival from usurping his authority.

Then Lysias made a bargain with the Jews, granting them religious freedom. This was accepted by the Hasidim but not by Judas. He wanted political freedom for his people as well as religious freedom and refused to cease fighting until he had his desire. He led his armies against Nicanor, who was sent by the king to destroy the rebellion led by Judas, and defeated him on the battlefield between Bethhoron and Adasa. This victory led to a period of peace during which Judas made alliances with powerful neighbors and sought to assure the safety of Judah among the nations of the world.

In time the king sent other hosts against Judas so great and powerful that the armies of Judas were unable to maintain themselves. In the heat of the battle which followed, Judas was slain and his armies routed. For him the fight was completed. His brothers, Jonathan and Simon, took him to the sepulcher where his father lay; and there, along with all Israel, made great lamentation for him, "and mourned many days, and said, 'How is the mighty fallen, the savior of Israel!' And the rest of the acts of Judas, and his wars, and the valiant deeds which he did, and his greatness, they are not written; for they were exceeding many."

PART TWO

STORIES FROM THE NEW TESTAMENT

The Birth of Jesus

IT WAS when Caesar Augustus ruled the mighty Roman Empire and Herod reigned in Judea that an order went out for a census of all inhabitants of the empire. Everyone was to travel to his own city and there sign the royal register—men, women, and children.

Among the multitude that took their way to Bethlehem was a righteous man called Joseph and his wife, Mary. Now, when Mary was betrothed to Joseph she was found with child, though he had not been with her. This troubled him greatly so that he was minded to put her away privately, not wishing to shame her before her people.

While he was thinking on this matter an angel of the Lord came to him and said, "Joseph, thou son of David, fear not to take unto thee Mary thy wife, for that which is conceived in her is of the Holy Spirit. She shall bring forth a son and thou shalt call his name Jesus, for it is he that shall save his people from their sins." Then Joseph arose and took Mary to wife.

When Joseph and Mary reached Bethlehem the city was already crowded so that they could find no place to rest except a stable. Here was clean hay, and Mary was big with child, so they spread their cloths and were soon fast asleep, exhausted by the trip from Nazareth, their home.

During the night Mary's time was upon her, and she brought forth her firstborn, a son whom she called Jesus. She wrapped him in swaddling clothes and laid him in a manger.

"There were shepherds in the same country abiding in the

field and keeping watch by night over their flocks. And an angel of the Lord stood by them, and the glory of the Lord shone round about them, and they were sore afraid. And the angel said unto them, 'Be not afraid, for behold, I bring you good tidings of great joy which shall be to all the people; for there is born to you this day in the city of David a Savior, who is Christ the Lord. And this is the sign unto you: Ye shall find a babe wrapped in swaddling clothes and lying in a manger.'

"And suddenly there was with the angel a multitude of the heavenly host praising God and saying: 'Glory to God in the highest, and on earth peace among men in whom he is well pleased.' "

When the angels went away, the shepherds arose and went immediately to Bethlehem where they found Mary and Joseph and the babe lying in the manger.

While the angels were singing to the shepherds of the birth of a Savior, there appeared a great and shining star in the east and wise men, seeing it, knew that the Savior was born and came immediately to worship at his feet.

But they were unable to find the place of his birth and went to Jerusalem seeking him. They made inquiries throughout the city: "Where is he that is born King of the Jews? We have seen his star in the east, and are come to worship him." The chief priests and scribes of the people were gathered together and they searched their sacred writings for an answer to the questionings of the wise men. After much study and thought they answered, "In Bethlehem of Judea, for thus it is written through the prophet: 'And thou Bethlehem, land of Judah, are in no wise least among the princes of Judah; for out of thee shall come forth a governor, who shall be shepherd of my people Israel.' "

When Herod heard about the visit of the wise men, he called them to his royal palace and made inquiry of them regarding the exact time that the star appeared. Then he said to them, "Go and search out exactly concerning the young child. When ye have found him, bring me word that I may also come and worship him."

Having heard the king, the wise men set out for Bethlehem, "and, lo, the star which they saw in the east went before them, till it came and stood over where the young child was." When they saw the star, they were filled with great joy and "came into the house and saw the young child with Mary his mother; and they fell down and worshipped him. Opening their treasures, they offered unto him gifts, gold and frankincense and myrrh."

When they were prepared to leave, they were warned of God not to return to Herod and tell him where the child could be found, for Herod was jealous and sought to slay the child lest he grow to challenge his rule. So they departed into their own country by another way.

John the Baptist and Jesus

JOHN, called "the Baptist," came from "the hill country" where he lived on locusts and wild honey and dressed himself in garments of camel's hair caught round the waist by a leathern girdle. His father was Zacharias, a priest of the "course of Abijah." Elizabeth, his mother, was also of priestly descent and was a relative of Mary, the mother of Jesus.

As a babe of only a few weeks, John had known the wrath of Herod who was fearful for his crown and his power. Elizabeth knew that Herod had vowed to destroy all newborn children and sought to hide from the king's soldiers but was discovered and pursued into the hills. About to be overtaken by the assassins, she cried, "Mount of God, receive a mother with her child," and suddenly the mountain was divided and hid her from the enemy.

When, years later, John came out of the hills and the wilderness he bore a message of accusation and challenge which he hurled in the teeth of the multitudes who flocked from Jerusalem and all Judea and all the regions about Jordan to hear him preach. "Repent ye, for the kingdom of heaven is at hand," he cried with biting eloquence, "for this is he that was spoken of through Isaiah the prophet, saying, 'The voice of one crying in the wilderness, make ye ready the way of the Lord, make his path straight.' "

Many believed and were baptized in the waters of Jordan, repenting of their sins.

So popular was the preaching of John that a great many of the Pharisees and Sadducees, men who trusted in their descent from Abraham to save them, came to him and begged for his baptism. But John questioned their honesty and sensed hypocrisy in this act. "Ye offspring of vipers," he accused, "who warned you to flee from the wrath to come? Bring forth therefore fruit worthy of repentance. Think not to say within yourselves, 'We have Abraham to our father,' for I say unto you that God is able of these stones to raise up children unto Abraham.

"Even now the axe lieth at the root of the tree. Every tree therefore that bringeth not forth good fruit is hewn down and cast into the fire. I indeed baptize you in water unto repentance, but he that cometh after me is mightier than I, whose shoes I am not worthy to bear. He shall baptize you in the Holy Spirit and in fire; whose fan is in his hand, and he will thoroughly cleanse his threshing-floor. He will gather his wheat into the garner, but the chaff he will burn up with unquenchable fire."

These were hard, prophetic words and many cried out in terror, rushing down to the waters to escape if they might through John's baptism. As this holy man from the wilderness cried to the multitudes about him to repent and searched their souls with his strange, piercing eyes, and his more piercing words, a young man from Galilee, Jesus, stood and watched. He knew that what his cousin said was all too true and listened with growing interest. At last he stepped from the crowds and expressed a wish to be baptized of John.

The prophet recognized this humble carpenter from Nazareth as the Christ of whose coming he had been preaching and was afraid. "I have need to be baptized of thee," he said, "and cometh thou to me?"

Jesus saw further than John and answered him, "Suffer it now, for thus it becometh us to fulfill all righteousness."

In this John and Jesus found a common understanding. Both stood at the culmination of a long prophetic tradition. John was "the voice" of whom Isaiah spoke, the forerunner of prophetic lore. Jesus was the "Coming One" of all Jewish hope and preaching. Now, as the prophets of old had predicted, these two strains had met and prophecy was to be fulfilled. John saw all this in Jesus' answer and led him into the water to be baptized.

As the multitudes waited in silent awe, the two men walked into the waters of Jordan and John pronounced the absolution of baptism as he performed the ritual. Then, as they were coming up from the water "the heavens were opened unto him and he saw the Spirit of God descending as a dove, and coming unto him. And lo, a voice out of the heavens, saying, 'This is my beloved Son, in whom I am well pleased.'"

Jesus went from that experience to the hills and to his great work on earth. John continued to preach and accuse the evil of his day wherever he found it. It was inevitable that, in time, he would find evil in high places, even in the palace of the king. Herod, the king, had married Herodias, his brother's wife. John spoke out without reserve against this incestuous marriage, for which he incurred the wrath of the royal pair and was imprisoned. But, fearful of the multitude, who counted John a prophet, Herod hesitated to sentence him to death. Herod, however, pleased at the dancing of Salome, daughter of Herodias, "promised with an oath to give her whatsoever she would ask" and she, "being before instructed of her mother," asked that John's head be brought to her. Though still fearful of the mob, Herod nevertheless acceded to Salome's hideous request and sent his guards to the prison where, at his orders, John the Baptist was beheaded.

The Temptations in the Wilderness

AT HIS baptism Jesus caught a vision of his mission and of the work that lay ahead. He heard a voice from heaven and knew that his would not be an easy duty to perform. Perhaps he had sensed it before, but this moment had awakened him fully to the part he was to play during the years to come.

As with many men in times of great crisis, Jesus stole away from others to be alone for a while and think through the vision that had burst upon him. He journeyed into the wilderness, there to fast and think.

When he had fasted forty days and forty nights, he hungered. Then it was that the tempter came to him with a challenge: "If thou art the Son of God, command that these stones become bread." Bodily hunger possessed him, and he was sorely tempted to use the power that was his to his own good.

After a struggle, Jesus answered the tempter, "It is written, 'Man shall not live by bread alone, but by every word that proceedeth out of the mouth of God.' " Jesus saw that his mission was not to be that of a miracle-worker, nor was his power to be used selfishly.

Then the tempter took Jesus to Jerusalem and stood with him on the pinnacle of the temple, high above the passing throngs below. As they stood there together and watched people passing on the streets and going in and out of the temple, the tempter said to Jesus, "If thou art the Son of God, cast thyself down, for it is written: 'He shall give his angels charge concerning thee,' and 'On their hands they shall bear thee up, lest haply thou dash thy foot against a stone.' "

Here was the tempter suggesting to Jesus that he use his power as the Son of God to awe the people, to strike them with wonder at his miracle-working ability.

Jesus listened, but was not impressed. "Again it is written," he reminded the tempter, " 'Thou shalt not make trial of the Lord thy God.' "

The tempter was not foiled at this. Again he took Jesus to a place of temptation. This time it was an exceedingly high mountain from which it was possible for him to see "all the kingdoms of the world, and the glory of them." As they stood there watching, the tempter said, "All these things will I give thee, if thou wilt fall down and worship me."

To this Jesus gave the only possible answer, "Get thee hence, Satan, for it is written, 'Thou shalt worship the Lord thy God, and him only shalt thou serve.' "

Jesus had stood the test. He had considered the power that was his as the Son of God and had resisted every suggestion that he come before his people as a common miracle-worker able to perform for their amusement and wonderment. He had also decided that this power could never be used for himself. In this moment of victory, the tempter fled from him "and, behold, angels came and ministered unto him."

☆

Nicodemus Comes to Jesus

NICODEMUS was a Pharisee, that sect among the Jews given more to upholding the forms and observances rather than the spirit of religion. He was also a leader of the Jews, a man in high position.

Jesus had caught his imagination. Here was something new in the life of his people, a teacher with a high and challenging message. Something in Nicodemus responded to Jesus' teaching.

Seeking to understand Jesus better, Nicodemus came to him by night, for he feared to be seen entering his abode, and asked, "Rabbi, we know that thou art a teacher come from God. No one could do these signs that thou doest, except God be with him."

Then they talked for some time about Jesus' work and his mission among men. Nicodemus listened and was deeply impressed with the wisdom and spiritual insight which this lowly carpenter's son showed.

In the course of the conversation, Jesus said, "Except one be born anew, he cannot see the kingdom of heaven."

Nicodemus was a ruler, an administrator of great ability, a practical man. He could not fathom the meaning of this statement. "How can a man be born when he is old?" he asked. "Can he enter a second time into his mother's womb, and be born?"

Jesus saw at once that Nicodemus lacked that spiritual insight necessary to understand his mission. To help him, he began a careful and lengthy explanation of what to him was central in all his teaching.

"Verily, verily, I say unto you," he began, "except one be born of water and of the Spirit, he cannot enter into the kingdom of God. That which is born of the flesh is flesh, and that which is born of the Spirit is spirit. Marvel not that I said unto thee, 'Ye must be born anew.' The wind bloweth where it will, and thou hearest the voice thereof, but knowest not whence it cometh and whither it goeth. So is everyone that is born of the Spirit."

Nicodemus was mystified. "How can these things be?" he asked Jesus.

His inability to understand spiritual things surprised Jesus. "Art thou the teacher of Israel, and understandest not these things?" he asked. "Verily, verily, I say unto thee, *John 3:11* we speak that which we know and bear witness of that which we have seen, and ye receive not our witness. If I told you earthly things and ye believe not, how shall ye believe if I tell you heavenly things? No one hath ascended into heaven, but he that descended out of heaven, even the Son of Man, who is in heaven.

"As Moses lifted up the serpent in the wilderness, even so must the Son of man be lifted up that whosoever believeth may in him have eternal life."

Then Jesus gave Nicodemus a new view of God, one that showed him that God was more than a lawgiver and ruler. "For God so loved the world," he said, "that he gave his only begotten Son, that whosoever believeth on him should not perish, but have eternal life."

Long into the night these two men talked. One the teacher, and the other earnest and devout but hearing for the first time things which taxed his understanding. God sent his son, Jesus explained, not as a judge to call man to task for his minute sins, "but that the world might be saved through him." Judgment comes not from the divine bench nor according to a set and inexorable law, but because men refuse to follow the light that is in the world.

Jesus sought to show Nicodemus a new kind of God, one that he had never dreamed of before. It was hard for him to understand a God of love and forgiveness, for he was a ruler who knew law and law only. He had been too long steeped in the legal tradition.

As they talked, Nicodemus' inner eyes were opened and he began to understand more clearly than before the God of Jesus. He went out from there as the dawn was lighting the skies, and in his heart the dawn of understanding was lighting the dark recesses and driving out the shadows. Nicodemus saw the light that night. *John 3*

The Gadarene Demoniacs

FAME, like a haunting shadow, followed Jesus wherever he would go. It was a sorry world that he visited, where sickness and death waited at every door and where men and women cried for deliverance. He had the power to heal and power to raise from the dead. As the story of this man of power spread and grew, he could find no place where he could be alone.

Although he traveled to "the other side of the country of the Gadarenes," two unfortunates possessed of demons accosted him. They had been cast out by their people and lived among the tombs on the edge of town. Wild and maddened by their affliction, they attacked all who passed that way so that it was unsafe for travelers to come near to the garden of tombs.

As Jesus approached, these demented ones cried to him, "What have we to do with thee, thou Son of God? Art thou come to torment us before the time?" With such ravings they followed Jesus and cursed his presence.

Afar off from there a herd of swine was feeding and grunting contentedly. The demons knew that they could no longer hold their victims, for Jesus had come to rescue them. In their despair they cried unto him, "If thou cast us out, send us away into the herd of swine."

Jesus gave them permission, and they came out and went into the swine. At their coming the whole herd of swine rushed down the steep embankment to the sea and perished in its waters.

Naturally, this strange happening frightened the men who had been set to feed and care for the swine. They fled the scene and went into the city where they told everything that had befallen those possessed of demons and concerning the swine which they had been keeping.

This news set rumors flying throughout the city and many went out to see this Jesus who had power to cast out demons. The curiosity of the crowd was mixed with fear. Had not the demons destroyed the herd of one of them? What more might happen if Jesus remained among them? They were fearful and begged him to depart from their borders. Their swine were more important than their men. Let those possessed by demons rave among the tombs where they bothered no one, but the swine were food and income. These must be protected.

So Jesus took the boat and crossed over to his own city, leaving the Gadarenes alone with their wild men and their swine, each in its proper place, as they believed.

The Transfiguration

THREE men from among the disciples were closest to Jesus. They seemed somehow to understand him better than all the rest. Then, each one, in spite of his faults, possessed a virtue which Jesus admired.

There was Peter, great, impulsive Peter, the "rock" upon which Jesus could found his church. There was James, the meek and devoted follower of the Master. And there was John, whom Jesus loved more than all the others.

Jesus took these three, his inner circle, and went with them to the top of a high mountain away from the crowds and from friends who did not fully understand. There, in the quiet and serenity that is the mountain's, Jesus was transfigured before them. His face shone as the sun, and his garments became white as the light.

And with him stood two saints of yesteryears, Moses, the great leader of his people, and Elijah, who had been taken up into heaven in a whirlwind and in a chariot of fire drawn by steeds of fire. There they stood, the three, Jesus, Moses, and Elijah.

Peter was overcome at the sight and was carried away by enthusiasm. While the others were dumb with awe, he made a suggestion: "Lord, it is good for us to be here. If thou wilt, I will make here three tabernacles; one for thee, and one for Moses, and one for Elijah." He had no other desire, no plans beyond the moment. Why not, he thought, remain here always in the presence of these great? At the foot of the mountain the multitudes waited to harass the Master with their needs. They did not appeal to Peter at this moment. Here was the best, and he saw no reason why he should not remain in the presence of the best forever.

As he spoke a bright cloud overshadowed them and a voice spoke from the cloud, saying, "This is my beloved Son, in whom I am well pleased. Hear ye him." When the disciples heard the voice of God, they were afraid and fell on their faces and tried to hide themselves from the glory. But Jesus came and touched them and said, "Arise, and be not afraid." When they lifted up their eyes, they saw no one save Jesus only.

As they were coming down from the mountain, Jesus commanded them, saying, "Tell the vision to no man, until the Son of man be risen from the dead." This troubled his disciples much, for they knew not that he must suffer and die to fulfill his mission to mankind.

The Good Samaritan

AMONG those who sought to trap Jesus in some statement that might be used against him was a certain lawyer. This legalist stood up in the crowd around the Master and asked, "Teacher, what shall I do to inherit eternal life?"

Jesus recognized the man and answered him in his own terms, "What is written in the law? How readest thou?"

His questioner was not prepared for this simple answer and was taken aback for a moment. But he could not afford to back down now, so he answered from the law, "Thou shalt love the Lord thy God with all thy heart, and with all thy soul, and with all thy strength, and with all thy mind; and thy neighbor as thyself."

"Thou hast answered right," Jesus told him. "This do, and thou shalt live."

Jesus had the better of the argument, and the lawyer knew it. The crowd knew it also and some began to murmur against him. Wishing to justify himself and save his face, he asked, "And who is my neighbor?"

Jesus' answer was a story. "A certain man was going down from Jerusalem to Jericho, and he fell among robbers who both stripped him and beat him and departed, leaving him half dead.

"By chance a certain priest was going down that way. When he saw him, he passed by on the other side. In like manner a Levite also, when he came to the place and saw him, passed by on the other side.

"But a certain Samaritan, as he journeyed, came where he was. When he saw him, he was moved with compassion and came to him and bound up his wounds, pouring on them oil and wine. Then he set him on his own beast and brought him to an inn and took care of him.

"On the morrow he took out two shillings and gave them to his host saying, 'Take care of him, and whatsoever thou spendest more, I, when I come back again, will repay thee.'"

This was the end of the story. After a moment Jesus looked the lawyer squarely in the eye and said, "Which of these three, thinkest thou, proved neighbor unto him that fell among the robbers?"

The answer came, "He that showed mercy unto him."

When the lawyer had answered thus, Jesus said very quietly, "Go, and do thou likewise."

Mary and Martha

IN A certain village two women lived. They were sisters, but quite different in their ways.

Mary was leisurely in all she did. She had time to sit and talk with friends. When anyone visited the sisters, Mary would let other duties go to spend time with the guest, listening and talking.

Martha was the busy housekeeper. Her first duty was with the cooking and the cleaning. She was unhappy if one household duty was undone. Even when guests came, she felt the burden of her work and would not turn aside even for a moment.

When one day a special guest came to their home, Mary and Martha acted as they were accustomed. The guest was

Jesus. And Mary stopped her work and "sat at the Lord's feet and heard his words." She listened as he talked with her about his work and the people he had met and served. They talked of many things, and Mary was happy.

Martha wanted very much to sit down and talk with Jesus. She heard the murmur of voices in the other room as her sister and their beloved guest talked on, and she saw the housework that needed to be done,—cooking, cleaning, washing, and a great deal more.

Finally, Martha broke into the room and complained to Jesus, saying, "Lord, dost thou not care that my sister did leave me to serve alone? Bid her therefore that she help me."

This was a very natural request. Martha felt that the work had to be done and that Mary should help rather than leave all the work for her while she enjoyed the Lord's visit. But Jesus realized how warped was her understanding of important things.

"Martha, Martha," he said, "thou art anxious and troubled about many things. But one thing is needed. Mary hath chosen the good part, which shall not be taken away from her." As Martha thought about what Jesus had said, she realized how things that are so important at one time may be cast into the shadows at another.

The Woman Taken in Adultery

EARLY in the morning Jesus came into the temple and a great crowd gathered there to see and hear him teach. When he had seated himself among the multitude and began to speak, a group of scribes and Pharisees burst in, pushed through the throng, and dragged to where Jesus sat a woman.

Her clothes were torn and dirty and her hair was a tangled mass. On her face were scars and fresh scratches.

This woman had been surprised in the act of adultery and the Pharisees, purists in religious matters and unbending legalists, had dragged her straight to Jesus.

"Teacher," they shouted as soon as the confusion created by their presence had subsided enough for them to be heard, "this woman hath been taken in adultery, in the very act. Now in the law Moses commanded us to stone her. What then sayest thou of her?"

They thought this would trap Jesus. He had preached love and forgiveness, and most of those present had heard him. But here was the law of Moses. If he refused to give his verdict according to Moses' law, the people would see that he was a dangerous man, teaching others to disobey the most sacred and ancient laws of the people. If he ruled as the law required, he would convict himself of insincerity and lose the people's confidence. Indeed, Jesus' enemies thought they had pinned him on the horns of a dilemma.

Jesus stood quietly for a moment, looking first at the poor, unfortunate woman who cringed at his feet expecting to feel the first stone any moment, then at the crowd. Then he stooped down and drew meaningless lines in the sand.

When the accusers continued to taunt him and demand an answer and the crowd began to murmur against him, Jesus stood up and with fire in his eyes said, "He that is without sin among you, let him first cast a stone at her." Then he stooped down again and wrote in the sand.

There was silence in the crowd. The woman trembled, not realizing what had been said. She had heard Jesus say, "Cast a stone," and believed that death was the verdict. After a time her accusers began to steal away one by one silently. The crowd dispersed. At last Jesus was left alone with the woman.

And Jesus stood up and said unto her, "Woman, where are they? Did no man condemn thee?"

"No man, Lord."

"Neither do I condemn thee. Go thy way. From hence-forth sin no more." *John 8*

☆

Lazarus Is Raised from the Dead *John 11*

IN THE little town of Bethany, just fifteen furlongs from Jerusalem, lived three of Jesus' dearest friends,—Mary, her sister Martha, and their brother Lazarus. When Lazarus fell ill, the sisters sent word to their friend, saying, "Lord, behold, he whom thou lovest is sick."

When Jesus received this news, he told his disciples, "This sickness is not unto death, but for the glory of God, that the Son of God may be glorified thereby." So he did not hasten to the bedside of his friend, but remained where he was for two days.

Then Jesus suggested to his disciples that they go into Judea. The disciples were opposed to this since, as they pointed out, the Jews there were seeking to stone Jesus and to make such a trip at that time would be highly dangerous.

Jesus met their warning with, "Are there not twelve hours in the day? If a man walk in the day, he stumbleth not, because he seeth the light of this world. But if a man walk in the night, he stumbleth, because the light is not in him."

When his disciples continued to object to his trip into Judea, Jesus told them, "Our friend Lazarus is fallen asleep, but I go that I may awake him out of sleep." Not under-standing that Jesus spoke of Lazarus' death, the disciples said, "Lord, if he is fallen asleep, he will recover."

Then Jesus told them plainly, "Lazarus is dead." To calm their sorrow, he added, "I am glad for your sakes that I was not there, to the intent ye may believe; nevertheless let us go unto him."

Thomas, who is called Didymus, was overcome with grief and cried, "Let us also go, that we may die with him."

When Jesus and his disciples arrived at Bethany, they found that Lazarus had been dead and in his tomb for four days and that many of the Jews had come to Martha and Mary to comfort them in their sorrow. Hearing that Jesus was nearby, Martha came to him with, "Lord, if thou hadst been here, my brother had not died. And even now I know that whatsoever thou shalt ask of God, God will give thee."

Jesus answered, "Thy brother shall rise again."

"I know that he shall rise again in the resurrection at the last day."

Then Jesus told her, "I am the resurrection and the life. He that believeth on me, though he die, yet shall he live; and whosoever liveth and believeth on me shall never die. Believest thou this?"

Martha's answer was quick and sure, "Yea, Lord, I have believed that thou art the Christ, the Son of God, even he that cometh into the world." Then she ran to her sister and whispered to her, "The teacher is here and calleth thee."

Mary arose quickly and went to him. The Jews who were with her in the house consoling her, thinking that she was going to Lazarus' tomb to weep, followed her.

When Mary came to Jesus she fell down at his feet and cried, "Lord, if thou hadst been here my brother had not died."

Jesus, seeing her weeping and hearing the mourning of the Jews who came with her, was troubled and asked, "Where have ye laid him?" As they approached the tomb Jesus wept. Some of the Jews saw him weeping and said, "Behold, how he loved him!" Others speculated, "Could not this man, who opened the eyes of him that was blind, have caused that this man also should not die?"

When they came to the tomb, Jesus asked that the stone be rolled away from the door, but Martha objected, saying, "Lord, by this time the body decayeth, for he hath been dead four days."

Irritated, Jesus replied, "Said I not unto thee that, if thou believest, thou shouldest see the glory of God?" Then they rolled the stone away.

As Mary and Martha and the Jews gathered at the now opened tomb of Lazarus, Jesus lifted up his eyes and prayed, "Father, I thank thee that thou heardest me. And I knew that thou hearest me always, but because of the multitude that standeth around I said it, that they may believe that thou didst send me." When he had prayed, he cried in a loud voice, "Lazarus, come forth!"

As he spoke, "he that was dead came forth, bound hand and foot with grave clothes, and his face was bound about with a napkin."

Many who saw Lazarus walking from his grave believed on Jesus, but some went to the Pharisees to consider what might be done to get rid of Jesus, fearing that he would cause trouble among the people.

☆

The Triumphal Entry John 12

JESUS saw the climax of his career approaching. Keen of understanding, he knew that it would be a pattern of high triumph and deep humiliation, of intense loyalty and heart-breaking disappointments, of exaltation and suffering. Great multitudes had gathered to hear him teach and to bask in the sun of his miracles. But there was an ever-increasing under-current of official opposition which could lead only to the cross.

With this all clearly in his mind, Jesus made a hard de-cision. He could remain among the villagers, away from the center of Hebrew life and tradition. Here his work might go on indefinitely. Or, he could move directly into the center and thereby throw down the challenge of his mission to Jewish officialdom. This would lead inevitably to official condemnation and perhaps death.

Jesus chose the latter, and moved on toward Jerusalem. As he drew near to the city, he called two disciples to his side and gave them specific directions, saying, "Go into the village that is over against you, and straightway ye shall find an ass tied, and a colt with her. Loose them and bring them unto me. And if anyone say aught unto you, ye shall say, 'The Lord hath need of them,' and straightway he will send them."

The disciples did as Jesus instructed and found the ass and her colt tied. They brought them to Jesus and put their garments on the ass and Jesus sat thereon.

In this humble fashion Jesus set out for Jerusalem and the great feast that was soon to be celebrated there. As they rode along, some were reminded of an ancient prophecy of Isaiah: "Tell ye the daughter of Zion, behold, thy King cometh unto thee, meek, and riding upon an ass, and upon a colt the foal of an ass." They told others and soon the roadway was lined with multitudes spreading their garments in the way while some cut branches from the trees and spread them on the ground in front of the advancing party.

Then, as they came near to Jerusalem, voices began to take up a chorus, singing, "Hosanna to the Son of David. Blessed is he that cometh in the name of the Lord. Hosanna in the highest." The singing increased as people rushed from everywhere to see this strange thing, a prophet riding into Jerusalem on an ass with her colt following close behind. Soon the highway was packed with the devout and the curious so that the little party moved slowly and often had to stop for a time.

Naturally, news of this spread through Jerusalem and the city was stirred with conflicting notions. Many asked, "Who is this?" And the multitudes answered, "This is the prophet Jesus, from Nazareth of Galilee." Then greater and greater hosts took up the cry, "Hosanna in the highest! Hosanna to the Son of David!"

But the scribes and others of official Jerusalem were worried. Men and women were deserting their sacrifices and religious duties to crowd around this Nazarene whose reputation in Jerusalem was not of the best. He was disrupting the routine of tradition, and many a knee trembled lest he foment a revolution and seek to overthrow those in power.

Jesus rode meekly into Jerusalem, but his very meekness caught the imagination of the people and their ancient dream of a Messiah rose again before them. Here was prophecy fulfilled, and there were many in Jerusalem who saw this lowly Nazarene as the promised deliverer. Certainly, the powerful were afraid and took counsel among themselves how they might nip this in the bud.

The Last Supper

THE time of Passover was approaching and devout Jews everywhere were preparing for the traditional meal commemorating that awful night when the angel of death struck down the first-born of every Egyptian house but passed over the houses of the Jews who were held in slavery.

Great throngs had come to Jerusalem to celebrate the occasion in the holy city, the center of their faith. Among these was Jesus and his little band of disciples. They had come into the city in triumph and Jesus had spent the intervening days teaching in synagogues and on the streets and answering the challenges of numerous official bodies who sought to trick him into saying something that could be used against him.

Now the time of the feast was approaching. It was the first day of unleavened bread. Jesus' disciples came to him and asked, "Where wilt thou that we make ready for thee to eat the passover?"

Jesus answered, "Go into the city to such a man and say unto him, 'The Teacher saith, "My time is at hand. I keep the passover at thy house with my disciples."'" The disciples did as Jesus instructed, and prepared the passover in an upper room given them by the man they met.

The night came and Jesus was gathered with the twelve in the upper room, presiding at the feast. While they were eating Jesus startled them by declaring: "Verily I say unto you, that one of you shall betray me!" There was silence around the table. Sorrow was written on the faces of the disciples. When they had recovered from the first shock of Jesus' words, each one asked, "Is it I, Lord?"

Then Jesus answered, "He that dipped his hand with me in the dish, the same shall betray me." Then he added a word of explanation, "The Son of man goeth, even as it is written of him; but woe unto that man through whom the Son of man is betrayed! Good were it for that man if he had not been born."

Judas Iscariot had heard all this unmoved. When Jesus finished, he turned to him and asked, "Is it I, Rabbi?"

"Thou hast said," was Jesus' answer. Then Judas stole unnoticed from the group to prepare the betrayal as he had bargained earlier in the evening.

As the rest were eating, Jesus took the bread, broke it, and gave it to each of his disciples, saying, "Take, eat. This is my body." Then he took a cup and, after giving thanks, passed it to each one, saying, "Drink ye all of this. This is my blood of the covenant which is poured out for many unto remission of sins. But I say unto you, I shall not drink henceforth of this fruit of the vine until that day when I drink it new in my father's kingdom."

These were strange words and the disciples listened to

them without understanding. Body! Blood! Betrayal! What did it all mean? Jesus offered no explanation, nor did they seek any. But deep in the conscience of each there was something stirring, a vague realization that this was far more than just another passover meal. But what, no one could say.

After Jesus had spoken, they sang a hymn and went out into the mount of Olives.

Jesus in the Garden of Gethsemane

JESUS ate the passover meal with his disciples. While the little band sat about the table in that upper room, Jesus had seen Judas leave quietly and knew that one among his chosen twelve was a traitor.

The meal completed, Jesus and his friends went out into the inky darkness and to a garden called Gethsemane. As they walked along together strange thoughts must have filled their minds. A cloud seemed to be settling over the group and the disciples were confused. What had Jesus meant by his words at the table, words about body and blood, "this is my blood, drink ye all of it?" Who would betray him?

Thinking, questioning among themselves, scarcely daring to breathe the queries that hung on their lips, the disciples followed their teacher silently. When they had walked some distance into the garden, Jesus broke the silence with, "Sit ye here, while I go yonder and pray." Then he took with him Peter, James, and John, and walked deeper into the garden.

But even these, his closest friends, could give him no comfort. He talked with them, pouring out his heart to the three from whom he might have expected some understanding of the crisis he was facing. They were not able to rise to the occasion, but remained earthbound.

At last, almost in despair, Jesus turned to the three and said, "My soul is exceeding sorrowful, even unto death. Abide ye here and watch with me." With this plea for companionship Jesus went forward a little and fell to the ground and prayed.

"My Father," he cried, "if it be possible, let this cup pass away from me. Nevertheless, not as I will, but as thou wilt." The task was almost too great for him. He prayed for a way out. But this prayer was followed by an avowal of faith, "not my will, but thine."

Rising from the ground with new courage coursing through his body, Jesus would have told his disciples of the victory that was his. He rushed to where he had left his friends, and found them sleeping. "Peter," he cried, "could ye not watch with me one hour? Watch and pray that ye enter not into temptation. The spirit indeed is willing, but the flesh is weak."

Twice more Jesus went aside and prayed, "My Father, if this cannot pass away except I drink it, thy will be done." And each time he returned to his friends to find them sleeping. At last, finding them asleep for the third time, he said, "Sleep on now and take your rest. Behold, the hour is at hand and the Son of man is betrayed into the hands of sinners. Arise, let us be going. Behold, he is at hand that betrayeth me!"

As the sleepy disciples stirred themselves and opened their heavy eyes, they saw a great multitude with swords and staves, and Judas in the lead. He stepped from among the crowd and kissed Jesus, the sign of betrayal which he had planned with Jesus' enemies among the chief priests and elders of the people.

Of course some of those with Jesus jumped to his defense, but it was too late. They had failed their Master when he needed them most. They had slept while he fought alone the greatest battle of his life.

Judas Iscariot Betrays Jesus

SILENTLY, Judas, who is called Iscariot, stole into the night. Inside the house, Jesus and his disciples ate the passover. Outside, in the dark, soldiers of the chief priests waited for final instructions from the arch betrayer.

Several days before the passover, Judas had gone to the chief priests with a proposition. "What are ye willing to give me," he had asked, "and I will deliver him unto you?" They knew that he meant Jesus whom they hated. A bargain was made and "they weighed unto him thirty pieces of silver." Since that time he had sought opportunity to deliver Jesus to them. The time had come and all was in readiness. While Jesus ate and drank with his closest friends, one whom he had trusted whispered directions to the soldiers who were to arrest him in the name of the chief priests.

Judas, we are told, came to Jesus with unclean hands but with an earnest but weak desire to wash them clean. Even before he was born, his mother, Cyborea, had a dream in which she learned that he was destined to murder his father, commit incest with his mother, and sell his God. This so frightened her that, when the child was born, she and her husband enclosed him in a chest and threw it into the sea hoping to destroy both the babe and the curse.

Picked up after the cask had drifted to a foreign shore, the young Judas was reared at court where he had every opportunity and the finest of training. But, in a moment of passion he committed a murder and was forced to flee for his life. Coming to Judea, he entered the service of Pontius

Pilate as a page. During the time he lived in the court of Pilate he was found by his father and felt forced to murder him to hide his identity.

Having learned the secret of his birth from his father, Judas was filled with remorse mixed with hatred for the treatment his parents had given him. After his father lay dead, remorse got the upper hand and he went to Jesus, a prophet who, he had heard, had the power to forgive sins. Jesus accepted him as one of his disciples and had promoted him to a position of trust in the little band of twelve.

Now the old curse had returned and Judas was about the business of selling his God. With the soldiers of the chief priests, he went to the mount of Olives where there was a garden called Gethsemane and waited.

Then Jesus came with the eleven. Judas watched as they talked beneath the olive trees. He saw Jesus leave the others and drop on his knees in prayer. He held the soldiers back until the prayers were finished and Jesus was about to leave the garden. Even Judas could not find it in his miserable soul to interrupt the master at prayer.

When Jesus and his disciples were about to return to the town, Judas signalled to the soldiers and the mob of ruffians that had come out with them. These crept among the trees until they had surrounded the little band of disciples. Then Judas stepped from the shadows greeting the Lord as though he had been absent on some legitimate errand and just found the party which he had been forced to leave. "Hail, Rabbi," he said, and kissed him.

Jesus knew the kiss of betrayal and said, "Friend, do that for which thou art come." Then the soldiers and ruffians appeared from all sides and laid hands upon Jesus to take him to the high priest. This action angered Peter so that he took out his sword and struck off the ear of a servant of the high priest. When Jesus saw this, he rebuked Peter, saying, "Put up again thy sword into its place, for all they that take the sword shall perish with the sword."

Then Jesus sought to explain what had happened to his dazed disciples. "Thinkest thou that I cannot beseech my Father, and he shall even now send me more than twelve legions of angels?" he asked. "How then should the scriptures be fulfilled, that thus it must be?"

Jesus was led away to stand trial and eventually to be crucified. But Judas Iscariot stole away to suffer the full realization of his crime. The curse which his parents had sought to avert and which he, by turning to the master, had endeavored to block, had been fulfilled to the last bitter word. The silver he had received burned in his hands, for he had sold his God, and at a price so cheap.

He could stand it no longer. When men found him later, he was hanged, destroyed by his own hands.

The Trial of Jesus

THE MULTITUDE, armed with swords and staves, took Jesus in the darkness of night. He had eaten the passover meal with his disciples and had gone out with them into the garden of Gethsemane to pray. It was here that Judas and a band of fanatics found him and put him under arrest.

Since they wished no delay, they took Jesus immediately, even though it was late at night, to the house of Caiaphas, the high priest. Here the scribes and the elders were waiting. Arrayed in their robes of office and sitting or standing, whichever was in accord with rank, they were solemn-faced and with dignity when Jesus was dragged in. Witnesses were called, most of them false. But, try as they may, it seemed impossible to make a case against Jesus. The Jews wanted reason for putting him to death. All they could get were reasons for his living longer than all the rest.

When the accusers were almost despairing and the patience of the high priest was strained almost to the limit, two appeared who testified, saying, "This man said, 'I am able to destroy the temple of God, and to build it in three days.'" This was indeed blasphemy. The temple had taken years to build. It was sacred to all Jews. Here was talk of destroying it. And building it back in three days! A dangerous miracle-worker!

The high priest stood up and waited for Jesus to make answer to this accusation. When he remained silent, the high priest said, "Answerest thou nothing? What is it which these witness against you?" Jesus said not a word. "I adjure you," the priest pleaded, "by the living God, that thou tell us whether thou are the Christ, the Son of God?"

"Thou hast said," Jesus responded. "Nevertheless I say unto you, henceforth ye shall see the Son of man sitting at the right hand of Power, and coming on the clouds of heaven."

This angered the high priest so much that he rent his garments and cried with a loud voice, "He hath spoken blasphemy. What further need have we of witnesses? Behold, now ye have heard the blasphemy, what think ye?"

And the crowd answered as one man, "He is worthy of death!" Then they began to spit on him and kick and slap him as their anger grew. Some slapped at him and then said, "Prophesy unto us, thou Christ, who is he that struck thee?"

But this was the season of the passover and the Jews did not want the responsibility of killing Jesus on their hands at this time. So, the next morning, they took him before the Roman governor, Pontius Pilate, and began to accuse him bitterly. Pilate, a weak but fair man, wanted to hear all the testimony. After the accusers had finished their tirade, he asked Jesus, "Art thou the King of the Jews?"

"Thou sayest," Jesus answered, and was silent.

"Hearest thou not how many things they witness against

thee?" Pilate continued. But Jesus gave them no answer. He knew that nothing he could say would convince his accusers, and he knew that Pilate was subject to too much pressure to be swayed by anything he might say.

It was a custom at the feast of the passover for the Roman governor to release a prisoner, chosen by the Jews, as a token of respect for the ancient festival. There was at that time a noted prisoner in the Roman jail whose career had become known everywhere. Knowing that Jesus was accused because of envy and wishing to avoid the responsibility of making a decision, Pilate said to the accusers and the crowd that had followed them to his chambers, "Whom will ye that I release unto you, Barabbas or Jesus, who is called the Christ?"

At this moment Pilate's wife came in and whispered something very important to him. She had dreamed something dreadful and feared. "Hast thou nothing to do with this righteous man. I have suffered many things this day in a dream because of him," she warned.

This was no place for a weak man such as Pilate. It demanded strength to make the right decision in spite of all pressure, and Pilate did not have such strength. He hoped to escape by throwing the decision back upon the crowd. Certainly, he thought, they would not release Barabbas.

But he was mistaken. No sooner had he made the request than the crowd began to shout for Barabbas. Pilate then asked, "What then shall I do unto Jesus who is called the Christ?"

The priests and scribes had stirred the crowd to white frenzy so that this question brought great shouts of, "Let him be crucified!" Pilate sought to change their minds by asking for specific charges against him, but they were by that time in no mood to listen. "Crucify him! Crucify him!" they kept shouting.

In despair, Pilate took a basin of water and, in the presence of the multitudes, washed his hands. When he had finished, he said, "I am innocent of the blood of this righteous man. See ye to it."

The crowd cried back, "His blood be on us and on our children!"

Then Pilate set Barabbas free and turned Jesus over to the people to be crucified.

The Crucifixion

THIS was a great day for the enemies of Jesus. All their hatred of him and his teachings, all their cruelty were turned loose.

At the praetorium, where he was taken after Pontius Pilate had pronounced the verdict of death, the governor's soldiers stripped him and placed a scarlet robe over his shoulders. A crown of thorns was pressed on his brow until blood dripped from the wounds. Someone pushed a reed in his hand.

As Jesus stood there, quiet and serene, the crowd milled about him. Some dropped to their knees in front of him, mocking and crying, "Hail, King of the Jews!" Others spat at him, while some struck him with reeds or with their hands.

When the fury of the crowd was spent, the scarlet robe was taken from him and he was dressed in his own garments. Then began the procession to Golgotha, "the place of the skull." Jesus was in the lead, dragging on his back the heavy cross upon which he was to be crucified. Behind him were two criminals sentenced to die with him. They, too, dragged their crosses. Then came the soldiers and the shouting, jeering crowds. On the edge of the crowd were a few of Jesus' friends not daring to make themselves known lest the fury of the mob be turned on them.

A pious woman in the crowd called Veronica was moved

with pity by the spectacle of Jesus carrying his cross and handed him her kerchief to wipe the drops of agony from his brow. The Lord accepted the offering and, after using the cloth, returned it to her with the image of his face miraculously impressed on it. The "veil," as it came to be called, was preserved by sorrowing followers of the Christ and lies today among the sacred relics in Saint Peter's at Rome.

They were only a short way on the march when Simon, a man of Cyrene, was pulled from the crowd and forced to carry Jesus' cross. This was done to make Jesus' mockery more bitter, for, as some were saying, "Must a king carry his own cross? No! Let him walk in royal dignity!"

When they were come to Golgotha, one of the soldiers gave Jesus wine mixed with gall, very bitter, which he refused. Then, in solemn ceremony, they raised him upon the cross, drove the nails through his hands and feet, and pronounced their job done.

Some were fixing over his head the accusation, *This Is Jesus the King of the Jews;* others were casting lots for his garments.

The two robbers were crucified with him, one on the left hand and the other on the right. There they hung. Three men on three crosses! Those that passed by railed at him, saying, "Thou that destroyest the temple, and buildest it in three days, save thyself. If thou art the Son of God, come down from the cross!" The chief priests, with the scribes and the elders, mocked him, saying, "He saved others; himself he cannot save. He is the King of Israel. Let him now come down from the cross, and we will believe in him. He trusted on God. Let him deliver him now, if he desireth him; for he said, 'I am the Son of God.' "

Likewise the robbers, as they writhed in the agony of their crosses, cast reproach upon him.

Now, there was darkness over the land from the sixth to the ninth hour. About the ninth hour Jesus cried in a loud voice, saying, "My God, my God, why hast thou forsaken me?" Some of the crowd that lingered nearby heard him cry and thought he was asking for Elijah.

When he cried again, there was a great earthquake and the veil of the temple was rent in two from top to bottom. Tombs were opened, and many bodies of the saints who had fallen asleep were raised. When the soldiers who had been set to guard the place saw what was happening, they were exceedingly fearful and said, "Truly this was the Son of God."

Some women, who had followed afar off, ministered unto him and wept at the foot of his cross when at last he yielded up his spirit.

The Resurrection

AMONG the little band of broken-hearted men and women who watched Jesus die on the cross was a wealthy merchant from Arimathea named Joseph. He had been a disciple of Jesus, but secretly "for fear of the Jews."

This man had had a new tomb hewn out of a great rock that lay in a garden near the place where Jesus was crucified and he wanted to give it as the last resting place of the Master whom he had loved, but secretly.

So, he went to Pilate, the Roman ruler of Judea, and asked that he might have the body of Jesus for burial. This simple request was granted, but only after Pilate and his soldiers made sure that Jesus was dead by piercing his side with a spear.

With the help of Nicodemus, the one who had come to Jesus by night and been told the mystery of the new birth, Joseph of Arimathea carried the body to his new tomb. There they covered Jesus' body with a mixture of myrrh and aloes, as was the custom, and wrapped it in a clean linen cloth. A great stone was rolled against the door of the tomb, sealing it against any man or beast that might seek to disturb the dead.

Then Joseph and Nicodemus went away leaving Mary Magdalene and Mary, the mother of James, sitting by the sepulchre weeping.

This all happened on the day of preparation, or late on a Friday, as we reckon time.

On the day after the preparation, many important men, including the chief priests and the Pharisees, were gathered with Pilate and talking about the events of the day before. One of this august body remembered a strange prediction.

"Sir," said he, addressing Pilate, "we remember what that deceiver Jesus said while he was yet alive, 'After three days I rise again.' Command therefore that the sepulchre be made sure until the third day, lest haply his disciples come and steal him away, and say unto the people, 'He is risen from the dead.' "

Pilate was not overly concerned with this possibility. But, to satisfy the fears of these important Jews and to make doubly certain that he be not placed in an embarrassing situation, he said, "Ye have a guard: go, make it as sure as you can."

And they went and sealed the stone with the great seal of Roman authority and placed a guard before the stone that held the door. Then they went away, satisfied.

Now, "late on the sabbath day, as it began to dawn toward the first day of the week," Mary Magdalene and "the other Mary" returned to the tomb. But, as they walked along the way they began to wonder how they could roll the stone from the door and enter the sepulchre to care for their Lord's body. But, as they drew near, they saw in the dim morning light that the stone was gone and that the sepulchre stood open.

Frightened at what they had seen, the women ran to where Simon Peter and John, "the disciple whom Jesus loved," were walking, and cried out, "They have taken away the Lord out of the tomb, and we know not where they have laid him!"

Hearing this, the two disciples ran to the tomb and looked inside. It was true, just as the women had said. The tomb was empty. Where Jesus had been laid there was only the linen cloth in which his body had been wrapped. The napkin that was upon his head was rolled up in a place by itself.

The men were satisfied. Something had happened which they did not understand, "for as yet they knew not the scripture, that he must rise again from the dead." So they went away to their homes to meditate. But Mary lingered behind, weeping.

Then she turned to take one last look at the spot where her Lord had lain. But the tomb was not empty as before. Two angels were there sitting, one at the head and the other at the foot where Jesus had lain. And, as she looked, they said unto her, "Woman, why weepest thou?"

And she answered through her tears, "Because they have taken away my Lord, and I know not where they have laid him."

Then she turned away in despair. But, there in the path was one whom she thought to be the gardener. He, too, asked her, "Woman, why weepest thou? Whom seekest thou?"

And she answered, "Sir, if thou hast borne him hence, tell me where thou hast laid him, and I will take him away."

Then she heard a voice speaking softly, "Mary," and she knew that it was not the gardener but Jesus risen from the tomb, and she answered him in Hebrew, "Rabboni," which means teacher.

And Jesus said unto her, "Touch me not, for I am not yet ascended unto the Father. But go unto my brethren, and say to them, 'I ascend unto my Father and your Father, and my God and your God.'" And he was gone.

Mary Magdalene ran until she came to where the disciples were gathered together in sorrow, and to this sorrowing group she brought the greatest news of all, crying: "I have seen the Lord!"

On the Road to Emmaus

SORROW deeper than man had ever known was settling over the little band of Jesus' disciples. They had companied with him until each felt he knew the master's innermost thoughts. He had kindled in them a great hope, hope that he was the Messiah for whom their nation waited and of whom they dreamed.

But all this was dashed to the ground. They had seen him taken in the garden, tried before Pontius Pilate and the Sanhedrin, and crucified between two thieves. Now the tomb in which they had laid him so tenderly was empty. There was a rumor, started some said by Mary, that he had risen from the dead. Who could believe rumors? No, this was another dream too beautiful to last.

Two from among the disciples set off for a village called Emmaus, threescore furlongs from Jerusalem. On the way they talked about events of the last few days and wept as they remembered the tragedy of it all. Questions rose in their minds that they could not answer.

As these two walked, a stranger joined them, a traveler who happened, they thought, to be going their way and wished company on his journey. "What communications are these that ye have one with another, as ye walk?" he asked to begin a conversation.

At this they stopped for a moment and looked at the stranger with astonishment and sadness. "Dost thou alone sojourn in Jerusalem and not know the things which are come to pass there in these days?" the one called Cleopas asked.

"What things?" the stranger questioned.

"The things concerning Jesus the Nazarene, who was a prophet mighty in deed and word before God and all the people; and how the chief priests and our rulers delivered him up to be condemned to death, and crucified him," they answered. Then, plumbing the depths of sorrow and despair, one of them said, "But we hoped that it was he who should redeem Israel."

After they had walked on for a while in silence, the one who had spoken first, Cleopas by name, said, half to himself and half to his companions, "Besides all this, it is now the third day since these things came to pass. Certain women of our company amazed us, having been early at the tomb. When they found not his body they came, saying, that they had also seen a vision of angels, who said that he was alive. Certain of them that were with us went to the tomb, and found it even so as the women had said, but him they saw not."

This was the story, all of it; a story of hope and despair, and of credulous women telling a story with little evidence to sustain its truth.

Then the stranger, who they thought must be a rabbi or someone schooled in the prophets, upbraided them for their lack of understanding, saying, "O foolish men, and slow of heart to believe in all that the prophets have spoken! Behooved it not the Christ to suffer these things and to enter into his glory?"

Beginning from Moses and calling to witness all the prophets, one by one, he interpreted each saying concerning the Christ and showed them how it was fulfilled in the events of the last few weeks, happenings that had cast them down with sadness.

When they arrived at Emmaus the stranger "made as though he would go further," but they asked him to remain with them for the night. He consented, and they entered an inn where food was served and drink. "And it came to pass, when he had sat down with them to meat, he took the bread and blessed; and breaking it, he gave to them. And their eyes were opened, and they knew him." Then, as in a flash, he vanished out of their sight.

For a moment the two men were stunned beyond speech. Then, as they recovered from the shock, they said one to another, "Was not our heart burning within us, while he spake to us in the way, while he opened to us the scriptures?" They rose up immediately and hastened back to Jerusalem. There they found the eleven, for Judas had hanged himself, gathered with other sorrowing followers of the Lord. To these they broke the news, saying, "The Lord is risen indeed, and hath appeared to Simon." Then they told every detail of the trip to Emmaus and how they had talked with Jesus whom they knew not until he blessed the bread at the inn. This news brought happiness and hope to those assembled and a new confidence for the days that lay ahead.

Peter's Sermon at Pentecost

JESUS' DISCIPLES were alone. They had seen their teacher and master crucified. They had talked with him after his resurrection. They had seen him ascend into heaven and had returned to Jerusalem to "get hold of themselves" after the tragic experiences of the last few days.

Hitherto it had been possible for them to turn to Jesus for advice and comfort when defeat threatened or tragedy overwhelmed them. Now the worst tragedy they could imagine was upon them and there seemed nowhere to turn. Jesus had left them alone. There was danger that all his work would come to naught. It was highly probable that the same forces that had brought about the death of Jesus would turn on the disciples now and eliminate them. This was indeed a tragic moment.

As so often happens, when a leader is needed, he appears. This time it was Peter. Impulsive, loyal, repentent Peter stood in the midst of the disciples and said the words necessary to bolster their failing courage and fire them with enthusiasm for the task ahead. Peter was the source of strength and courage so necessary at this moment.

It was on the day of Pentecost, the Feast of Weeks. The disciples, and some others who were loyal to the cause, were gathered in one place praying and talking of events of the last month. Of a sudden there came from heaven a great sound like that of the rushing of a mighty wind. Then tongues appeared, like as fire, touching each one present and filling all with the Holy Spirit so that each could speak in a different tongue.

There followed a thing most miraculous. The devout Jews from all nations under the sun who were in Jerusalem heard men speaking in their own tongues and telling of Jesus and his salvation. Naturally they listened. Here were Galileans standing and speaking the language of Parthians, Medes, Elamites, of men dwelling in Mesopotamia, Judea, Cappadocia, Pontus, Phrygia, and in numerous other parts of the world. The people were amazed and said one to another, "What meaneth this?"

Some, who could not understand these languages and spoke only their own, believed these men to be "filled with new wine" and thus thick of tongue.

When a great crowd had gathered, Peter stood among them and said, "Ye men of Judea and all ye that dwell at Jerusalem, be it known unto you, and give ear unto my words. These are not drunken, as ye suppose, seeing it is but the third hour of the day." Rather, he told them, this that they saw was but the fulfilling of the words of the prophet Joel who predicted that in the last days the Spirit would be poured out upon the righteous and they should prophesy and show many wonders in the world.

Then Peter told the story of Jesus and of the resurrection, a story already familiar to many who listened. The people, he said, had killed Jesus, but God had raised him from the dead. Now Jesus sits upon the throne of God and will rule the world in righteousness.

This powerful sermon struck home to many and a great cry went up when he had finished, "What shall we do?" Peter was ready with an answer, "Repent ye, and be baptized every one of you in the name of Jesus Christ unto the remission of your sins, and ye shall receive the gift of the Holy Spirit."

About three thousand souls received the word and were baptized on that day. A great many joined with the apostles to preach and minister to those in need. Others sold their possessions and gave the money to the poor, and a great host "continued steadfastly in the apostles' teaching and fellowship, in the breaking of bread and the prayers."

The Work of Stephen

THE ASCENSION of Jesus marked the beginning of widespread preaching which resulted in a host of new disciples from among all nations and all walks of life. The little group that Jesus left grew rapidly, due to the inspired preaching of Peter and the apostles.

Such rapid growth often breeds trouble. In this instance the apostles were so busy preaching and teaching that they neglected the widows in the daily ministration. The Grecian Jews murmured against the Hebrews because of this, and the apostles realized that they were right.

To solve this problem the apostles called together the multitude of disciples and, with their help, chose seven men from among them to have charge of all charity. One of those chosen was Stephen, "a man full of faith and of the Holy Spirit."

The work of this Stephen was outstanding among all the Jews. He did great wonders and signs among the people. Not only did he minister to their bodily needs, but he preached the new gospel of Jesus so convincingly that many believed and were baptized.

So successful was Stephen that there arose certain men from the synagogues of Jerusalem and other cities who argued with him. When he defeated them in debate, they turned against him and sought to convict him by false witnesses. They hired men to testify, "We have heard him speak blasphemous words against Moses, and against God." Others testified, "This man ceaseth not to speak words against this holy place and the law. We have heard him say that this Jesus of Nazareth shall destroy this place, and shall change the customs which Moses delivered unto us."

Stephen was arrested and brought before the high priest for trial. His accusers appeared and spoke their lines as they had been instructed. The high priest listened to them until they had finished, then, turning to Stephen, he asked, "Are these things so?"

Then Stephen made testimony in his cause. He traced the history of the Jews from Abraham unto his own day and told how the people had refused in each age to listen to their leaders when they spoke the true words of God. He concluded with these words: "Ye stiffnecked and uncircumcized in heart and ears, ye do always resist the Holy Spirit. As your fathers did, so do you. Which of the prophets did not your fathers persecute? They killed them that showed before of the coming of the Righteous One, of whom ye have now become betrayers and murderers; ye who received the law as it was ordained by angels, and kept it not!"

This angered the multitudes greatly. The high priest and the others of the synagogues flew into a rage and "gnashed on him with their teeth." The fury of the mob grew and swirled about Stephen. In its midst, he looked up into heaven and said, "I see the heavens opened, and the Son of man standing on the right hand of God."

The crowds cried out with a loud voice and stopped their ears, and rushed at him with one accord. They cast him out of the city and, in a mad rage, stoned him to death as he called upon the Lord, "Lord Jesus, receive my spirit. Lay not this sin to their charge." With this "he fell asleep."

The Work of Philip

Signs and miracles fascinated the people of Samaria, in central Palestine. Everywhere were doers of strange things. Competition was keen and only the best dared appear before the people. A poor performer would reap bitter contempt for his efforts.

The early apostles and disciples were workers of wonders. Many of them had high reputations for their skill and people followed them wherever they went, to see the strange things they did.

When, after the stoning of Stephen, a great persecution broke out in Jerusalem and a young man named Saul "laid waste the church, entering into every house and dragging men and women out to commit them to prison," some of the faithful fled to Samaria. Among these was Philip, skillful with signs and wonders.

When the people of Samaria saw the wonders which he did, they listened attentively to him and his message. They saw unclean spirits come out of those who had housed them for years and heard the spirits cry with a loud voice. They saw the palsied and the lame healed. They marveled at the many signs which he worked so skillfully.

One man among them, however, was more impressed than the others. And well he might be, for he had a great reputation as a sorcerer and a worker of signs. For many years he had amazed the people of Samaria with his sorcery. Some said, as they watched him work, "This man is that power of God which is called Great." Now, here was one from Jerusalem whose works fascinated him. He reasoned that this Philip must have something worth investigating.

Simon, for that was the sorcerer's name, joined himself with Philip, was baptized, and continued with Philip "beholding signs and great miracles wrought," and was amazed.

When the apostles, who remained in Jerusalem despite the persecutions, heard of Philip's successes in Samaria, they sent Peter and John to pray with the Samaritans and endow them with the Holy Spirit. When Simon saw them receive the Holy Spirit, he was much impressed and offered the apostles money if they would place their hands on his head and give him the Holy Spirit. This angered Peter and John, who told him, "Thy silver perish with thee, because thou hast thought to obtain the gift of God with money. Thou hast neither part nor lot in this matter, for thy heart is not right with God."

Then they proceeded to deliver a sermon, saying, "Repent therefore of this thy wickedness, and pray the Lord, if perhaps the thought of thy heart shall be forgiven thee. I see that thou art in the gall of bitterness and in the bond of iniquity."

This impressed Simon greatly so that he cried, "Pray ye for me to the Lord, that none of the things which ye have spoken come upon me."

After this the apostles returned to Jerusalem and left Philip and his converts to work with the Holy Spirit in

Samaria. But Philip was needed elsewhere and an angel came to him in a dream with instructions. "Arise," the angel ordered, "and go toward the south unto the way that goeth down from Jerusalem unto Gaza."

Philip obeyed the angel and set out along the Gaza road. He had not gone far in this direction when he chanced to meet a man of Ethiopia, a eunuch who had great authority under the queen of the Ethiopians, Candace. He was in charge of all the queen's treasures.

This eunuch was returning from Jerusalem where he had gone to worship. When Philip found him he was sitting in his chariot and reading from the book of the prophet Isaiah. "Understandest thou what thou readest?" Philip asked, when he approached.

The eunuch answered, "How can I, except someone shall guide me?" Then he asked Philip to come into the chariot with him and explain the passage. Together they discussed the passage and many other matters of which the eunuch was uncertain. At last Philip began to tell the story of Jesus. The eunuch listened attentively and was much impressed.

When they came to a place where there was water the eunuch said, "Behold, here is water. What doth hinder me to be baptized?" There was nothing to hinder him, so he ordered the driver to stop. The two men, Philip and the eunuch, went down into the water and the inquirer was baptized as he wished. As they came up out of the water the Spirit of the Lord caught Philip away so that the eunuch saw him no more. His work had been completed here and the eunuch went on his way rejoicing, while Philip was carried to Azotus where he was needed to preach the gospel.

☆

The Conversion of Saint Paul

SAUL OF TARSUS, later named Paul, had studied at the feet of Gamaliel, the greatest Jewish teacher of his day. This training and the careful and thorough instruction received in his home made him one of the most intelligent and devout of Jews.

He saw in the Christian movement a great danger to all that he considered most sacred in Judaism. These Christians were, to him, dangerous radicals bent upon destroying the law and tradition. Thus, he found a great deal of satisfaction in watching the stoning of Stephen and in hunting out Christians wherever they might be found.

In discharge of this, which he considered his sacred duty, Saul went everywhere "breathing threatening and slaughter against the disciples of the Lord." One of his trips turned his face toward Damascus where he went with letters from the chief priests to bring bound to Jerusalem all whom he might find "of this way."

As he and his party journeyed near to Damascus, "suddenly there shone round about him a light out of heaven." He fell on the ground and lay in a stupor for some time. As he lay thus he heard a voice saying unto him, "Saul, Saul, why persecutest thou me?" Saul was curious and asked, "Who art thou, Lord?" And the voice replied, "I am Jesus whom thou persecutest."

After a pause the voice returned, saying, "Rise, and enter into the city, and it shall be told thee what thou must do."

Saul lay on the ground, stunned and overcome by this strange happening. The men who were with him heard the voice but could behold no one. This frightened them so that they stood motionless, unable to come to the aid of their leader or to flee from the voice.

When at last Saul arose from the ground and opened his eyes, he could see nothing and had to be led by the hand during the remainder of his journey. For the next three days he was blind and touched neither food nor drink.

In Damascus there dwelt a good man and loyal disciple by the name of Ananias. In a vision the Lord appeared to him and commanded, "Arise, and go to the street which is called Straight, and inquire in the house of Judas for one named Saul, a man of Tarsus. He prayeth, and he hath seen a man named Ananias coming in and laying his hand on him, that he might receive his sight."

Ananias was not happy with this mission. He knew Saul by reputation and felt that blindness was but just for him. He could see no reason for the Lord to be interested in this arch enemy of the Christians. And he told the Lord how he felt, saying, "Lord, I have heard from many of his men, how much evil he did to thy saints at Jerusalem. Here he hath authority from the chief priests to bind all that call upon thy name."

This was all too true, but the Lord had a mission for this persecutor. "Go thy way," he said to Ananias. "He is a chosen vessel unto me, to bear my name before the Gentiles and kings, and the children of Israel. I will show him how many things he must suffer for my name's sake."

Ananias listened and a new understanding filled his mind. The Lord was going to take the most violent persecutor of the Way and turn him into his most loyal evangelist. And Ananias had been chosen to play a part in this conversion. He went out from his house at once, and came to that where Saul was praying.

When he entered, Ananias placed his hands on Saul and said, "Brother Saul, the Lord, even Jesus, who appeared unto thee in the way which thou camest, hath sent me that thou mayest receive thy sight and be filled with the Holy Spirit."

Immediately the scales fell from Saul's eyes and he saw

clearly. He arose and was baptized at once. After this he took food and received back his strength.

From this moment Saul of Tarsus, arch enemy of the Christians, became Saint Paul, the greatest of Christian missionaries, the disciple to the Gentiles, founder of churches throughout the Roman world, servant of the Lord for the rest of his days.

Paul's Voyage to Rome

WHEN Paul appeared in Jerusalem to report to James and the elders regarding his recent missionary journey in Cyprus and Syria he found the rumor widespread that he was teaching Jews living in Gentile countries to forsake the laws of Moses. Despite all that he could do to show his loyalty to this law, Paul was set upon by a mob and would have been killed had not Claudius Lysias, chief captain of the Roman garrison in Jerusalem, rescued him.

Once in the hands of the Romans, who had to determine whether he was guilty of any crime against Roman law, Paul leaned heavily on the fact that he was a Roman citizen by birth. At last, realizing that the Roman authorities in Jerusalem and at Caesarea, where he was taken to appear before the governor, were seeking favor with the Jews and would not give him a fair trial, Paul appealed to Caesar. This took the matter out of all lesser authorities' hands and made it necessary for the king to send Paul to Rome, where he could present his case before Caesar himself.

Setting sail from Caesarea in a ship of Adramyttium, Paul, with several other prisoners, was put in charge of a centurion named Julius, a member of the Augustan cohort. The first part of the voyage was without incident. Julius was kind to Paul and permitted him to go ashore at Sidon and visit with friends and refresh himself. From Sidon the ship sailed across the Mediterranean Sea, "under the lee" of Cyprus, to Myra, a city of Lycia. Here they changed ships and took one from Alexandria bound for Italy. Sailing, with some difficulty because of the contrary winds, they came after many days to Fair Havens, a harbor near Lesea on the island of Crete.

Here it became evident to Paul that further sailing would be dangerous because winter was near and the winds would be most unfavorable. When he told the centurion of his fears, he was ignored since the master and the owner of the ship wanted to get their cargo to Italy as quickly as possible. Thus they moved out of Fair Havens and set their course for Phoenix.

For a few days the south wind was favorable and it seemed that the voyage would be completed without any of the dangers predicted by Paul. But, "after no long time," a tempest blew down upon them and the ship was tossed helplessly in the stormy waters. Fearful of being destroyed, the sailors began to throw overboard first the freight and then the ship's gear. This made the boat lighter and easier to handle, but the storm was so severe that it seemed to all only a matter of time before they would be drowned in their ship.

Paul cheered the mariners on and gave them hope with the assurance that an angel of God had appeared to him the night before, saying, "Fear not, Paul, thou must stand before Caesar." This was evidence enough for him that he would not perish in the sea but would complete his journey to Rome.

For fourteen days they sailed, no one knew where. The storm beat their ship unmercifully and all that the sailors could do seemed of no avail. Then they were about to abandon the ship for their small boats when Paul argued that only by staying with the ship could they be saved. The men harkened to his advice, mindful of the fact that had they listened at Fair Havens they and their ship would have been safe for the winter.

On the morrow they found themselves near a bay which had a wide beach. Here they ran the ship aground and made their way to the beach. This they found to be the island of Melita, a place inhabited by some "barbarians" who treated them kindly. While Paul was helping gather wood for the fire which the "barbarians" had kindled for them, a viper crawled out of the bushes nearby and "fastened on his hand." When the "barbarians" saw this, they were certain that Paul was a murderer or some other criminal, and they commented to each other, "No doubt this man is a murderer whom, though he hath escaped the sea, yet Justice hath not suffered to live."

Paul surprised everyone by shaking off the creature into the fire and going about his work unharmed. Those nearby expected him to fall down dead suddenly. When nothing happened, they were astonished and changed their minds toward him, saying that he was no criminal, but rather a god.

After three months on the island of Melita, Paul was taken on a ship from Alexandria which had wintered there and carried north to Syracuse, thence to Rhegium and to Puteoli, and to Rome. At each stop along the way Paul found Christians who greeted him joyously and whom he encouraged with words of counsel and praise.

At Rome, Paul was permitted to live in a house he had rented, but was forced to remain chained by one wrist to a praetorian soldier night and day. Here for more than two years Paul awaited trial. During this period he worked with the Roman Christians and wrote letters to churches which he had founded and to the many friends he had made during his long and eventful life.

As time dragged on, it became evident to Paul that his case would inevitably end with a conviction. In his second letter to Timothy he expresses this fear. This is a cry of despair for his life but an expression of faith in the cause for which he had given his life. His work is done and he is about to be "offered." So he writes to Timothy, his companion and friend, whom he now longs to see. Others have deserted him and he is alone save for Luke. So he urges Timothy to come to him with all haste, picking up a few other friends on the way.

Tradition says that Timothy did reach Rome in time to share Paul's last days but not in time to do anything to save his friend from condemnation under Roman law. Paul was tried, but had no independent evidence to rebut the charges against him and had to bow to the executioner's sword. The traditional date is June 29 of the year 62 and the place of execution is said to be the Ostian Way some three miles from Rome, probably at the modern Tre Fontane.

PART THREE

STORIES OF SAINTS AND RELIGIOUS LEADERS

The Later Years of Saint John

JUST OUTSIDE the Latin Gate in Rome, the gate leading to Latium, stands the church of Saint Giovanni in Olio. This church has stood there since the days of the first Christian emperors of Rome, and was built to commemorate the deliverance of Saint John the Evangelist from the persecutions of Domitian.

Domitian feared and hated the Christians. He told the people that he was divine and ordered them to refer to him as "Our Lord and God." The Christians refused to give him this honor and even preached that there was only one God, the God of Our Fathers.

Chief among these was the aging John, the disciple whom Jesus loved and who had devoted himself since the ascension of Jesus to preaching the gospel, even at Rome. This angered the emperor, who was slowly going mad from an incurable mental malady, and led him to prescribe a horrible and certain death for John.

Domitian called his most trusted guards and ordered them, "Go, find John, that Christian who has been telling the people false tales of another god. Bring him to me, or I will have your heads."

Finding John was not difficult. John did not hide, but went about the city preaching and talking with any who would show interest in what he was saying. So the guards very quickly found him and dragged him before Domitian. The very sight of the old man drove the emperor into a mad frenzy.

"I am the only god," he shouted. "You do not speak the

truth when you talk of other gods. The people have one god and that god is Titus Flavius Domitianus! I am god!"

John never took his piercing blue eyes from the raving emperor. When he had finished his ranting, John answered in a firm but quiet voice, "Titus Flavius Domitianus, I know no other God than him spoken of by Jesus, the Christ. Him I worship, and no other."

This made the emperor more angry than before. Trembling with rage, he shouted to his guards, "Take him away! Throw him into a cauldron of boiling oil! I will hear no more of this!"

And the old man was dragged away, outside the Latin Gate, where the prescribed torture had been prepared. When the oil was boiling and the fire had reached a great heat, three burly soldiers seized the old man and threw him into the oil. They waited until the fire had burned out and the oil had ceased to bubble.

Then they saw Saint John, not burned as they had expected, but standing in the oil as one coming from a refreshing bath. At first they thought their eyes were deceiving them. This was some trick of the imagination! But, when the old man walked from the cauldron and spoke to them, they knew that he was alive and ran in fear to tell the emperor what strange thing had happened.

Domitian was more angry than before, but he was also afraid. "By what strange magic does this Christian work?" he asked. But no one could give him an answer.

Then one of the guards suggested, "I know not the magic by which this old man was saved from the boiling cauldron, but it must be great and he may turn it on us to destroy us all."

This threw the emperor into a fit of trembling so severe that he fell to the floor where he lay for some time shaking and whimpering. When he had recovered enough to pull himself back on his royal couch, he gave orders that John should not be tortured further but should be banished to the island of Patmos.

This order was carried out. And it was during John's stay on the island of Patmos that he saw the vision which is recorded in the last book of the New Testament and which is called "The Revelation of Saint John." After the death of Domitian, John returned to Ephesus and continued preaching until the day of his own death.

Saint Clement and the Lamb

DURING the reign of the Emperor Trajan in Rome there broke out a persecution of the Christians more fierce than usual and many were martyred while others suffered ingenious torture at the hands of Roman officials or lawless mobs. At the height of the persecution a young man by the name of Clement was brought before the authorities.

Clement was no ordinary fanatic or rebel against the established Roman religion. He was well-known because of his holy life and his many kindnesses to the poor and needy. His life was an example to many in Rome of self-denial and personal sacrifice, so that he was honored and loved in the homes of the lowly and in many of the mansions of the rich and powerful.

When Clement was brought before the tribunal and accused of the high crime of dishonoring the Roman gods, there were many who did not wish to see him suffer. Indeed, Mauritius, the prefect who examined him, could find no fault in him and was so impressed by his earnestness and self-effacement that he pleaded for him with the Emperor Trajan.

The emperor listened to Mauritius' plea, and then handed down his decision: "No doubt this Clement is a holy and good man, as you say. But here in Rome everyone must make his sacrifice before the altar of our gods. If this Clement will make the sacrifice as ordered, he shall go free to continue his good works. If he refuses, he must leave Rome at once and spend the rest of his days in the Tauric Chersonese. This is my command. Go, and tell it to Clement."

Mauritius brought the news to Clement and begged him to obey the emperor. "What does it matter," he argued, "if you make a sacrifice at the Roman altar? It is merely a form, a ritual. You can throw a pinch of salt on the sacred fire with one eye closed. It matters little, and you will be able to stay in Rome where there are many who need you."

But Clement would not listen. "It is written," he said, "that one shall have no other god before the God of our Lord and Savior Jesus Christ. Even a pinch of salt would be a sin. No, I cannot obey the emperor."

When Mauritius saw that Clement was determined, that all his pleading was in vain, he wept as he pronounced the sentence of the emperor upon his friend. Then he added, "God will not abandon thee."

Thus, by order of the emperor, Clement was banished to the Crimea where a great many Christians who defied the Roman government had been sent to work in the mines until death. Here Clement found much suffering and hardship, for the Roman authorities did not care for the health or welfare of their charges. Work was all they wanted of them, and, when they were no longer able to work, they were left to die.

One thing the captives needed most of all was water, since the nearest source of supply was some ten miles away and it was a difficult task to carry water over such a distance. They had looked everywhere, but could find no water nearer. Then Clement encouraged them to pray for help. He knelt to pray with them.

As they prayed, Clement lifted up his eyes and saw on a nearby mountain a lamb pointing with its right foot to a spot not far away. No one saw the lamb save Clement, but he was certain that it was the Lamb of God sent to help these distressed people.

At once Clement arose from his knees and, taking some of the men with him, went to the spot where the lamb had been pointing. They sank spades into the ground, and there gushed up a great spring of water, enough for all the needs of the captives.

As the days and months went by, Clement worked among the Christians in the Crimea, teaching them the words of the Lord and helping them when they were in distress. Many who were not Christians heard him and saw his good works and were converted to the way of the Lord.

When the emperor heard of the work of Clement and that many non-Christians were being won over by his kindness and his preaching, he became very angry and sent soldiers to seize and punish these new converts as an object lesson to others who might be tempted to follow Clement. But these people gave themselves up to martyrdom joyfully, singing praises while they were being tortured or being led to death.

Realizing that Clement must be destroyed, the emperor ordered that a heavy anchor be tied about his neck and that he be tossed into the sea to drown and be eaten by the fishes. He did this to be certain that no relic might be left for the people to worship. All memory of him was to be wiped out forever.

But the Christian captives and the many who had become Christians under the preaching of Clement prayed that they might recover his body and give it due honor. As they prayed, suddenly the waters of the sea were rolled back for three miles and there, on the dry bottom of the sea, was the body of Clement in a beautiful marble shrine which the angels had built. And near the body lay the anchor, the instrument of his martyrdom.

For many years after this, at the festival of Saint Clement, the sea would roll back and leave the ground dry for seven days so that the Christians who had known and loved this holy man might come and worship at his shrine.

Ignatius, Bishop of Antioch

THE Roman emperor Trajan seemed on the point of conquering the world. Everywhere he went, nations and people fell under the power of his armies until there seemed none who could withstand him or resist his will.

But, everywhere he went, amidst all his conquests, there were the Christians, a small religious society whose members had formed churches throughout the Mediterranean world. These people worshipped a sovereign other than the Roman emperor, and they dared to claim that their ruler was superior to the ruler at Rome and that his kingdom was greater than all the far-flung Roman empire.

Conquest could not be complete, Trajan felt, so long as the Christians succeeded in defying his authority. They must be broken and forced to acknowledge him the greatest of all rulers. As the Christians continued to resist his authority, he felt forced to take drastic measures against them. As he was marching his armies from victory over the Scythian Dacians to other victories over the Armenians and the Parthians, he threatened dire persecutions unless these Christians worshipped as did all the other nations under his power.

This threat aroused Ignatius, the reverend bishop of Antioch. He had guided his people through other persecutions and realized that his advice and counsel was needed in this crisis. So he presented himself before Trajan to argue the case of the Christians and attempt to soften the heart of the emperor.

When Ignatius was brought into the presence of the mighty Trajan, he was asked, "Who are those evil demons hastening to transgress our commands, persuading others also that they should miserably perish?"

The bishop's answer was confusing to the emperor, for he replied, "No one calls Theophorus an evil demon, for all the demons have departed from the servants of God. But if indeed I am grievous to thee, and if thou callest me evil to the demons, this I confess; for having Christ, who is the heavenly King, I do indeed dissolve their devices."

"And who is this Theophorus?" Trajan asked in some bewilderment.

"He who has Christ in his breast," Ignatius explained.

"Do we, then, seem to thee to have no gods in our minds," Trajan asked, "we on whose side the gods fight against our enemies?"

This question gave Ignatius the opportunity for which he had been waiting. He explained to Trajan, "The demons of the nations, in an illusion, thou proclaimest to be gods. But there is one God who made man and the earth and the sea and all things therein, and one Christ Jesus, the only be-gotten Son of God, for whose kingdom I am longing."

"Dost thou speak of him who was crucified under Pontius Pilate?" Trajan questioned.

"I speak of him who has crucified my sin, with him who devised it, and has put all delusion and evil under the feet of those who bear him in their hearts."

"Then thou bearest the crucified in thy heart?" the emperor asked.

"Yes," Ignatius affirmed, "for it is written, 'I will dwell in them and walk in them.'"

Trajan had asked many questions and assumed the ap-pearance of interest in the doctrines of the Christians. But he had done all this merely to lead Ignatius on until he should convict himself out of his own mouth. What the good bishop had thought was an honest desire to know about

Christ and the Christians was only a clever trap, and he had walked blindly into it.

Now that Ignatius had confessed his allegiance to the crucified one, Trajan threw off the cloak of pretense and gave a royal decree to his soldiers, saying, "This Ignatius, who says he bears about within him the crucified, we condemn to be taken, bound, by soldiers to Great Rome, to become the prey of wild beasts for the festivity of the people."

Though he knew that his end was near, Ignatius was not afraid, nor was he disheartened. On the contrary, he was overjoyed at the prospect of suffering martyrdom for his Lord. "I thank Thee, O Supreme Lord," he cried out, "that Thou hast deigned to honor me with the perfecting of love to Thee, permitting me, like Thine Apostle Paul, to be bound with chains."

Bound and on his way to Rome and death, Ignatius wrote a letter to the Roman church in which he poured out his heart. "Now I begin to be a disciple," he rejoiced. "Fire and cross, troops of wild beasts, rending of every limb, dire torments of the devil, let them come to me, if only I may follow Jesus Christ. . . . Living, I write to you, longing to die. My love is crucified. I long for the Bread of God, the Bread of Heaven, the Bread of Life, which is the flesh of Jesus Christ, the Son of God. I long for the wine of God, His own blood, which is love incorruptible, and eternal life."

At Rome the people had gathered in the Circus Maximus to witness another of the now oft-scheduled extravaganzas, part of which was always an act in which some Christians were thrown to the lions. The crowd was in a holiday mood, shouting and singing and praising the work of the entertainers.

At last came the major event of the day. A band of Christians was led into the arena. Among them was one who seemed to have the respect of all, a man tall and straight and with a glow about his person which everyone saw but no one understood. As the lions were turned in upon them, the little band knelt in prayer led by this strange figure, Ignatius.

It was soon over. The lions were hungry that day and ate fast and furiously. Only a few hard bones remained when they had finished, and the crowds went away satisfied with the day's entertainment. During the night, when all was quiet and deserted in the arena, a few Christians stole into the Circus Maximus to gather up the bones as relics of the sacred martyrs.

Ignatius was dead. Some said that all that remained of him were a few bones. But others knew that the memory of his good works and many kindnesses would remain forever to tell men of a true Christian whose greatest joy was martyrdom for his Lord.

Polycarp, Bishop of Smyrna

SOMETIME during the third quarter of the second century a violent persecution of Christians and Jews broke out in the Roman world. This persecution was especially frenzied in Asia where, whenever there was a public festival of any description, the crowds would cry out for martyrs to enliven their entertainment.

In Smyrna there lived an aging servant of the Lord called Polycarp. For some time he had been the bishop of the Christian community of that city. In early life he was taught by some of those who had known the Apostles of Jesus. In fact, the historian Irenaeus tells us that he "lived in familiar intercourse with many that had seen Christ."

This Polycarp had often stirred the populace to murmur against him because of his work and his preaching of the Christian gospel. But usually these murmurings amounted to nothing or were quieted when the bishop retired from public view for a time.

But this newer persecution was different. It had been going on for some time and the lust of the people for Christian and Jewish blood was rising steadily to unheard of violence. Soon there came time for a great festival in Smyrna and people gathered from far and wide to see the games and participate in the many contests staged by the authorities. The city was a mass of sweating, cheering humanity seeking every possible thrill. Among the visitors to the festival was the proconsul Statius Quadratus. The Asiarch Philip of Tralles presided over the games.

On one particular day of the festival eleven Christians, mostly from Philadelphia in Peraea, were put to death in the arena. This sight whetted the appetites of the crowd for more Christian blood, so that they quickly took up the cry of some in the stands, "Away with the atheists. Let search be made for Polycarp!"

News of the temper of the crowd quickly reached the old bishop and he was persuaded to take refuge on a farm in the country. Neither he nor the church which he served believed in fanatically seeking martyrdom. "We do not commend those who give themselves up," they maintained, "since death often brings to an end the leadership of an individual."

But Polycarp was discovered and brought back to Smyrna to stand trial. At his trial the magistrates sought to have him recant, or at least to offer a public sacrifice. The proconsul urged him to "revile Christ," and promised, if he would consent to abjure his faith, that he would set him at liberty. The dignity and gentleness of the bishop touched his enemies deeply and they did not want to see him die.

Indeed, the soldiers who were sent to arrest him stood for two hours while he prayed. At the end of his prayer many were sorry that "they had come forth against so godly and lovable an old man."

We are told that the Irenarch and his father permitted the bishop to ride in their chariot and attempted to persuade him that there was no real harm in sacrificing to Caesar. But, when they saw that Polycarp would not listen to them, they pushed him out of the rolling chariot so that he sprained his ankle and had to limp along to his trial.

At the trial the proconsul urged him to recant, saying, "Swear and denounce the Christ, and I will set thee at liberty."

To this Polycarp responded, "Eight and sixty years have I served him, and he has done me no injustice. How, then, can I blaspheme my King, who has saved me?"

This answer infuriated the mob. Cries went up for the lions to be turned loose on this Christian. The proconsul was equally angered and sent the herald to proclaim throughout the city and in the stadium: "Polycarp has professed himself to be a Christian."

But the Asiarch refused to feed Polycarp to the lions, arguing that the games were officially over. Then the crowds demanded that he be burned at the stake and the authorities did not protest, but ordered that it should be done.

When Polycarp was led into the stadium the crowds cried out, "This is the master of Asia, the father of the Christians, the enemy of our gods."

To this Polycarp replied, "Away with the godless!" Then he told the people of the "enduring fire" of the spirit of Christ, a fire so different from that "transitory flame" to which they had condemned him. While he was speaking, the authorities were preparing the pyre. When they were ready to nail him to the stake, as was the custom, he resisted, saying, "He who gives me to suffer by fire will enable me to stand unmoved by the pyre."

Then Polycarp knelt to pray and the guards waited until he had finished. He prayed, "Lord God omnipotent, Father of Thy beloved and blessed Son, Jesus Christ, through whom we have received the knowledge of Thee; God of the angels and the heavens, and of the whole creation, and of all the generations of the just ones who live before Thee, I bless Thee that Thou hast thought me worthy of this day and hour, that I should have a part in the number of Thy martyrs, and the cup of Thy Christ, unto the resurrection of eternal life, of soul and body, in the incorruptible life of the Holy Spirit; among whom I desire to be received today before Thee, a ripe and acceptable sacrifice, as Thou hast prepared and foreshown and fulfilled, Thou the true God who canst not lie. Wherefore for all things I bless Thee, I glorify Thee, with the eternal and heavenly Jesus Christ, Thy beloved Son, with whom to Thee and the Holy Spirit be glory now and in the ages to come. Amen."

When he had finished, he remained kneeling upon the timber and faggots as the soldiers put flame to the pyre. Many who saw him there told how the flames formed into a triumphal arch about him and how his body shone like silver. The fire could not burn him. Seeing this, one of the soldiers struck Polycarp with his sword and his blood flowed out to extinguish the flames.

Some say that a dove, gentle as was his spirit, rose from the pyre and flew into the heavens.

Fearful lest the Christians would rescue the body of Polycarp and worship it, the Roman authorities rekindled the fire and threw what remained of the old bishop back on the pyre where it was wholly consumed. But a few of his charred bones were gathered up by the faithful and laid away as treasures to remind those of future generations of the sainted Bishop of Smyrna who endured fire rather than renounce his Lord.

The Legend of Saint Christopher

SAINT CHRISTOPHER, the patron of ferrymen and the protector of all who travel by water, was a pagan of great stature and powerful body, but he was hideously ugly. Those who saw him could think of nothing else but a very ugly dog. Indeed, they whispered that this ogre was a man-eater, and everyone feared to come near him.

Since he was so big and strong, he worshipped strength and roamed about seeking someone bigger and stronger than himself whom he could serve.

The King of Canaan seemed to him to be just the man he was seeking. He was powerful, a ruler of vast lands and many people, with great armies at his command. So Christopher attached himself to this king and swore everlasting loyalty. But, one day he noticed that the king seemed to tremble when one of his priests mentioned the devil.

"Why do you tremble?" Christopher asked.

"Because the devil is very strong and his evil ways will destroy me and my kingdom if I make him angry," the king replied.

This was enough for Christopher. His idol had fallen. No more could he follow the king. He had to set out to find the devil and serve him, for, he reasoned, "If the devil is able to make this powerful king afraid, he must be the strongest man there is."

He found the devil and served him for many years. Indeed, he had great fun serving the devil. Everywhere he went he found that people feared his master and that everything the devil planned succeeded because he had many strong and mighty people working for him.

Then, one day while he and the devil were walking along a country lane bent on a mission of evil, they came to a little church, on the steeple of which was a cross. Christopher wanted to destroy that building, but the devil would not let him.

"Never touch a cross," the devil explained. "It is the symbol of the Prince of Peace, and its power is greater than mine."

Christopher was surprised and bewildered. For a long time now he had been devoted to the devil, for he thought him to be the strongest being alive. But this idol was afraid of the cross and Christopher could no longer follow him.

So he set out alone again, to find this Prince of Peace whom even the devil feared. On his journeys he came upon a hermit who told him the story of the Christ, how he was born a babe in a lowly manger, how he healed the sick and raised the dead, and how, when men sought to kill him, he conquered death and came from the tomb to live forever.

This story fascinated Christopher, especially that part where the Christ had conquered death. For Christopher was growing old and he did not want to die. "If I can find this one who conquered death, perhaps he will show me how to live forever as the hermit says he lives," Christopher reasoned.

So he set out to find the Prince of Peace. He roamed here and there, looking and inquiring. But, though men told him many stories of this great one, and though he found evidence of his work everywhere, he was always just a little too late. The Prince of Peace had been there, but had gone.

At last, almost in despair, Christopher came to a river full of rapids and dangerous whirlpools. There was no bridge and only the very strongest of men could cross safely. Here Christopher stopped, built a rude hut to protect himself from the cold, and spent his time helping people across the river on his back. It became known everywhere that a great, ugly giant was living on the river's edge and was always ready to help people who had to cross the river, and his fame spread throughout the land. Indeed, many who had seen him and been helped by him felt that his countenance was changed and that the old dog-face was now beautified with a light that seemed to shine from deep inside.

One cold and stormy night Christopher was warming himself by his fire and thinking that his services would not be required in such a storm, when he heard the voice of a child crying outside, "Christopher! Christopher! Come, and help me across the river!"

Though he was old now and not so strong and sturdy as in the past, Christopher could not refuse. So, he put on his warmest clothing and went out into the bitter winds and rain. He set the child on his shoulders and started to wade the whirling stream. The child grew heavier and heavier and it seemed to Christopher that he would never reach the other bank. Several times he stumbled and almost fell. But, at last, weak and exhausted, he stumbled up the far side and placed the child on dry land.

Then he upbraided the child for putting him in such peril. "Had I borne the whole world on my back," he said, "it could not have weighed heavier than thou."

"Marvel not!" the child replied. And Christopher, looking up from where he lay resting, saw a great light shining and in its center not the child he had been carrying, but a man in white robes and with a crown of thorns about his head.

"Thou hast borne upon thy back the world and him who created it," the Christ explained. "You have found me now and can come with me to eternity."

Christopher's face was lighted by a new light and his heart was happy. But he knew that he was about to die and this made him sad.

"Master," he said, "I have searched everywhere for you, to serve you and you alone. Now that I find you, my years are spent and I have no more strength to do your bidding."

"Be not sad, Christopher," the Christ replied. "You have been serving me from that day when you first helped others across this stream. Now you have your reward and can dwell with me forever."

Saint Cecilia and the Angels

IN THE DAYS of the early Christians, when to tell the story of Christ and his death openly was a crime punishable by death, there was born to the noble house of Caecilii a baby girl named Cecilia, of unusual sweetness and beauty. Though she grew up in the Campus Martius and in a pagan home surrounded by the trophies of her war-loving ancestors, this child turned early to the Christian faith.

Cecilia's parents did not oppose her faith, but so loved her that they gave her every opportunity to grow into a fine and talented Christian woman. Under her gold-embroidered robe she wore a garment of hair, and under her dress, close to her heart, she carried the Book of the Gospels.

Day and night Cecilia went among the catacombs and where the sick and needy lived, ministering to them and singing the hymns of the early church. Her voice was ravishingly sweet, and her talent for music so great that she was able to play almost any instrument. Tradition tells us that she invented the organ to have an instrument that would give forth music truly expressive of her deep religious feeling.

As she approached the full bloom of young womanhood, she was betrothed to Valerian, a young man of wealth and fine character, but a pagan. After their marriage, Cecilia told Valerian that she had vowed to serve Christ and that an angel always guarded her. He wanted to see the angel, but was told that before this was possible, his eyes of faith had to be opened.

"Go," Cecilia told him, "to the Appian Way and say to the poor there that I have sent you to find Urban the Old. He will purge you from sin. Only then shall you see the angel."

Valerian went as she had directed and was shown to the abode of Urban. Suddenly, as he told the old man of his wish, there appeared before them one clad in white and holding in his hand a book written in letters of gold. Valerian fell to his knees and buried his face in his hands, but the shining stranger lifted him up and began to read from the book of the Lord, and faith, and God, and Christianity.

And when he had finished he asked, "Believest thou this thing?"

And Valerian answered, "I believe all this."

Then the stranger vanished and Urban baptized Valerian and sent him on his way with a blessing.

When Valerian returned to Cecilia and entered her room, he saw there an angel with two crowns, one for the head of his wife and one for him. Then the angel said, "Because you have accepted the will of God, you may ask anything and it will be given you."

"I have a brother whom I love as I love no other man," Valerian answered. "I pray, then, that my brother may have grace to know the truth as I do."

No sooner had he spoken than his brother came into the room. When he smelt the sweet fragrance of the celestial crowns, he asked, "I wonder whence the sweet smell of roses and lilies comes at this time of the year. I find the fragrance in my heart, and it hath changed me into another kind. Is it a dream?"

"All our life till now has been a dream; now we are in the reality," Valerian replied. "We have two crowns, snow white and rose red, that shine clearly, which your eyes have no power to see. But, as you smell them, through my prayer, so shall you see them clear, if without sloth you will believe aright and know the truth." Then he told his brother about the Christ, and Cecilia spoke with such eloquence that the young man was converted and hastened to Urban, who baptized him in the faith.

After this, the three went about doing good works so that many were turned to the Christ and those who suffered were cared for and comforted. And Cecilia sang sacred hymns with such sweetness that the angels came down to listen.

In time news of their work reached the ears of the prefect of the city, Almachius, who ordered their arrest. When the brothers were brought before him, he gave them the alternative of sacrificing to the gods or being put to death.

"Every day we offer sacrifices to God," they said.

"To which of the gods?" Almachius asked.

"Is there more than one God?" Valerian questioned.

"Then the whole world is wrong and you and your brother alone are right!" said the prefect.

"Deceive not yourself," Valerian warned. "The Christians who have embraced this faith can no longer be numbered. It is you who are as the planks which float in the water after a shipwreck."

This angered the prefect, and the brothers were sentenced to die. But they were to be given one more chance to sacrifice. When they were brought to the palace and offered incense for the sacrifice, they refused and fell on their knees in prayer and devotion. In that position they were beheaded by the soldiers. Maximus, one of the soldiers whom they had converted, said that he saw their souls glide to heaven with the angels, "full of beauty and light, as if going to a nuptial feast."

As Maximus told of the saintliness of Cecilia and of the death of the brothers, many were converted. But he was beaten to death by the guards.

When Cecilia was brought before the prefect and the tribunal, many found their hearts melted by her gentle and gracious ways and begged her to save her life by obeying the order of the authorities to sacrifice to the Roman gods. But she answered them, "To die for Christ is not to lose youth but to renew it."

Then Almachius asked, "What manner of woman art thou?"

"I am a gentlewoman born," she said. "Among men I am called Cecilia, but my noblest name is Christian."

"Knowest thou not," he warned, "that I have the power of life and death?"

"Not of life," she said, "but thou canst indeed be a minister of death."

The prefect then ordered her to death, but not the death

of public execution. She was to be taken to his house to die by heat and suffocation in the calidarium of the baths. But though the heat was severe, she was unaffected and "sat all cold, and felt it no woe."

At last the headsman came and struck her neck three times with the sword, but failed to sever her head from her body. Since more than three strokes was not lawful, he had to leave her, with neck half bent, to die. Cecilia continued to teach the faith to all those who came to see her and many were converted to the Christ before death came to relieve her of pain.

Today a church rises where her house stood and in it is a marble statue over her tomb. The spotless marble represents her lying, not as one dead and buried, but on her side, as one asleep. Great artists have painted her at the organ playing the sweet hymns of the church while angel faces gather about her shoulders. In the church, Cecilia is the patron of music and of the blind.

Cyprian, Bishop of Carthage

FOR forty-six years Cyprian, of noble lineage and comfortable wealth, lived as scholar and teacher in the African provinces. He was a trained rhetorician and a professor of philosophy. And he loved his gardens. Men respected him and among those in high position he claimed many close friends. Cyprian had all that man could desire.

But not quite all! He knew, though his friends scarcely sensed it, that there was something lacking. "I was still lying in darkness and gloomy night, wavering hither and thither, tossed about on the foam of this boastful age, and uncertain of my wandering steps, knowing nothing of my real life, and remote from truth and life."

Then the aged presbyter Caecilius found him and led him

to the Christian faith. For Cyprian this was truly a "new birth." His wavering was gone and the darkness of night was illumined with a heavenly light that shone through him to all men.

The first act of the new Cyprian was to sell his beautiful gardens and two of his estates for money to distribute among the poor. This act was lasting testimony to the faith that had possessed him, for he loved his gardens and found them places of solitude and contemplation so necessary to his happiness. Of these gardens he wrote, "This vintage festival invites the mind to unbend in repose. Moreover, the place is in accord with the season, and the pleasant aspect of the gardens harmonizes with the gentle breezes of a mild autumn, in soothing and cheering the senses. In such a place as this it is delightful to pass the day in discourse. That no unrestrained clatter of a noisy household may disturb our converse, let us seek this bower; the neighboring thickets secure us solitude, and the trailing of the vine branches, creeping in pendant mazes among the reeds that support them, have made for us a porch of vines, a leafy shelter."

But Cyprian gave up his gardens, as he eventually gave up his wealth, his health, and finally his life, for the cause of Christianity and for the souls of men and women who needed him.

Cyprian had not been long baptized when the Bishop of Carthage died. To succeed him was far from the mind of the new convert, but the people of Carthage were of a different mind. They crowded about Cyprian's house and begged him to become their bishop. At last they prevailed and the Christian community at Carthage chose one of its greatest leaders.

For the church was to face dark days, days in which the leadership of men like Cyprian was sorely needed. The Decian persecutions, which broke out soon after Cyprian's election, caused many to fall away from the church in fear of their lives. Others were hounded by the authorities, persecuted, and in many cases killed after horrible torture. When some of those who had deserted the church repented and wanted to return to its fold, there were those in high places who wished them punished. But Cyprian understood them, and begged that they be reinstated, for, he argued, "They have suffered and been weak. Now they are repentant. It is not for us to deny them the comfort of our Holy Church. We should open our arms to them and give them our strength so that, when the evil one strikes again, they will be strong to resist his wiles."

This position won out and many were taken back into the church to become strong in the future, even strong enough for martyrdom.

Also, many who had suffered for the church were so unbeholden of Christ that they wanted places of prominence in the Christian community. Some even would become dictators and lord it over those who had not suffered, or who had suffered less. Cyprian fought this. To some who were flaunting their martyrdom, he wrote, "With what praise can I commend you, most courageous brethren, the strength of your hearts and the perseverance of your faith! . . . Nor let any one of you be saddened as if he were inferior to those who have suffered tortures. . . . Now let each one strive for crowns, white as of labor, or purple as of suffering. In the heavenly camp both peace and strife have their flowers, with which the soldiers of Christ may be crowned for glory."

When the Berbers, native African tribes, attacked the rim of the African provinces and carried away many Christians, Cyprian was ready with consolation and financial help to redeem the captives. When the dreaded plague broke out in Carthage and everywhere people were dying while the living feared to touch the sick or the suffering, Cyprian directed the Christians to minister unto all the people, Christian or pagan, and thereby show that they were not as other men.

Both Christian and pagan came to love Cyprian deeply. But the emperors Valerian and Gallienus did not bear this love for the Bishop of Carthage. They dispatched a letter to Paternus, the proconsul, ordering that "those who do not observe the Roman religion must recognize the Roman ceremonies."

When the proconsul informed Cyprian of this order, he answered, "I am a Christian and a bishop. I know no other gods than the one true God, who made heaven and earth, the sea and all things that are therein. This God we Christians serve; to him we pray day and night for ourselves and for all men, and for the prosperity of the emperors."

Then Paternus demanded that Cyprian reveal the names of the presbyters of the church so that he might bring them to trial. To this Cyprian answered, "In your laws you have well and usefully judged that there shall not be informers. Therefore these cannot be revealed and given up by me. But they will be found in their own cities."

For this, and for being a Christian, Cyprian was ordered banished to Curubus. From exile he carried on his work in the church, writing to the leaders of Christian groups throughout the empire, encouraging, advising, accusing, and exhorting as the need arose.

Then he received a summons to return to Carthage and stand trial. Many of his friends urged him to retire to a secluded spot and live out his days in peace, but he refused. Rather, "he went forward with a lofty and erect bearing, gladness in his countenance and courage in his heart."

When the trial began, Galerius Maximus said to him, "The most sacred emperors have commanded thee to sacrifice."

Cyprian replied, "I do not."

After Maximus had urged Cyprian to take counsel with himself and realize the results of his action, and after Cyprian had refused several times to sacrifice, the proconsul said, "Long hast thou lived with a sacrilegious mind, and many men hast thou gathered to conspire with thee, and hast constituted thyself an enemy to the Roman gods and the sacred laws; nor have the pious and most sacred princes Valerian and Gallienus been able to recall thee to the observance of the ceremonial due to them. By thy blood, discipline will be restored." Then he pronounced sentence, "It pleases that Thascius Cyprian be beheaded with the sword."

To this Cyprian cried, "Thanks be to God!"

The appointed day dawned bright and clear. A great multitude had gathered in the field of execution to await the ceremonies. When Cyprian was brought forth, he laid aside his upper garments and prostrated himself in prayer before the Lord. When he had finished, he divested himself of his dalmatic and stood in his linen garment.

Many in the crowd begged to be beheaded with their beloved bishop while others jeered and cried against him. When quiet had been restored, the aged bishop asked that twenty-five gold pieces be given to the executioner. Then Cyprian bound his eyes with his own hands and bent himself to the sword of the executioner "who could scarcely clasp in his trembling hands the weapon which was to bring about the death of that man so dearly prized."

It was over in a moment. The head of the beloved Bishop of Carthage tumbled in the dust while fear and trembling smote the soldiers and there arose from the crowd a refrain of Cyprian's last words, "Thanks be to God!"

The Story of Saint Agnes

FROM earliest childhood, Agnes, daughter of a noble Roman family, was devoted to Christ and his Way. Her parents, also Christians, encouraged her and were happy when she announced, at the age of thirteen, that she had pledged her life to the Savior's service.

But the son of the Roman governor Sempronius had seen the beautiful child and fallen madly in love with her. As was the custom in those times, he visited her parents and asked for her hand in marriage. Respecting the feelings of their daughter but not wishing to anger the governor, they received his advances with hesitation.

At last, impatient of delay, the young man sought an interview with Agnes and begged her to become his bride and the daughter-in-law of the governor. Agnes was pleased that he should honor her so, but explained that she was already pledged to one "by whose love alone my soul lives. Such is his beauty that the brightness excels all the brightness of the sun and the stars; the heavens are ravished with his glory and say in their language that they are as darkness to his light. He has given me a treasure beyond all the wealth of the Roman Empire. Those who serve him are loaded with riches. He is so powerful that all the forces of heaven and earth cannot vanquish him; the sick are healed by his touch, the dead rise at his voice, and I love him more than my life and soul and am willing indeed to die for him."

Although the young lover did not know his rival, he became very jealous and his anger increased as Agnes repeatedly refused to honor his suit. Even all the pleadings of Sempronius were of no avail. Then someone told the governor that Agnes was a Christian and that it was the Christ to whom she had given her heart.

This news gladdened the governor. He reasoned that, if Agnes continued to refuse his son's advances, he would avenge her disdain of his position without seeming to vent his personal resentment. So he had her brought before him in private.

"Agnes, you must marry my son immediately," he ordered. "If you refuse, you must sacrifice in public to the goddess

Vesta and serve her all your life. You shall be one of the virgins who keep the sacred fires of Rome."

Agnes understood, even at her tender age, what the governor meant, but she refused. At this Sempronius grew very angry and threatened to have her ravished by one of his guards and in public. To this threat Agnes answered, "If I will not be faithless to my Lord for thy son, who nevertheless has my esteem and who is a living creature of God, still less will I abandon his service for lifeless forms which can neither hear nor see. And as to thy threatened wrongs, my Lord Jesus can send his angels to protect me, or he himself will build an impenetrable citadel about me."

Seeing that threats were of no avail, the governor ordered her to be outraged before the crowds of the city, but her trust was rewarded and she was preserved inviolate in the midst of every attempted outrage. A heaven-sent robe whiter than snow enfolded her and shone with such brightness that the darkness of night was turned into heavenly day and those who approached to do her harm grew pure and chaste in heart by the sweet purity of her presence and went away penitent.

At last the governor's son, blinded by rage and passion, rushed upon her intent on doing her bodily harm. But the wrath of heaven smote him and he fell in the dust, blinded and in hideous convulsions. In a moment he was stiff in death at her feet.

Sempronius was mad with grief and anger and accused her before all the people of being a sorceress and murderess worthy only of death. This aroused the multitudes to demand her execution without delay.

Agnes was able to make the father see that it was not she who had caused his son's death but the anger of heaven. When he was convinced by her tender pleading, he fell at her feet begging in tears for her prayers. And she prayed so fervently to God for the life of the son that he was returned to his father. This miracle turned the son into a herald for God, so that he went throughout Rome preaching and proclaiming that there was no other god than the God of the Christians. And the governor would have gladly pardoned Agnes.

But it was too late for pardon. The people were afraid and were running through the streets crying, "She is a sorceress, a witch! She must die!" So great was the cry that the governor could do nothing but turn her over to the populace. A pyre was built on the edge of the city and Agnes was placed in the center and the faggots kindled. But the flames divided and encircled her as a rainbow while they reached out and consumed those who had attempted to destroy her.

At last, when the fire was extinguished and Agnes was not dead, the executioner mounted the ashes as was the custom. He was pale and trembling at what he had witnessed, but at heart he was a Roman soldier and knew his duty. After praying fervently, Agnes bent her head to the fatal blow and gave up her mortal life for one eternal.

The Christians, among whom were her mother and father, laid her body in a tomb in the catacombs and went daily to her bier to pray. On the eighth day of her martyrdom, while her parents were praying at the grave, they saw a vision. A company of virgins appeared clothed in cloth of gold, with precious stones, crowned with garlands, pearls, and diamonds. In the midst of the company, they saw Agnes with a lamb whiter than snow by her side.

When the virgins came close, they stopped and Agnes comforted her parents, saying, "My beloved parents, weep not for me as for one dead, but rejoice rather with me that I have now in heaven the crown of glory in such a holy company, and that I am with him whom when on earth I loved with all my heart and soul and strength."

Then she passed on, but her parents rose from their knees, happy and full of love for Christ and his gospel.

Since then, Saint Agnes has become the patron of young

girls; and each year on Saint Agnes' Eve, January 20 to 21, maidens in rural districts often indulge in quaint rites to discover the names of their future husbands. This belief has been immortalized by the poet Keats in "The Eve of Saint Agnes."

Today the saint's bones rest in a church named for her in Rome, where each year on January 21 two lambs are blessed after a pontifical high mass and their wool is later woven into the pallium of the archbishop.

The Story of Saint Agatha

QUINTIANUS, governor under the Emperor Decius, was a man wicked beyond compare. Nothing was sacred to him and no crime was too vile for him to commit.

Soon after he came to the governor's palace, he heard of the beauty and charm of Agatha, child of an illustrious family then living in Catania, and determined to seduce her from Christianity and purity. But nothing that he could do would attract her. His invitations and special favors were ignored, and his threats were of no avail.

When it became evident to Quintianus that Agatha could not be tempted, he grew very angry and ordered her placed in the keeping of a wicked old hag and her nine yet more wicked daughters. These women knew all vice and cursed everything good and pure. But, although they kept Agatha for nine days and used all of their wiles and temptings upon her, they were unable to tear Christianity from her heart or trick her into committing even the least sin.

When they had failed and admitted that Agatha's power was stronger than theirs, Agatha explained how it was that she resisted them successfully. "My soul," she told them, "is founded and built on Christ. Your words are but wind, your persuasion like a stormy rain, your threats like a rushing river. But this wind, this rain, this river, let loose against the foundations of this house of mine, cannot shake it, for it is founded on a rock."

Quintianus was angry beyond words. Not only had Agatha successfully resisted his advances, but she had challenged his authority and hurt his vanity. In his wrath he ordered her brought before him. When his soldiers pushed her into his presence, he asked, "What is your condition?"

Quietly but firmly she replied, "I am free-born,—indeed, of noble birth."

This, of course, the governor knew, but he asked it so that he might ask another question, "Why, then, if of noble and illustrious family, do you show by your conduct the baseness of a slave?"

"Being a servant of Christ," Agatha explained, "I am in this sense of servile condition."

"If you were indeed noble," the governor asked, "would you take the name of slave?" He could not understand how one born of the nobility could debase herself so far as to join with the Christians.

"The service of Christ is perfect freedom and the highest title of nobility," she told him.

"Are not we, then, who despise the service of Christ and worship the gods, of noble birth?" he asked, thinking that nobility could be attained only by birth and knowing not of the "new birth" of which Jesus told Nicodemus.

But Agatha had experienced the governor's vile attempts to seduce her and answered his question with a firm voice, knowing that she was inviting the burning anger of a Roman ruler, "Your nobleness has sunk to a slavery so low that not only are you slaves of sin but subjected to wood and stone."

Quintianus could hardly contain his anger. He threatened Agatha with extreme torture unless she would sacrifice to the gods, and even had her led to a door through which she could hear the cries of pain of those who were being stretched and burned.

But Agatha warned him, "Take care that you do not become like the gods you worship—thyself like thy Jupiter, thy wife like Venus. What more curse could we wish to anyone than to wish them to follow those execrable lives?"

The argument had reached a white heat on both sides. "To what end this torrent of words?" he shouted. "Take her away and begin her torment."

Agatha was dragged from the presence of the governor and subjected to the most horrible of tortures. But she did not cry out in pain. Rather, she sang hymns of praise and repeated verses of thanksgiving to God. Only once, when in the agony of her wounded breast, she asked if no mother's breast had nurtured her persecutors.

When night came and her torturers grew tired, Agatha was thrown into a dungeon to die. But, near midnight there appeared to her an old man carrying a wreath and offering to heal her wounds. Agatha was suspicious of his offer and told him, "If it is the will of my savior Christ to heal me, he will heal me himself."

Then the old man told her that he was Peter, the apostle of Jesus, and explained, "Fear not, my daughter, for Christ has sent me to minister to thee." At that the prison was filled with so brilliant a light that the jailers fled and Agatha's fellow prisoners urged her to escape.

With her wounds healed, Agatha stood before the assembled prisoners and said, "Tempt me not to lose my crown and be a cause of trouble to my guards. With the aid of my Lord Jesus Christ, I will keep my confession to the end."

After four days, Agatha was summoned to appear before the judges. They had not heard of the miracle of the dungeon and expected to see a broken and diseased body but, to their great astonishment, the prisoner who appeared before them was fresh and strong and healed of all her wounds.

"Who has healed thee?" Quintianus inquired.

"It is the Christ, the Son of God," Agatha answered.

In spite of his surprise at seeing Agatha healed and strong, Quintianus grew angry at this answer and cried, "Dost thou dare speak of thy Christ?"

"My lips shall never cease to confess him nor my heart to call upon him," she answered.

At this, Quintianus ordered his soldiers to kindle a great fire outside the city. When the fire was burning fiercely, Agatha was bound and thrown into the flames. Just then a severe earthquake shook the city and extinguished the fire that had only partly burned the maiden. This convinced the people that the gods were angry at Quintianus for his treatment of Agatha, and they rose against him, crying: "Down with the Roman devil!"

In the confusion that followed, Agatha was taken back to prison where a bed of live coals was prepared for her torture. But, before she could be laid on them, she lifted up her hands to heaven and prayed, "O Thou who hast won my heart from earth and made me victorious over torture, and given me courage and patience, I pray Thee now to receive my soul."

With this prayer, Agatha rendered up her spirit to God.

As they were about to bury her, a young man appeared suddenly, clothed in rich raiment and followed by a troupe of more than a hundred beautiful children dressed in golden robes. He and the children followed the funeral procession to the tomb singing praises to God. After her body had been laid to rest, the young man placed a marble tablet at her head. On this tablet was written these words: "Holy, devoted soul, the glory of God, the protector of the city." Then he disappeared and with him the children, and neither was ever heard of again.

Among the relics left by Agatha was a veil of great beauty and fine workmanship. It was the veil in which she had wrapped herself in the prison and by which she hid her wounds from the strange visitor who proved himself to be the Apostle Peter. This veil was kept in the church dedicated to her memory at Catania, and was brought out only on special occasions.

Many years later, Mount Etna, near the city, began to throw out flames, smoke, and tons of burning lava which flowed down the side of the mountain and across the bay toward the city. It seemed certain that the city would be completely covered and destroyed to the last man. In desperation, the townspeople brought the veil of Agatha from the church and spread it on the beach in the path of the lava. Immediately, the flow of lava ceased and the city was spared.

The Miracle of Saint Valentine

While Saint Valentine was a young priest at Rome, his good works, especially his kindness and care for those who suffered because of their faith, made him popular throughout the Christian communities of the empire. In fact, even the Emperor Claudius II heard often of him and came to respect and even admire him secretly.

But not even an admiring emperor could overlook the fact that Valentine was a Christian who did not worship the established gods of the Roman Empire. So he had Valentine brought before him for examination.

"Why is it," he asked, "that you refuse to worship the gods of our people?"

To this Valentine replied, "If you, sire, knew the gift of God, you would abandon the worship of these impure beings, and you and your empire would be happy."

This answer struck at a tender spot, for all was not well in the vast Roman Empire. The powerful Claudius was unhappy. Half believing at times, but bound by his exalted position and training to the gods of the Roman cult, he was torn between loyalty to the tradition of his people and a secret yearning for whatever it was that made the Christians happy even in death.

To fill an awkward pause that followed Valentine's answer, a judge asked, "What do you think of the great gods Jupiter and Mercury?"

"They appear to have spent most of their time in low pleasures not even worthy of a good Roman," Valentine answered.

How true! There were many Romans who secretly felt ashamed of the stories of their gods and tried to explain them away as legends or poetry, not really true. Claudius was moved by these answers, realizing their truth, and was on the point of sending Valentine back to his flock when the prefect of the city asked, "Shall we forsake the religion of our people?"

Mild as was this question, Claudius saw that it pointed to the danger of sedition in the empire, for the religion of the empire was the essence of patriotism. To permit Christians to defy the Roman gods was as good as allowing them to be disloyal and unpatriotic. The emperor knew that he could not sanction this.

So Claudius gave Valentine over to the prefect who ordered him placed in the custody of Asterius, the judge. He was taken to the judge's house and held there as a prisoner. Upon entering the house, the good bishop offered a prayer that God would make those who were still in darkness see Jesus as the light of the world.

Asterius heard him praying, and when he had finished, he asked, "How do you know that Jesus Christ is the light of the world?"

"Not only the true light," Valentine replied, "but the only light, who lighteth every man that cometh into the world."

The judge, thinking that he would silence his prisoner forever, offered him a test. "If what you say is true, listen to this test, and prove it to me. I have a little adopted daughter who has been blind for two years. If you can restore her sight, I will believe that Jesus Christ is the light and is God, and I will do all you command."

The child was brought to Valentine who placed his hands on her eyes and prayed, "Lord Jesus Christ, who art the true light, enlighten this thy servant."

Immediately, at these words, the child's eyes were opened and she saw clearly. Asterius and his wife threw themselves at the feet of the bishop and begged to be told how they could be saved. He ordered them to destroy all the idols that adorned their home, to celebrate a three-day fast, forgive all who had injured them, and then be baptized.

Asterius obeyed Valentine to the letter, and even set free the Christians who had been entrusted to his keeping by the emperor. Then he and all his household of forty-six persons were baptized.

Upon hearing of this, Claudius ordered Asterius and all his household destroyed. But so firm was their faith that not one flinched even at the presence of torture and death. Valentine also suffered. He was thrown into a dungeon and beaten with rods until death put an end to his suffering.

Years later a church was built near the Ponte Mole in Rome to do him honor. For a long time the gate, which is now known as the Porta del Popolo, near this church, was called the Gate of Valentine. He has been honored, also, by being called the patron saint of young girls, and a pagan festival for boys and girls in honor of Juno which occurred at the time of his martyrdom has been transformed into Saint Valentine's Day.

☆

The Story of Saint Margaret

AEDESIUS, pagan priest of Antioch, had a beautiful daughter whom he loved devotedly. He called her Margaret and dreamed of her growing into a sweet and charming woman, the comfort of his old age.

But Margaret's mother died while she was very young and her father had to place her with a poor woman who lived just outside the town. Here the child grew up among the fields and the flocks and came to love the simple life of the country. More than all, she came to love her foster mother and the Christ in whom the old woman believed. As she approached womanhood, Margaret gave herself to her Lord as her only master.

When Aedesius heard that his daughter had become a Christian, and when he realized that all his pleading and threatening was of no avail, his devotion turned to deep anger. He cast her out and refused even to see her again. She was no longer his daughter, but one strange and unknown to him.

Margaret remained with the old woman of the fields, serving her as a menial and thinking no more of her noble birth. She tended the few sheep of her foster-mother and often occupied herself, while the sheep grazed, with contemplating the love of God and the passion of his son. Thus, browned by the summer sun and strengthened by the cold of winter, she grew into a girl of unusual beauty and grace.

One day Olybrius, the pagan governor, happened to pass that way and saw her in the fields watching the flocks. Struck by her grace and gentle beauty, he fell deeply in love with her and ordered his attendant, "If she is a slave by birth, she must be purchased for me. If she is free-born, I will make her my wife."

The attendant went immediately to seize Margaret and bring her to the governor's house. Fearful of what might be in store for her, she prayed fervently to God begging that he keep her from all evil and strong in her faith. Her prayers were heard by the attendant who lost no time in informing the governor when they arrived at his house. "This young maiden is an enemy of the gods of the empire," he said. "She adores Jesus Christ, and no promises nor threats of ours can move her."

Olybrius would not believe his officer, so greatly was he smitten by love for the maiden. When she was brought before him he told her, "Fear nothing, young maiden; tell me whether thou art slave or free-born."

"My family is well known in the city and I am of no obscure house," she answered. "But, since thou speakest of freedom, know that I am bound to no man. I am a servant of Jesus Christ. From my earliest years I have learned to revere and honor him, and him I will adore forever."

"What is thy name?" the governor asked.

"Men call me Margaret," she replied, "but in holy baptism I received a more illustrious name. I call myself a Christian."

These answers to his questions angered the governor greatly. The warning of his captain was true, a warning he had refused to honor. But Olybrius still hoped to win the girl from her Christian faith and to love for him. So, he ordered that a great tribunal be gathered and invited all the people of the city to come and witness the trial of this young girl. He hoped that in fright at all this notoriety and show of power, she would turn from her new-found faith and sacrifice to the gods of Rome.

The day of the trial dawned, and Margaret was brought into the great trial hall. There were assembled all the high dignitaries of the city,—the judges, captains, generals, and priests of the local religions. The place was thronging with people, both great and small, come to witness the spectacle.

The governor, after telling in a long speech of the girl's devotion to Christianity, threatened her with torment and death if she refused to sacrifice to the gods. He held up to her the choice between life and death, joy and torment. But to all this Margaret replied, "Life and joy, thanks to God, I have indeed found. They are in the strong citadel of my heart."

Then she began to tell the assembled multitudes of her faith and of the Christ who had died for their sins. So eloquent was her speech and so gentle her manner that many believed and were converted. But the governor swore that such thoughts and fine words could not be hers. "She is bewitched by some strange sorcery," he said. "There is magic enchantment about her that can come only from the Evil One."

Then he realized that no manner of persuasion could change her or win her over to his belief. So he ordered her to be tortured until she either confessed to the gods of Rome or died.

Torture after torture was applied to her body, but the power of God within her strengthened her and her faith was not weakened. Finally she was thrown into a dungeon and the governor summoned the Evil One to torment her. But even his most cruel terrors did not avail and she resisted his every wile.

As a last resort, the Evil One rushed at Margaret in the form of a dragon, breathing out sulphurous flame, grabbed her in his hideous jaws and soon had devoured her completely. But, as he lay back to rest and enjoy the memory of his victory, he began to hurt violently and to writhe about the dungeon screaming and bellowing. At the height of his pain he burst into nothingness and there stood the maiden unhurt and shining with a holy light which penetrated even to the darkest corners of the prison. Beside her stood the cross and resting on it was a dove whiter than snow.

On the morrow her tortures were renewed, but nothing

hurt her. Throughout all her torments she continued to speak to the people assembled to watch her suffer, and many fell on their knees and confessed Christ.

At last, she was borne outside the city, to the place of execution, and there, as she knelt to pray, the swordsman severed her head from her body and the eloquence of her preaching was silenced forever.

Saint Catherine of Alexandria

ONE of the wisest women of ancient times was Catherine, daughter of Konetos and Sabinella, King and Queen of Egypt. As a mere child she was noted throughout the land and in foreign places for her beauty and wisdom.

To encourage her studies, Catherine's father built a great tower for her in which were many large rooms filled with books and mathematical instruments. From its top she could study the stars and make all kinds of astronomical observations and predictions.

When Catherine was only fourteen, her father and mother died and left her Queen of Egypt. Though scarcely more than a child, she was the wisest person in the kingdom and the most beautiful in all the world. But she cared nothing for royal pomp and dress and precious stones. The stars of the heavens and the wisdom of Plato and the many wise men of the East occupied all her interest.

In time the people of Egypt became worried and sent a mission to beg that she marry so that she might have someone near her to share the cares of government and lead the people in glorious wars. When the spokesman of the mission told her the wish of her people, she was much troubled and asked, "What manner of man is it that I should marry?"

"Madam," the emissary said, "you are our most sovereign lady and queen, and you have four notable gifts. First, you are come of most noble blood. Second, you are a great inheritor. Third, in wisdom you surpass all others. Fourth, in bodily shape and beauty there is none like you. Wherefore we beseech you that these good gifts with which you are endowed may induce you to take a husband, to the intent that you may have an heir to the comfort and joy of your people."

Being very wise, Catherine answered the spokesman discreetly. "I will do as you suggest, O noble Sir," she promised. "But the one whom I shall marry must be of blood so noble that all men shall worship him; so great that he shall never think I have made him king; so rich that he shall pass all others; so full of beauty that angels shall desire to behold him; and so benign that he will gladly forgive all offenses done to him. When you have found such a man, I will take him for my lord and husband."

This answer startled the queen's counsellors and all those who had come from the people. "There never was nor never will be such an one as you desire," they replied.

But the queen was wise, and she gave them answer, "If I do not find him, he shall find me, for other will I none."

Near the palace of the queen there lived an old hermit devoted to Christ and to the Holy Virgin. In his sleep that night the Virgin appeared to him to tell him that the king should be her son. When the Virgin had disappeared, the hermit arose and went immediately to the palace and presented Catherine with a picture of the Virgin and Child and told her what he had seen in a dream. This filled the queen's heart with holy joy and made her forget her books and the stars.

When the hermit had returned to his cave, Catherine had a dream. She was met on the top of a high mountain by a company of glorious angels who took her by slow stages to the presence of the Blessed Lady, who led her into the presence of her son. But, when she had entered, he turned from her and said sadly, "She is not fair enough for me."

She awoke with those words ringing in her ears: "She is not fair enough for me." What could they mean? At last, when she could not reason out an answer, she sought the hermit who had come to her from the cave. She told him her dream. He understood at once and explained how it was necessary for her to become a Christian and be baptized.

When Catherine was baptized, the Blessed Virgin appeared to her in a dream and presented her with the Lord of Glory, saying, "Lord, she hath been baptized, and I myself have been her godmother." The Lord smiled and held out his hand and plighted his troth to her. When she awoke from the dream, the ring was on her finger and her heart was full of joy and blessedness. She had found the only one who could rule as king with her and who could be lord of her heart and soul.

Soon thereafter, Maximinus, ruler of the Roman Empire, came to Egypt from Italy breathing rage against the Christians and under oath to exterminate all he could find. He ordered that the people were to appear at a great public sacrifice to the gods and take part in the festivities. Any who refused were convicted by this very act of being Christians and worthy of instant death.

Catherine the Queen did not wait until the festival, but went immediately to the Roman ruler to plead the case of the Christians. Her beauty so attracted Maximinus that he called a great assembly of the people and permitted the queen to argue the case of the Christians against the priests and philosophers who were to champion the gods of the empire.

When the assembly was convened, fifty of the greatest sophists were called to defend the gods. They began with scorn and many sneers. Soon they realized that their opponent was no mere woman but the wisest in the land. She quoted their own books to prove that there could be only one

God, the God of the Christians. So complete and unanswerable were her arguments that the sophists surrendered and admitted that Christ the Lord was God. And many thousands in the assembled multitude believed with them.

Maximinus was violently angry. He ordered the new converts to be massacred and Catherine beaten and thrown into a dungeon. But the words of the queen had touched Faustina, the emperor's wife, and Porphyry, the emperor's chief captain. These stole to the dungeon at night and listened while Catherine told them of the Christ who died for all and of the salvation which he offered all who would believe. So convincing was her pleading that they believed and left the dungeon singing praises. But three days later, the emperor, enraged beyond words at finding the Christian poison in his own household, had both his wife and his chief captain put to death.

For her part in this crime, Catherine was placed among four wheels made with spikes, to be torn to pieces. But an angel came down and broke the wheels to pieces. Many were injured by flying bits of the wheels, but Catherine was unhurt.

At last she was led outside the city of Alexandria and beheaded by the public executioner. As she yielded up her spirit to God, angels flew down and lifted her body tenderly and carried it over the Red Sea and the sandy desert to Mount Sinai, where hundreds of years later she was found, her raiment old but her body folded in the silken tresses of her hair and a heavenly perfume about her tomb.

☆

Saint George and the Dragon

SAINT GEORGE, patron of England and protector of soldiers, was born of Christian parents in Cappadocia at a time when many Christians were high in the service of the Emperor Diocletian. His father was a trusted soldier who had gained some wealth and no little position because of his strength and talent. Although he died while the boy was still young, it was possible for George's mother to give him a good education.

At seventeen George chose the profession of arms. Being of goodly proportions and handsome of mien as well as intelligent and highly skilled in fighting, he pleased the emperor, who quickly promoted him. While yet very young, George was made military tribune of the emperor's guard, a position of high honor and great trust. Here the young Cappadocian served with distinction and honor.

While on one of his knightly tours, George came to a town in Libia called Silence. As he approached the town, he noticed the way covered with human bones and, as he came nearer, he met a beautiful maiden clothed in royal raiment. When she saw the handsome knight approaching she cried out to him to go away and not risk his life. But George was not one to run at so slight a warning, and came closer to ask her trouble and why she cried for him to go away.

She told him of a dreaded dragon living in the marsh outside the city that came out of hiding to devour the flocks and herds of the people. She told how, to prevent him from coming near the walls of the city and poisoning the air with his breath, the people had given him two sheep each day to satisfy his hunger. When the sheep were all gone they were forced to feed the dragon two children each day. Now these were chosen by lot. The lot had fallen on her and she was to be eaten by the dragon.

George listened to her story and then answered, "Fear not, for I will deliver you from this dragon."

But she warned, "Oh, noble youth, tarry not here, lest you perish with me; but fly, I beseech you."

"God forbid that I should fly. I will lift my hand against this loathing thing, and I will deliver thee through the power of Jesus Christ."

Just then the dragon appeared from the marsh, leaping and flying as he came. At the sight of him the princess trembled and cried to George, "Fly, I beseech you, brave knight, and leave me here to die."

Paying her no heed, but making the sign of the cross and calling on the name of Christ, he charged toward the dragon. A mighty battle followed, with the dragon breathing fire and lashing out at George with its claws and tail. George fought back with all his strength and skill until he pinned the dragon to the ground with his spear and held him there writhing but thoroughly beaten. Then he asked for the girdle of the princess, with which he bound the dragon securely and led him, as one would a dog, back to the town.

When the people saw this strange party approaching and knew that their princess was unharmed, they were happy but terrified at the might of the stranger. But he called to them, saying, "Fear nothing; only believe in that God through whose might I have conquered this adversary, and be baptized, and I will destroy him before your eyes."

The king and all twenty thousand of his subjects were baptized and professed faith in God and his son, Jesus Christ. Then George killed the dragon and cut off his head to convince the people that they had nothing further to fear. In appreciation of his valor, the king gave George much money and many treasures, and the rich people of the town added to these. George gave it all to the poor and went on his way leaving the town in peace.

But all was not well in the empire. The emperor was a devotee of Apollo and often consulted the oracle of this god on matters of state. During one visit to the oracle the emperor heard a voice from the cave say, "The just who are on the earth prevent my telling the truth. By them the inspiration of the Sacred Tripod is reduced to a lie."

What did these strange words mean? The emperor asked, "Who are the just?" And the priest of Apollo answered from the depths of the cave, "Prince, the just are the Christians."

Diocletian believed that this was a command from the god to renew persecution of the Christians, persecution that had died down and been neglected in many places. The Roman Senate issued new decrees against the Christians, and governors and rulers everywhere were ordered to be ruthless with all who were even suspected of being Christian conspirators.

George was much disturbed by these persecutions and denounced the whole matter boldly. In vain did his friends plead with him to be prudent lest he lose favor with the emperor, but he was not to be dissuaded. Having distributed his property and wealth among the poor, and having set free all his slaves, he went directly to the emperor to plead the case of the Christians. He begged that Diocletian give them liberty, for, he argued, "liberty can hurt no one."

The emperor warned him, "Young man, think of your own future." But George was interested in the Christians and cared nothing for his own advancement. This angered the emperor, who condemned him to the most horrible torture. He was thrown into prison, his feet placed in stocks, and a great stone rolled onto his chest. When he endured this torment without repenting, he was stretched on a wheel with sharp spokes which cut him deeply.

Then a voice came to George from heaven saying, "George, fear nothing, for I am with thee." There also appeared a man shining as brightly as the sun and wearing a white robe. He encouraged him and healed his wounds. The guards who saw the man fell down in the dust and swore allegiance to Jesus.

Seeing that George endured the torture without flinching, Diocletian urged him to make even a small sacrifice to the gods of the temple. When George asked to be taken to the temple, the emperor thought it was for the purpose of sacrificing and ordered the Senate and the people to assemble at the temple to witness the act.

When all were assembled and George was led before the statue of Apollo he crossed himself and said to the idol, "Wouldst thou that I should offer sacrifices as to a god?"

To this question the idol answered, "I am not god, and there is no other god but him whom thou preachest."

At this very moment all the idols in the temple began to cry and shriek terribly and one by one they crumbled into dust before the eyes of the assembled masses.

The priests and the emperor were angered beyond words. And the people were in a panic. The high priest of Apollo warned the emperor, "Sire, you must destroy this magician at once or he will destroy you and the empire. No one could do this unless he was in league with the demons."

Diocletian knew that he was in danger and feared for his life. So, he ordered that George be taken to the place of execution and there beheaded. This was done, but there were many, especially those in the little town of Silence, who remembered the good works of the martyr and worshipped his memory.

Saint Denys, Patron of France

IN THE YEAR 250 a missionary named Dionysius came to Gaul, then an outpost of the Roman Empire, where Christianity had made little headway, charged by Pope Clement with the task of converting the French to the church. Dionysius set about his mission with unsparing zeal and determination and in a short while began to see the results of his efforts in the smaller towns and villages of France.

But when he came to Paris he found the people unwilling to accept the gospel and Dionysius was forced to undergo extreme anguish before the Parisians would believe in the faith that he brought them. Outraged by his preachings, the Parisians, urged on by their Roman rulers, first cast Dionysius into a pit of wild beasts, expecting him to be rendered asunder, but the beasts came and licked his feet. Still unbelieving, and infuriated at the failure of their plan, they cast him into a fiery furnace. But, like the three Hebrew children who had been put to the same test hundreds of years before, Dionysius emerged unharmed. Dionysius was then taken from the furnace and crucified, but he preached to his tormentors from the cross and they were forced to take him down and they returned him to prison. He was then summoned before the Roman governor who ordered him and two other Christians of the city to be executed.

The three believers were led to a hill overlooking the city and there beheaded. This hill, now known as Montmartre, or the mount of the martyrs, was named for them. The bodies of Dionysius and his two fellow-Christians were then ignominiously thrown into the river Seine, but a Christian lady named Catalla had them pulled from the river and buried reverently near the place of execution. Several years later a chapel was erected over the remains of these martyrs.

King Dagobert, who died in 638, founded at this spot the great Abbey of Saint Denys, dedicating it to the memory of Dionysius who had come to France and whom the French had so taken unto themselves as to change his name to Denys and make him their patron. This abbey was for generations the burial-place of the kings of France until, during the French Revolution, the tombs of the rulers were opened by

the mobs and the royal remains strewn about as a gesture of
their contempt for royalty.

The Story of Saint Nicholas

SOMETIME during the fourth century a very remarkable child
was born to two old people of Panthea, in Lycia. They called
him Nicholas and, as soon as he was born he stood upright,
faced the east, and joined his baby hands in prayer.

While Nicholas was still a small boy his aged parents died
and left him a considerable inheritance. Obeying the voice of
Scripture, he sold all that he had and began distributing his
wealth among the poor.

Once, it is recorded, he heard of a nobleman of the city
who had become so poor that he saw no way for his three
daughters to exist except through a life of shame. Nicholas
heard of this and, filling a bag with money, crept silently to
the house at night. As he peered into an open window he saw
the old man weeping bitterly. Nicholas tossed the bag of
gold in at the window and stole away before he could be discovered. The old man was very happy and went immediately
and gave his eldest daughter a dowry.

On the next night Nicholas repeated his visit and left another bag of gold. But on the third night, when Nicholas was
about to toss the bag of gold into the room, the father, who
had been watching to discover his benefactor, rushed upon
him and threw himself at his feet in gratitude.

This incident has led, after many centuries, to the legend
that Saint Nicholas, or Santa Claus, steals down the chimney
on Christmas Eve to leave presents while the receivers are
asleep.

But Nicholas did many other good things during his long

life. At one time, when he was on a voyage to Egypt and the Holy Land, a storm broke and threatened to destroy the ship and those on board. All was given up for lost when, at his prayers, the storm ceased. A sailor who had fallen overboard was rescued and Nicholas restored him to life. Hence Saint Nicholas is also the patron of sailors.

Though Nicholas loved the life of a monk and sought to dwell in solitude and prayer, the people would not permit him to desert them. The citizens of Myra, where he had a monastery, chose him as their archbishop. Soon thereafter a dreadful famine laid all the land waste and the people were begging for grain.

Nicholas heard of some grain ships at a port in Sicily. He appeared to the merchant who owned them and, in a dream, urged him to bring the grain to Myra. He left three gold coins under the merchant's pillow as security. When the merchant awoke and found the coins, he hastened to bring his cargo to the starving people.

During this famine, Nicholas discovered an innkeeper who had been tempted to murder little children and feed their flesh to his patrons. One day he was passing the inn when he heard voices crying to him from the cellar. He went down immediately and found a tub full of brine and floating in the brine were pieces of the bodies of murdered children which were to be used as food. Nicholas fell on his knees in prayer and almost immediately the children stood up alive and whole and gave thanks to God.

This incident has given rise to the practice of picturing Saint Nicholas with three children standing in a tub.

Saint Nicholas is today universally honored. He is the patron of Russia, of little children, of friendless maidens, of the oppressed, of sailors, scholars, and of strangers. His story has been combined with Dutch legends and customs to make up a great part of the Christmas celebration.

☆

Saint Blaise, Bishop of Sebaste

BLAISE was born of wealthy parents, residents of the little community of Sebaste, in Armenia. From his earliest childhood he was quiet, modest, and unassuming. People who knew him liked him and many came to love him dearly. And he returned their love.

In fact, when he became a young man, his great desire was to study medicine in order to cure sickness and help those who were suffering. He was able to satisfy this desire and became a trusted doctor in his home town.

Blaise was also a Christian, a member of the band of devoted souls who worshipped the Christ and made the sign of the cross. So beloved was he by the people that when the time came he was chosen bishop of the Christian community and entrusted with the leadership of the people whom he loved and had so often helped as a physician.

It was Blaise's custom to retire to a cave in Mount Argus, a wooded peak near his city. There he would enjoy the beauty of the place and spend his time contemplating the greatness of God and his love that would sacrifice his Son for man's sins.

The good bishop was so kind and understanding that the beasts and birds came to trust him and many of them came every day to his cave to do him homage and be cured of their diseases. If, as often happened, they found him at prayer, they never disturbed him but waited until he had finished before making their presence known. And, always, when they left him they would express their appreciation of his help. Blaise loved the wild life of the place, and all the birds and beasts loved and trusted him.

After a time they made a language by which they could talk to each other. The beasts could express their thoughts to the bishop and he could tell them what he was thinking. Often he preached sermons to them in this language and they would say, "Amen."

One day the governor, Agricola, came to Sebaste bearing instructions from Emperor Licinius to destroy all Christians in Armenia by whatever method he thought best. Being a cruel man himself, Agricola decided to throw all the Christians he had arrested to the wild beasts in the arena.

But he needed wild beasts. So he sent his soldiers into the surrounding hills to capture a number of wild lions and tigers and other fierce animals. As they wandered through the woods, they came to the cave of Blaise and were astonished to find him in the company of a great number of ferocious wolves, tigers, and lions. But these animals sat quietly watching the good bishop meditating and when he would utter a prayer all would say, "Amen," in their own language.

This strange sight so astonished the soldiers that they left the cave and returned to the city to tell their governor what they had seen. Of course, he did not believe them and sent other soldiers to bring Blaise before him. When these arrived at the cave on Mount Argus and told Blaise what the governor had demanded, he replied happily, "My children, you are welcome. I have long sighed for your coming. Let us go in the name of God."

The people heard that the good bishop of the cave was coming down into the city and they lined the pathway along which he was being led, shouting encouraging words to him and often begging for his help or blessing. One woman pushed through the crowd to lay at his feet a child who was dying from swallowing a bone. The bishop placed his hand over the child's heart and prayed, and life was restored.

Farther on a poor woman brought him the story that her one pig had been carried off by a wolf. Blaise told her not to worry, that he would see that her pig was returned. This was not difficult, for all he had to do was ask the wolf to return the pig, and he did. The old woman was so happy and thankful that she killed the pig and brought it to Blaise for food while he was in prison.

When the bishop and his captors entered Sebaste, they went directly to the governor's house where Agricola greeted Blaise with, "I am charmed to see you, Blaise, dear friend of the immortal gods."

To this sneer Blaise replied, "God keep you, O governor. But give not the name of gods to those miserable spirits who can do *you* no good." And he pointed to the idols all about.

This so angered Agricola that he had the bishop scraped all over with a comb used in carding wool and then beaten for half a day with sticks. But through all the ordeal Blaise continued to be happy and to sing praises to God. To the soldier who was beating him he said, "O senseless deceiver of souls, dost thou think to separate me from God by torments? No, no; the Lord is with me. It is he who strengthens me. Do with me therefore what thou wilt."

During all this torment many women and children gathered about the open space praying and singing. To break up the crowd, the soldiers ordered them to sacrifice to the gods or be killed. The women asked that they be allowed to take the gods from their places to the lake and wash them clean. "If we first wash them," the women said, "they will be pure and we can sacrifice to them better."

The soldiers, thinking the women were in earnest, allowed them to take down all the idols and carry them to the lake. But instead of washing the idols, the women threw them in the lake where they sank immediately. This so enraged the governor that he had all the women burned to death.

When the fires that burned the women had died down and the tortured Blaise had seen the last of the women die, the governor ordered the bishop to be thrown into the lake to drown with the idols. But Blaise made the sign of the cross and walked quietly over the waters. When he had reached the middle of the lake, he sat down as on a throne.

When Agricola and his soldiers saw that it was vain to

torture Blaise or try to drown him, they did not know what to do. Then Agricola decided to try one last thing. When Blaise floated back to shore, he was seized by the soldiers and beheaded. His blood mingled with the waters of the lake and each spring the shores of this lake are a mass of rich, red roses to commemorate the death of the good Blaise. And it is said that the wild animals who drink from the lake are made tame and gentle by its waters.

Saint Anthony and the Desert Fathers

THROUGHOUT the ages there have been those who found it difficult to live in this day-by-day world of human frailties and temptations and, to preserve the integrity of their souls, have left the society of their fellows for the solitude of the desert or the hills.

The Roman world of the third and fourth centuries was especially difficult for the sensitive Christian soul. Its temptations were many and everywhere sin was flaunted and ideals were derided. Some devout souls invented ways of living in this world physically while denying it spiritually. Others found this impossible and turned their backs upon the company of men to find peace in being alone with their God.

A leader of this new way of life was Saint Anthony. Born in Egypt around 250, he very soon found the world about him inhospitable to his cherished ideals. At twenty this sensitive boy began the practice of an ascetic life while still living in his native town. He denied himself all luxuries and took only the bare necessities. He refused intercourse with friends who spent their time in shallow conversation and useless amusement and passed his time in holy conversation, prayer, and meditation.

After fifteen years, during which he was never wholly satisfied, Anthony withdrew from society altogether and went to live in an old fort far in the mountain of Pispir. The mountain, a high spot on the edge of the desert, supported little vegetation, but it was enough for his needs. Here Anthony lived all alone for twenty years. Here he disciplined his body by exposure and torture. And here, freed from physical cares, he was able to devote himself to the care of his soul. He was often set upon by temptations sent by the Evil One, sometimes in the form of a friend, or an unknown woman, or a dragon, but he resisted them all.

Many derided Anthony and laughed at his strange ways of life. "Anthony is wild," they would say. "He lives with the wild beasts and eats their grass. He has lost his reason." But there were others who felt that he had discovered a way to protect one's soul from the temptations of the world. Some of these followed Anthony into the mountain or took up their abode in the desert which stretched out from the base of the mountain. They lived in caves or built rude huts in which they could find solitude. The number of these hermits grew as the years passed.

At last Anthony emerged from his solitude and sought to organize these hermits into colonies of worshippers. Although each one lived alone and spent the greater part of his day and night in prayer and contemplation, little groups would gather at stated times under the leadership of Anthony to discuss religious matters and pray. In this way the first monastery was born among the fathers of the desert. Much later, others, inspired by the work of Anthony, drew together his ideas of a true monastic life and discipline into a "rule" which bears his name.

But Anthony was not happy except in solitude. So, after a time he withdrew from the companionship of other hermits, left the leadership of the small monastic groups which he had organized to others, and went to a remote mountain near the Red Sea. Here, for a few years he found the solitude he coveted. But even to this remote place devout men came to be near the holy Anthony and receive his help and counsel.

Sometime near the middle of the fourth century this first monk and originator of monasticism, which was soon to sweep over all Europe, died and was buried in solitude among the quiet hills where he had sought salvation for his soul. There, years later, a monastery bearing his name,—Der Mar Antonios,—was erected in honor of the first of that great host of devout men who sought the Way of Life alone in the hills and the desert. Today many Coptic Syrian and Armenian monks live by Anthony's rule and find joy in his way of serving his Lord.

Saint Martin of Tours

IN SAINT MARTIN we have the peculiar combination of a soldier in the service of pagan Roman emperors and a devout servant of the Christ. Born at Sabaria in Hungary, of pagan parents, Martin early heard the call to follow Christ and, at ten years of age, fled to the desert to become a catechumen.

But Martin's father was one of that host of old Roman soldiers who believed passionately in the virtues of army service and wished to pass on to his son the family tradition. In deference to his father's wishes, at fifteen Martin enlisted in the Roman army and strove to be a good soldier.

When a youth of eighteen, Martin was in Amiens with part of the Roman army. One day, when he was riding out of the Roman gate on the hillside swept by a bitter winter wind, he met a poor ragged man who begged for alms. The young soldier took off his warm military coat and, in obedience to Scripture, cut it in two parts and gave half to the beggar, who wrapped it about his bare shoulders and went away praising his benefactor.

The bystanders jeered or admired according to their turn of mind. But that night Martin dreamed that he saw the Lord among his angels clad in the half cloak which he had given to the old man. And the Lord said to his angels, "Know ye who has thus arrayed me? My servant Martin, though yet unbaptized, has done this." And Martin arose and was baptized immediately.

For fourteen years Martin served the Roman army, part of the time under the rule of Julian the Apostate. Then he left military service to devote himself to Christian service.

After the death of Saint Hilary, the Christians of Tours chose Martin as their bishop in spite of his wish to remain a simple Christian monk. As bishop he served his people and maintained a semi-monastic existence. Two miles outside the city he built himself a monastery to which he could retire in secret and meditate and pray in his own little wooden cell. Many other devout men came out to live in cells nearby and partake of the Christian strength that was Martin's. Soon a thriving monastery took form. Here everyone lived in poverty and in Christian devotion.

Martin made many missionary trips with his disciples from the monastery through Burgundy and around Autun and Chartres. These earned him the title of "Apostle of Gaul."

Once Martin went to the court at Trèves to plead for the followers of the murdered Gratian and also for the hunted Priscillianist heretics of Spain. He was bitter in his denunciation of the sins of the emperor and empress. He warned and rebuked them, and they could not do him honor enough. The emperor prepared a great feast for him and gave him the place of honor at the table and the empress cooked a meal for the bishop. Both professed to be won over by his pleadings and begged his blessing. But no sooner had he left the court than Priscillian and many of his followers were beheaded.

A year later Martin returned to the court to plead for Leucadius and Narses, two officers of the murdered Gratian. The emperor treated him royally but was angry because he refused to communicate with the bishops who were leading the persecution of the Priscillians in Spain. At last Martin weakened and consented to communicate with the bishops if the emperor would spare the two officers.

This satisfied the emperor, but Martin's soul was in turmoil. He had compromised with his conscience and was sore of heart. While meditating upon what seemed to him now to be a sin, Martin saw an angel before him who said, "Martin, with reason thou art pricked in heart; but no other way was open to thee. Retrieve thy virtue, resume thy firmness, lest indeed thou risk not thy renown, but thy salvation."

But Martin had lost his supernatural gifts. He lived for eleven years after this compromise in misery and weakness. To his friend Sulpicius Severus he confessed with tears, "I have lost the power to rescue those who are possessed of the devil."

Toward the end of his life, while Martin was praying in his cell, the Evil One appeared to him clad in royal robes and crowned with a gold and jewelled diadem and professing to be the Christ. When this vision proclaimed himself the Christ and asked that Martin fall down and worship him, the bishop gave answer, "Jesus, the Lord, announced not that he would come in glittering clothes and radiant with a diadem. I will not believe that the Christ is come, save in that state and form in which he suffered, save with the show of the wounds of the cross."

At this the Evil One vanished in a cloud of smoke and the cell was filled with the horrible odors of his presence.

As the aged bishop lay dying on a bed of ashes the Evil One appeared to him again, but this time in all his hideousness, taunting the holy man. Martin knew that his end was near and rebuffed all advances of the tempter. At last, turning to his adversary he cried out, "Beast of blood, deadly one, thou shalt find nothing in me. Abraham's bosom is receiving me." And with these words he died.

Saint Jerome and the Lions

SAINT JEROME "is one of the few Fathers to whom the title of Saint appears to have been given in recognition of services rendered to the Church rather than for eminent sanctity. He is the great Christian scholar of his age, rather than the profound theologian or the wise guide of souls."

There is a legend which, in a way, tells more about Jerome than a book of words. It was in the desert of Chalcis that he sought victory over the evil memories of his youth. "There, withdrawn in this vast solitude, burnt with the sun," he tells us, "I kept far from men; my soul filled with bitterness; covered with hideous sackcloth, my skin black as an Ethiopian's. I spent days in tears; my bones scarcely held together. When overcome with sleep, I fell on the bare earth. My flesh was already dead, and yet my passion surged upon me. I threw myself at the feet of Jesus. I bathed them with tears. If I found some dark ravine, or steep precipice, that was the place I chose to pray in, and to imprison this wretched body."

One morning, while this troubled soul was praying in his rude cell and "washing the dirt of the floor with tears," he saw a wounded lion with fiery eyes and wide open mouth at the entrance. The beast was holding up his bleeding paw and mutely begging for help. Jerome went to him, caressed him, and staunched his wound. From this moment the lion became his faithful slave and companion.

And so it was with Jerome throughout life. Often the wounded and bleeding in heart and spirit came to him and he cured them. Ever after they were devoted to him with a passion which most people could not understand.

Paula was one of these "wounded lions" whom he cured and who became his slave. She, the daughter of a high-born Greek of Athens and a lady of the house of the Scipios, was an enthusiastic student of the Scriptures and a devoted friend of Marcella, Jerome's pupil. One of her daughters, Eustochium, was a member of that little group of devout women from patrician families who met daily at Marcella's palace for the reading of the Scriptures and for prayer. Through Eustochium, Jerome became acquainted with Paula.

When Blesilla, another of Paula's daughters, died, Jerome wrote the mother a letter of comfort and remonstrance at her excessive grief. "Leave these senseless self-tortures to a proud philosophy," he wrote. "The Spirit of God descends only on the humble, not on those who are in revolt. These tears, which bring thee to the threshold of death, are full of sacrilege and of unbelief. Thou utterest piercing cries, as if being burnt alive. But at thy cries the compassionate Jesus comes to thee and says, 'Why weepest thou? The child is not dead but sleepeth.' Thou castest thyself in despair on the tomb of thy daughter. But the angel is there who says to thee, 'Seek not the living among the dead.' "

Thus he bound up her wounded heart and she became his lifelong slave. She divided her wealth among her children and, with Eustochium and a company of consecrated virgins, joined Jerome at Antioch. They traveled over the Christian world, visiting holy places, doing good works, and making many converts to Christianity. At Bethlehem Paula founded a community of four monasteries, three for nuns and one for monks. Here, in a cave nearby, Jerome spent the last thirty-four years of his life in study and teaching.

When news reached Paula that her daughter, Paulina, had died while giving birth to a baby girl, she and Jerome insisted that the child be sent to Bethlehem where she could have the benefit of their care and instruction. Jerome especially begged for the child.

Their request was granted, and the baby Paula came to live with her grandmother Paula. It was for this child that Jerome wrote his famous treatise on the education of young girls.

But the grandmother was worn out by toil and service to the many who crowded her community and death soon took her to her reward. Jerome lost all interest in work and was overwhelmed with grief. Only Eustochium could persuade him to work. She assumed all the responsibility for directing her mother's religious community and of taking care of Jerome. In both she was successful. Together, she and Jerome reared the little Paula and, when sixteen years later Jerome passed away, it was this grandchild of his most devoted convert who knelt by his bed and closed his lifeless eyes.

Jerome was buried, as he wished, in the hollow of the rocks of Bethlehem where, even today, his name may be seen traced in the rock.

☆

Saint Ambrose of Milan

BY THE MIDDLE of the fourth century the worship of the Christ had so penetrated high places that bishops forced rulers to repentance and the battles between paganism and Christianity were fought in the open with the gods of wood and stone coming off a poor second.

Into this new world of Christian ascendency was born Ambrose, youngest child of Ambrosius, praetorian prefect of the Gauls under Constantine the Younger. The family was most powerful and of high esteem. The powers over half of Europe, save those of military command, were in the hands of Ambrosius. He was second only to the emperor. And he was a Christian whose ancestors had endured persecution for the faith.

Ambrose was the youngest of the three children in the family. His sister, Marcellina, was the eldest, and his brother, Satyrus, was only a little older than he.

Marcellina, being the oldest, had been consecrated to God in infancy and baptized in the faith. When she reached the age of nineteen she heard, while resting at her father's country home, the voice of Sotheris, a martyred maiden of her house, calling to her to renounce the world and devote herself to the service of God. She obeyed and the following Christmas received the veil from the aged Pope Liberius.

Soon thereafter Ambrosius died, and the widowed mother with her three children went to live with a friend of Marcellina's, also dedicated to the church. As was the custom, girls who took the veil lived with their parents. Marcellina's influence in her home was felt by both her brothers who came to adore her and to depend upon her for advice and comfort.

The society of Rome, in the days of Ambrose, reflected the decaying pagan civilization, peculiarly mixed with the young and vigorous Christianity. Pagan temples were open throughout the city. Many high officials were pagan and among the friends of Ambrose and his family were a great number who worshipped the old gods. Julian the Apostate was attempting a pagan revival. But, in the midst of all this pagan splendor and activity one could see a steady flow of great minds toward Christianity and it was not an uncommon sight to behold a noted pagan leader, such as, for example, Victorinus, translator of Plato and teacher of many noble youths in Rome, ascending the steps of the tribune of the Christian basilica and making public renunciation of paganism.

But, while still a young man, Ambrose was called away from this corrupt society to become consul of what is now

Piedmont and Lombardy. The seat of the government was Milan, then under the rule of the Arian bishop Auxentius and in turmoil over the Arian controversy. When Ambrose had been governor for only a year, Auxentius died. This brought the controversy to a head. The clergy assembled for the election of a new bishop and crowds gathered throughout the city, disputing and crying for their favorites. Milan was in a state of near riot.

Ambrose, as governor, came to the basilica to see that rioting did not break out and to assure a fair election of the new bishop. His position, faith, and just character had become well-known in the city so that great numbers believed in his ability. Thus, as he entered the basilica the crowd took up the cry, "Ambrose is bishop!" So great was the enthusiasm that both the clergy and Ambrose had to yield and the new bishop was elected by popular appeal.

The years that followed proved the wisdom of this chance choice. Ambrose fought brilliantly for Christianity. Wherever he went, whatever he did, there was only one idea in his mind,—the rule of the principles of Christ.

One of Ambrose's greatest victories was over the Emperor Theodosius. There was a charioteer in Thessalonica who had caught the people's fancy because of his skill in the races. But he was of low character and was given just punishment for one of his crimes by a high government official. This angered the people and they murdered the official.

The emperor was at Milan at the time. When news of the murder reached him, he flew into a violent rage and swore that he would avenge the death of his officer. So, he sent out an order inviting the populace of Thessalonica to the arena to witness the games. When the place was crowded to capacity and all were intent upon the games, the soldiers poured in on the people and a horrible massacre followed. News of this affair struck the entire empire with fear and trembling. But the emperor was convinced that he had done what was right and felt no remorse.

Ambrose felt differently about the matter. He refused to go to the palace of Theodosius and refused to admit the emperor to the church before he had made public confession of his sin and made as much reparation as was possible.

Though Ambrose wrote in a most earnest and tender manner pointing out the sin of the emperor and pleading with him to repent, Theodosius was unrepentant. His advisers persuaded him that Ambrose meant well but would not refuse him admittance to the church if he presented himself at the door. So, with all his imperial suite, he came. But Ambrose met him in the vestibule of the penitents and catechumens.

"Emperor," Ambrose said, "you know not, I see, the gravity of the murder you have committed. Do you forget that you are made of dust like the rest of us? Perhaps absolute power blinds your eyes. Take care lest the purple make you lose sight of the infirmities it covers. Those you rule are men, your brothers, your fellow-servants, for there is but one emperor, the creator of all. How, with the stains of blood unjustly shed on your hands, can you come to the body of Jesus Christ? Rather fear to add to your crimes the crime of sacrilege."

Theodosius protested, but to no avail. For eight months the battle between emperor and bishop went on. Then came Christmas. The emperor wanted to attend services at the church, but Ambrose stood his ground even though Rufinius, his minister, visited the bishop and begged that he relent.

Finally Theodosius reached a conclusion. "I will go to Ambrose," he said, "and accept the affront I deserve."

Ambrose met him in the court of the basilica and heard his confession. The emperor accepted his rebukes. He made reparation by enacting a law imposing a delay of thirty days between a sentence of death and its execution. Then, admitted at last to the church, he lay prostrate on the floor, in tears, crying, "O Lord, I cleave to the dust of Thy house;

restore life to me according to Thy word." This was a great victory of the church over temporal power.

Years passed and Ambrose continued to battle for the right and the power of the church. Meantime Theodosius died and Ambrose delivered an eulogy in which he said, "He is gone, this great man, to take possession of a kingdom greater than that he has left. He has made his entry into the Holy Jerusalem whither for his piety Jesus Christ has summoned him."

During the years that followed Ambrose brought the great Augustine to the Christ, wrote much of the beautiful church music that we hear today, and served his Lord and his people as a faithful bishop and a good shepherd.

Then came Good Friday, in the year 397. Those gathered about the bed of the bishop, who had worn himself out in service of the Christ, saw him "extend his arms in the form of a cross to pray." He moved his lips but was too weak to make a sound. After he had finished, the body of the Lord Jesus was brought and "when Ambrose had received it into his heart he yielded up his soul." Easter dawned for him on high, and on earth a host of worshippers throughout the Roman world praised God for a life of unutterable sweetness and truth.

Saint Augustine

ON THE thirteenth day of November in the year 354 there was born to the Christian Monica and her pagan husband Patricius, burgess of the Numidian town of Tagaste, a son whom they named Augustine. This simple statement of fact begins a story unmatched in Christian history of mother love and devotion and of a great man's struggle to find his own soul.

Monica was deeply devoted to the Christian faith. Her tender piety was known by all in Tagaste, and there was scarcely a home into which she had not gone at some time to bring healing or comfort or to strengthen the courage of one whose spirit was low.

Her love for Patricius was as true and rich. And, though a pagan, he loved her with all his heart. Thus, Augustine was born into a home of pure and true affection and great understanding.

Monica's one great mission in life was to bring her beloved husband and son to the Christ. Her "beautiful faith and enthusiasm and patient prayer for both her husband and son . . . have made her a type of womanly saintliness for all ages."

From his birth Augustine was instructed and nurtured in the faith of Jesus Christ and, while yet a boy, was on the verge of being baptized. Falling ill with "a sudden oppression of the stomach" and believing himself near to death, he begged to be baptized. But, when the illness passed, his baptism was put off because of fear that he would commit such sins after baptism as would pollute his confession. Monica knew her son better than he knew himself. Later he wrote, "But how many great waves of temptation seemed to hang over me in my boyhood. These my mother foresaw, and preferred to expose to them the clay whence I might afterwards be moulded rather than the cast itself when made."

Augustine's young manhood was dominated by two great passions, one of the flesh and another of the intellect. Inheriting from his father a passionate nature, he early found himself leading a promiscuous life which was terminated only when he formed an irregular union with a woman who was devoted to him and whom he came to love deeply. She bore him a son to whom he gave the name Adeodatus, meaning "by God given," and for whom he formed a great love and admiration. The boy became keen-minded and intellectually gifted. Augustine's book, *The Master,* is a dialogue between himself and his son.

His other passion was for knowledge and understanding. Blessed with one of the great minds of medieval times, he was given every opportunity possible to develop it. His parents, "beyond the ability of their means," furnished him the money necessary for travel and study. Indeed, this desire to develop the boy's mind led to excesses which Augustine came later to condemn. Monica urged him not to marry lest a wife would hinder his mental growth and ruin her hopes for him, "not the hopes of the world to come, but of learning in this world, which both were too anxious I should attain."

When he was seventeen his father died and Augustine took an allowance from his mother and left home to continue his studies at Carthage. Here he threw himself into the intellectual life of the city. He was the prize student at the school of rhetoric and began to show great talent as an orator.

At this time he turned to a study of the Christian Scriptures, but found them lacking in literary value and unworthy to be compared with the writings of the great Latin masters.

From this he turned to Manichaeism, a strange mixture of Zoroastrianism and elements from Gnosticism, and, for a time, believed he had found satisfaction for his soul. But, in arguments and discussions with Faustus, "a bishop among the Manichaeans," he saw the weaknesses of this position and turned away from it with much disappointment.

Being by this time a man of considerable repute as a teacher of rhetoric, Augustine traveled to Rome, hoping to ply his trade and possibly satisfy his intellectual thirst for truth. Here he associated with the academicians and developed a liking for Plato as interpreted by the Neo-platonists. But Rome was as unsatisfactory to him as Carthage had been.

Thus, when the people of Milan sent to Symmachus, the

prefect of Rome, for a teacher of rhetoric, Augustine applied for the position and was successful. This was the turning point of Augustine's life, for Symmachus was a close friend of Ambrose, Bishop of Milan, and he gave him a note of introduction to the bishop.

"That man of God received me as a father," Augustine recounts in his *Confessions,* "and showed me episcopal kindness on my coming. Thenceforth I began to love him. At first, indeed, not as a teacher of the truth (which I utterly despaired of in Thy Church), but as a person kind towards myself. And I listened diligently to him preaching to the people, not with that intent I ought, but as it were testing his eloquence, whether it flowed fuller or lower than was reported; but as to the matter I was a careless and scornful looker-on."

Meantime Monica, who was at her home in Africa and was continually praying for her son's conversion, heard that he had at last consented to become a catechumen with Ambrose and hastened to join him in Milan. She found him "in grievous peril through despair of ever finding truth" and redoubled her efforts to bring him to the Christ.

Two young men, former pupils of Augustine's at Carthage by the name of Alypius and Nebridius, shared his struggle and his earnest search for truth. They studied together, discussed problems of religion, and compared the Christian doctrine with all the philosophic and religious theories which they could gather. And Monica was praying for him and trying as best she knew how to win him from his past. She arranged a marriage for him and was able to force him to send away the mother of his son. This was a terrible blow to Augustine who, though recognizing the evil of his relationship with this woman, loved her deeply.

At length, broken in spirit and heavy of heart, he turned to a study of Saint Paul. Through friends he heard of many simple and ignorant people who had found conversion and peace. "What ails us?" he asked Alypius. "The unlearned take heaven by force, and we with our learning, without heart, we wallow still."

He and Alypius went into a little garden near the house. Augustine was deeply troubled of soul and he felt a great struggle going on within him. "When a deep consideration had, from the secret bottom of my soul, hunted up all my misery, there arose a mighty storm, bringing a great shower of tears," he tells us. "I rose from Alypius. Solitude seemed fitting for the blessedness of weeping. I cast myself down under a fig tree. I sent up these sorrowful words, 'How long? how long? tomorrow? tomorrow? Why not now?'

"So was I speaking and weeping in the most bitter contrition of my heart, when lo, I heard from a neighboring house a voice of one, boy or girl, I knew not, chanting and oft repeating, '*Tolle, lege,* Take up and read.' Instantly my countenance altered; I began to think intently whether children were wont in any kind of play to sing such words, nor could I remember ever to have heard the like."

Checking his tears, he returned to where Alypius was sitting and where he had left a copy of the writings of Saint Paul. He opened the book and his eyes fell upon the Scripture: "Not in rioting and drunkenness, not in chambering and wantonness, not in strife and envying; but put ye on the Lord Jesus Christ and make not provision for the flesh." He read no further.

Together, he and Alypius went to Monica and told her the good news,—her prayers had been answered and her son had become a Christian. Her joy was beyond bound and her thanksgiving for this miracle poured out with her tears.

The days that followed were spent in prayer and study of the Scriptures. Mother and son communed together about the God of Jesus Christ and his love. Then, late on Easter Eve in the year 387, he was baptized in the Basilica of the Baptistry at Milan by his friend and teacher, Ambrose.

Thus began the career of one of the greatest fathers of the early church. His mother's work was done, and she died later that year, happy in the thought that her son belonged wholly to her Christ. During the forty-three years that followed, this son of her tears and prayers rose to the bishopric of Hippo, led the church to many glorious victories, wrote volume after volume for the guidance of Christians, preached hundreds of sermons, and in many other ways carved his name in letters of fire across the history of early Christianity.

Then came the Vandals, invited by Count Boniface, a Christian and a friend of the aged bishop of Hippo, to avenge himself against the ingratitude of the Imperial Court of Ravenna. They burned villages and killed the innocent until at last they arrived at the gates of Hippo behind which great hosts had taken refuge.

Augustine would not desert his people. Old and greatly weakened by a strenuous life of service to God, he continued to preach and minister to the frightened multitudes until his strength began to fail. When he knew that the end was near, he asked to be left alone by all save his physician and those who brought him food, so that he could devote all his remaining time to prayer.

As the enemy pushed the siege of his beloved city, Augustine was taken by the Christ whom he had loved and served for so long to the City of God which no enemy can besiege and into which no evil can creep. On August 28, 430, his friends folded his lifeless hands in prayer, knowing that he was safe from all vandals, material or spiritual.

Saint Patrick, Patron of Ireland

"I, PATRICK, a sinner, the rudest and least of all the faithful, and the most despicable among most men, had for my father Calpurnius, a deacon, son of the late Potitus, a presbyter, who was of the town Bonaven Taberniae, and he had a farm in the neighborhood, where I was taken captive. I was then nearly sixteen years old."

This statement from the *Confessions* of Saint Patrick reveals that he came from a family high in Christian circles in the British Isles. But he was not religious. Indeed, his captivity by a band of Irish marauders was, he believed, punishment "because we had gone back from His commandments, and had not been obedient to our priests."

As a captive of Miliucc, a chieftain living near the mountain called Slemish in county Antrim, Patrick tended cattle and did other menial services. During the six years of his bondage, he became subject to religious emotions and saw visions which encouraged him to escape. His attempt being successful, he fled to the coast and boarded a vessel engaged in the import of Irish wolf-dogs. This took him to Gaul from whence, after some years of wandering, he went to his home in Britain.

"And there," he writes in his *Confessions,* "in the dead of night, I saw a man coming to me as if from Hiberio, whose name was Victoricus, bearing innumerable epistles. And he gave me one of them, and I read the beginning of it, which contained the words, 'The voice of the Irish.' And whilst I was repeating the beginning of the epistle, I imagined that I heard in my mind the voice of those who were near the wood of Foclut, which is near the Western Sea. And thus they cried, 'We pray thee, holy youth, to come and henceforth walk amongst us.' And I was greatly pricked in heart and could read no more; and so I awoke. Thanks be to God, that after very many years the Lord granted unto them the blessing for which they cried."

Patrick experienced a number of other visions, each calling him back to the land of his captivity and to the service of the Lord in that land. The result was that he went to Ireland and there devoted his life to the conversion of these people to Christianity.

Saint Patrick sought to adopt as many of the Irish customs and traditions of those he was seeking to Christianize as he could. Wherever he found anything which seemed to him good in their culture, he translated it into Christian terms, as far as possible, and made it part of his teaching. He sought to enlist on his side the Druids,—the priests, teachers, and poets of the people. These Irish bards often became his most faithful disciples.

At one time Patrick expressed fear that the too piratical and profane warriors whose glory the bards celebrated might be in hell. To this one of the bards replied, "If thy God were in hell, my heroes would rescue him thence."

Slowly Patrick won the bards to his cause and the monasteries founded by him became the homes of Celtic poetry. As one writer points out, "The song of the bards, blessed and transfigured, became so beautiful that the angels of heaven stooped down to listen, and the harp became the badge of Catholic Ireland."

In this way Patrick sought to make holy many of the pagan customs and festivals of the Irish people by adapting them to Christian ideals. But, wherever he found pagan practices which were wholly un-Christian, he fought them violently. He destroyed the famous idol, Cenn Cruaich, in county Cavan and had many contests with the Druids over the power of his God and their gods.

But Patrick was able to gain the good will of the tribal rulers of Ireland and often to convert them to the faith. Their sons became his pupils and learned from him the secrets of the Christian gospel. In time, they went out to carry forward the work of the missionary. As a result Christianity spread over the land and Ireland became one of the great centers of the church.

Patrick died in 461, some years after he had resigned as bishop of Armagh and retired to Saul in Dalaradia. Here

Saint Bridget, daughter of a captive slave and one of his converts, ministered to him and, with her own hands, prepared his coffin and buried him.

Saint Simeon Stylites

MANY MEN have chosen ways of serving Christ which appear strange to their fellows but which express in some way their deep devotion. And often their methods have proved successful in winning others to the Christian life. One of these men was Saint Simeon Stylites, the saint of the pillar.

Simeon was born in northern Syria in 390. Very early he showed marked religious devotion and sought to excel all others in the austerity of his life. It is recorded that one time when he encountered a ragged beggar he not only gave him his purse and all his clothing, but lay in the dust and insisted that the filthy man walk on him.

He entered a monastery early in life and gave himself wholly to austere practices to defame his body and purify his soul. He would expose his body naked to both the sun and the cold and refuse any medical care even when he was burned by the heat almost to a crisp or blue from cold. "When God is ready," he argued, "He will take me to his bosom. If I live, it is his will; and if I die, it is his will."

These excessive austerities were demoralizing to the monastery. Monks refused to obey the rule of the place and spent all their time devising ways to torture their bodies and vied with each other in suffering pain. The monastery was fast becoming a voluntary torture chamber in which all work, study, and even prayer and worship were neglected. So demoralizing was the influence of Simeon that he was finally dismissed by the authorities at thirty years of age.

This gave Simeon the opportunity to dramatize his devotion. Near the monastery he built a pillar six feet high and established himself on its top, there to live. His friends brought him food and water and other necessities of life and hundreds came out to see him and listen to his preaching from the top of the pillar.

Dissatisfied with the height of the pillar, he soon built one higher. This continued for ten years, until he had a pillar sixty feet high. A ladder stretched from the top to the ground and friends scaled this as often as it was necessary to serve the monk.

As the pillar grew higher, greater and greater crowds came out to hear Simeon preach. When he was not preaching, the crowds would sit about the pillar and worship. A number of people built rude huts and other places of abode nearby until a small colony was established with the pillar as its center.

For thirty years Simeon lived atop this pillar, never descending for any reason whatsoever. Storm, wind, rain, or heat were as nothing to him. There he studied and prayed. Friends scaled the pillar and kept him informed about ecclesiastical affairs and politics. Thus his sermons were often pertinent to church matters and their influence was great. He swayed the opinions of the crowds that came out to hear him. Often there were many clergy among his listeners and they were deeply influenced by his oratory and reasoning.

Numerous imitators of Simeon sprang up in other places, but no one had the influence that was exerted by this first pillar hermit. Many heathens were converted by his preaching and his example and the power of his life was felt long after the strange figure atop the pillar had become but a memory to some and a legend to others.

☆

Saint Benedict of Monte Cassino

SAINT BENEDICT was born in luxury and before him stretched a life of ease, position, and Roman culture possible for only the few in the Roman world of the sixth century. He was born in 480 at Noricum in Nursia. His father was a member of the old and respected house of Anicii and his mother was of the race of the "seigneurs" of Nursia. No youth could ask for a better inheritance.

While a lad, he was sent to Rome by his father to attend the Roman schools and learn from the wisest and most scholarly men of his day. The gates were opened to him. He had but to enter and partake of all a young Roman could wish.

But Benedict was not happy. The "wise folly and holy ignorance" of the city disgusted him. Here he saw sin in its lewdest dress and temptation stalked on every street. Although he succumbed to both in his early years, he was too sensitive to be contented with what they offered, and fled from the vices with which he was unable to cope.

Forty miles from Rome, in the mountain districts of the Abruzzi, lay the ruins of Nero's palace and, nearby, a lake which Nero had built by impounding the waters of a river. Among the rocks on the side of the valley opposite the palace, Benedict found a deep hollow with no view except upward towards the sky. This became his home for three years. Romanus, a monk of a neighboring monastery whom he had met earlier and who had given him a hair shirt and a goat-skin cloak, brought him part of his own scanty meals. This food was lowered to him by a rope to which a bell was attached. When Benedict had finished his meal he rang the bell and the empty vessels were hoisted to the surface.

In this cave Benedict was haunted by the memory of a beautiful woman whom he had known in Rome. To tear away this memory, he rolled himself in thorn-bushes till his flesh was all torn and bleeding. Seven centuries later Saint Francis of Assisi came to this thicket of thorns and planted two rose bushes. Today the thorns are gone, but the roses of Saint Francis remain.

The monks of the neighboring monastery asked Benedict to become their abbot. He accepted, but found the lives of the residents irregular and dissolute. His demands for austerity fatigued many and made others hate him so that one attempted to give him a glass of poison. But Benedict made the sign of the cross over the glass, and it was shivered in pieces.

After leaving these treacherous monks, Benedict gathered about himself enough recluses to fill twelve monasteries with twelve monks in each. He founded the monasteries in the immediate area of the cave, but maintained general control of all. Although the monasteries thrived and many Roman patricians and senators sent their sons to be trained in them, the wicked priests of the neighborhood harassed the young communities in every way they could imagine. Finally, they sent a troop of dissolute women to tempt them by wild songs and dances.

This opposition eventually forced Benedict, with a small company of his disciples, to leave the monasteries he had founded and push farther away from Rome along the range of the Apennines. Coming to Cassino, a town halfway between Rome and Naples, he found a high peak just outside the city on which was a temple dedicated to Apollo. Here the peasants came to worship this pagan god. Benedict made known to the people the religion of Christ and persuaded them to cut down the sacred grove and destroy the statue of the sun god which adorned the temple. Then he established there a monastery which very soon became one of the great centers of Roman Christianity, the monastery of Monte Cassino.

Gradually the monastery grew in fame and service. A

great many came out from Rome and other Italian cities to find at Monte Cassino escape from the chaotic conditions of the crumbling Roman empire. Others sought the austerity of Benedict's rule to escape the chaos of the church, the wild reaction to Oriental paganism. Goths, who though they were rude invaders were repelled by the dissoluteness of the Roman world, sought sanctuary and peace in this monastery. Oppressed peasants, weary men of that weary old world, Roman nobles, and Gothic kings, came to inquire of this seer in his shrine among the mountains.

For fourteen years Benedict lived in the monastery atop Mount Cassino, teaching, praying, helping, often laboring with the other monks at masons' work or at tilling the soil on the slopes of the mountain. Here he prepared a "rule" for the governing of the monastery. He set aside regular periods for prayer and mental and manual labor. The monks were obliged to cultivate the land and also to spend time in literary pursuits. Much fine work was done in copying manuscripts. The "rule" was revised and expanded several times and eventually became the famous "Rule of Saint Benedict," now used wherever there is a Benedictine monastery.

Benedict devoted himself wholly and completely to his monastery, seldom leaving it for more than a few hours. His sister, Scholastica, lived in a convent on the slopes of Mount Cassino, but he would see her only once a year and then only for the few hours of the day, returning to his own monastery as the sun sank in the west.

At the last meeting of Benedict and his sister, the health of the old monk was failing and Scholastica feared that she would never see her brother again. So, when the shadows began to lengthen, she begged him to stay with her through the night, saying "My brother, leave me not tonight, that we may speak of the joys of heaven till tomorrow morning."

"What sayest thou, my sister?" he answered. "At no price can I stay a night outside my monastery."

At this Scholastica laid her head on her clasped hands on

the table and prayed. Scarcely had she finished her prayer when a violent storm broke, and the rain was so heavy that neither Benedict nor any of the monks who accompanied him could leave.

In the morning they parted, never to meet again on this earth. Three days later Benedict was standing at the window of his cell when he "saw the soul of his sister entering heaven under the form of a dove." He had her body brought to Monte Cassino and laid in the sepulchre which he had prepared for himself.

Forty days later he announced his own death to his disciples. A violent fever seized him and he knew that his end was near. Calling his monks to him, he asked that he be carried to the chapel consecrated to Saint John the Baptist. Here he had the tomb in which his sister lay opened and his own grave prepared.

Then, placing himself on the edge of the open grave, and thus also at the foot of the altar, with his arms stretched toward heaven, he died standing, breathing out his soul with his last prayer.

Soon after Benedict's death the Lombards destroyed the Abbey of Monte Cassino and the monks fled to Rome where they established the Lateran basilica. It was rebuilt in 720, but was again destroyed, this time by the Saracens, in 884. Forty years later it was restored and reached the height of its influence under Desiderius and Oderisius, from 1059 to 1105. At the dissolution of monasteries in 1866, Monte Cassino was spared because of a remonstrance by English well-wishers of United Italy.

In 1944 the monastery was destroyed by air bombardment because it was being used for military purposes by the German armies in Italy.

☆

Saint Gregory the Great

GREGORY, son of Gordianus and Silvia, was born to the purple. His father was a wealthy man of senatorial rank, owner of a large estate in Sicily and a palace on the Caelian Hill in Rome. His education was of the best and he attained high proficiency in the arts of grammar, rhetoric, and dialectic,—all that then constituted a liberal education. At thirty he became praetor of Rome and seemed on the road to a distinguished career in public service. He went among the people of Rome wearing the garments and emblems of his high office,—silken robes, purple stripes, and jewels.

When Gregory was thirty-four his father died. This was a stunning blow to both him and his mother. Silvia retired into a convent, and Gregory sold a large portion of his inheritance to found six monasteries, five in Sicily and one in Rome. In the last, the monastery of Saint Andrew, he became a monk and sought seclusion from all that he had known and honored before. His silken robes were exchanged for the black woolen Benedictine dress and hood.

But one so gifted and sensitive as Gregory could not remain long in seclusion. His was an age of mighty upheavals and the problems of church and empire were many and hard to solve. Africa was in Vandal hands and the church there was torn by schisms. Spain was under the Arian heresy. The Saxon invaders had driven the Christians of England into the mountains of Wales and Cornwall. The Catholic faith in Gaul was being daily dishonored by its professors. The Persians threatened the East. And Italy itself, the seat of the church, was almost constantly in the throes of war with Goths and Lombards contesting with the Byzantine Court for the right to plunder her and enslave her people.

Gregory was called back from his seclusion into this world

that so desperately needed him and his talents and in 578 he was ordained archdeacon of the Roman Church. The following spring Pope Pelagius II appointed him resident ambassador at the imperial court in Constantinople. When he returned to Rome, after representing the Roman see brilliantly, he was made abbot of Saint Andrew's monastery.

At Saint Andrew's his rule was severe and uncompromising. When one of his monks, who had much medical skill and had often assisted Gregory by his knowledge and kindness, lay dying, in his hand were found three gold pieces which he had concealed, contrary to the monastic vow of poverty. To Gregory this was dangerous disloyalty and must be punished severely. At his order, the body of the monk was cast on a dunghill with the three pieces of gold and every member of the monastery, instead of chanting the Benedictus at the funeral, was commanded to repeat the awful Apostolic sentence, "Thy money perish with thee."

But Gregory's heart softened later and he ordered that masses and prayers be offered daily for the poor monk's soul. At the end of thirty days the monk appeared to his abbot in a dream and told him that his soul had been in anguish but now was relieved.

Some time later Gregory was walking through the slave market in Rome when he was attracted by a group of fair-haired boys. Upon making inquiry, he was informed that they were Angli and pagans from the once Christian island of Britain. "They are well named," he said, "these fair strangers. Angels they are in countenance and should be co-heirs with the angels in heaven."

When he was told that they were from the province of Deira, he remarked, "Deira. Yea, verily, they shall be saved from God's ire and called to the mercy of Christ. How is the king of that country named?"

"Aella," was the answer.

"Then must Alleluia be sung in Aella's land."

Though Gregory wished to go personally to convert these

people, and although the pope permitted him to set out on the mission, so great was the protest of the people at losing their beloved leader that he was called back after only three days. But the desire to save England never died in Gregory's heart and he was eventually responsible for sending Augustine of Canterbury to this far-off land.

In 590 Pope Pelagius II died amidst one of the worst plagues ever to ravage Rome. The clergy and the people unanimously chose Gregory to fill his place. But this was not an honor sought by the abbot of Saint Andrew's. Indeed, he did everything to avoid this dignity, even to petitioning the Emperor Maurice not to ratify the election. When this was refused he contemplated going into hiding, but, "while he was preparing for flight and concealment, he was seized and carried off and dragged to the basilica of Saint Peter" where he was consecrated bishop.

The fourteen years that followed were marked by a phenomenal growth in the power and influence of the Roman Church. Gregory thought of himself as the head of the entire church of Christ on earth and acted accordingly. He saw the power of the Roman emperors declining and did his best to move into the gap which was left open. He dispensed charity widely, even to impoverishing the treasury of the church. Gradually he gained power over the bishops, removing the power of election from each district and placing it under himself.

In his view Rome was "the head of all the churches" wherever located. "I know of no one," he wrote, "who is not subject to the apostolic see." For the first time in history the bishop at Rome appeared as a political power, a temporal prince. He appointed governors to cities, issued orders to generals, provided munitions of war, sent his ambassadors to negotiate with the Lombard kings, and actually dared to conclude a private peace. In a real sense it is true that "of the medieval papacy, the real father is Gregory the Great."

During all these years and while Gregory was serving the

Roman Church with more vigor than any of his predecessors, he was ill and in pain. His powerful frame, injured beyond repair by his early fastings and austerities, could not endure the pace he had set. In many of his intimate letters a cry of pain bursts from his brave heart. "My body is dried up as if already in the coffin," he writes. "Death is the only remedy for me." In another place he cries, "For two years I have been confined to my bed by such suffering from gout that I can only keep up for three hours to celebrate mass at the great festivals. These maladies will neither quit me nor kill me."

Death came at last, on March 12, 604, in his sixty-fourth year. By this time the position of the Roman Church was established and the outline of its future career well drawn.

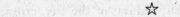

☆

Saint Giles, Patron of the Woodlands

THEODORE AND PELAGIA, both of royal Athenian blood, had a child whom they named Giles, born a cripple. His foot was turned in so that he walked with great difficulty, and awkwardly. His deformity made his parents love him all the more and he in turn was devoted to them beyond the power of words.

It is not surprising, then, that the death of both parents within a year was a blow almost too great for Giles to bear. He was but twenty-four years of age. Behind him lay a thorough training in Christian piety and love and an education in the schools of classical learning that could not be matched in the empire. The loss of his parents convinced him of the transitoriness of all human joys, and made him feel that the only things of eternal value were prayer and communion with one's God.

Thus, Giles sold all that he had, distributed his wealth among the poor, and set out to find solitude where he could devote the remainder of his life to his Master. Landing on a lonely island near Athens, he found human footprints on the shore. He followed these and came to a cave in which dwelled a venerable old hermit who had lived there for twelve years, eating herbs and roots. Giles shared the cave of the old man for three days of prayer and meditation. But, fearing that his friends would find him so close to Athens and force him to return to a life which he had come to hate, Giles hailed a passing ship and traveled until he came to the old Greek colony of Marseilles.

Here he spent much time healing the sick and ministering to the suffering and miserable. Indeed, his presence was so great a blessing to the city that he was invited to settle there and continue his work. But Giles was seeking solitude and, suddenly and secretly, he slipped out of the city, crossed the Rhone, and traveled toward the rocky steep watered by the river Garonne.

In this wild, out-of-the-way place Giles found a cave in which lived a solitary from Greece. For a time both were happy in being able to converse in their native tongue and to sing the praises of Christ in the language of their childhood. But in time Giles found the old fear returning, the fear that he would be forced back into the world from which he desired more than anything else to flee. So, the two friends parted with many a tear and Giles wandered deeper and deeper into the forest.

At last he came to a lonely and beautiful glade near a stream. Here he found a cave carved out of solid rock and shaded by four giant oaks. This became his abode for many years. He lived on the wild fruits and vegetation of the place and was happy.

In time Giles won the confidence of a hind who would come daily to the stream to drink. She spent much time in his cave and gave him her milk to drink. Here, with the creatures of nature and the wild life of the forest, the unhappy cripple worshipped God and prayed for the salvation of his soul.

One day, the quiet of the forest was pierced by the blare of horns and the baying of hounds, all the sounds of the chase. To the hunters who had ridden to this solitary and virgin woodland Giles' gentle hind was merely part of the wild game of the place.

The frightened creature took refuge in Giles' cave just as a hunter approached and aimed an arrow at her. The holy hermit threw up his hand to protect his friend and received the arrow through his palm. The hunters rode up and demanded that Giles give over the hind as their rightful prey of the chase, but he refused and began to preach to them about the vanishing clouds of this life and the eternal life with Christ.

His gentle dignity and sweet words touched their hearts and they believed. Being from the court, the huntsmen returned soon with Wamba, their king, who wanted to see the hermit in the cave with his hind. The king was impressed and offered to give Giles land and gold for any foundation he chose, but he refused all entreaties, preferring his life of solitude and prayer.

Finally, however, Giles was persuaded and consented to become the founder and leader of an abbey where charity was to be had in abundance and where the sick, the lonely, and the suffering could find help and understanding. For many years the Abbey of Saint Giles flourished and became famous throughout the land.

Then came the Saracens, burning and laying waste the land and fields. The Abbey of Saint Giles was in their way, and it was destroyed. The monks from the abbey took refuge with Charles Martel, aiding him with their prayers in the great battle for the Christianity of the West. At last these prayers were answered and the on-rushing tide of Mohammedanism was checked and turned back at Châlons.

One of the first things done after the victory was the restoration of Saint Giles' monastery and the good works of charity were continued as before the invasion.

With his monastery flourishing again and the poor and needy coming and going in a constant stream, Giles was happy and contented to turn over the work to others more able than he to continue. "Lord, now lettest Thou Thy servant depart in peace," he said. "Eighty and three years weigh on me, and I am tired." On the first of September, 720, his prayer was answered and he fell asleep among his monks to awaken in the life eternal.

But Giles lived on in this world in the good works which he began. Everywhere throughout the western world the poor are helped, wild life protected, and cripples given new hope and courage in his name and the light of Saint Giles burns brightly in many a human heart that would otherwise be dark with despair.

The Venerable Bede

BISHOP BISCOP, founder of the monasteries of Wearmouth and Jarrow in England, made frequent trips to Rome, Vienna, and monasteries throughout the Christian world, and always returned laden with books and other literary treasures collected from these seats of medieval learning. When he began to unpack his prizes, no one was more interested than a certain youth who was born in a home situated between the two monasteries and who had been entrusted by his parents to Biscop's care. This youth was Bede who was later called "Venerable."

At the age of seven, Bede had been sent to Biscop to be instructed in the learning of the day and in Christian principles. Early he showed great promise and became the bishop's favorite pupil. Later he tells us, "From that time I have spent the whole of my life within that monastery [Jarrow] devoting all my pains to the study of the Scriptures; and amid the observance of monastic discipline, and the daily charge of singing in the church, it has ever been my delight to learn or teach or write."

At nineteen, far under the accustomed age, Bede was admitted to the deaconate, and at thirty he was ordained to the priesthood. Then, until his death, he devoted himself to writing the story of the church and commentaries on the Scriptures.

The *Ecclesiastical History of the English Nation,* Bede's greatest contribution, has justly earned him the title of "Father of English History." In it we have the best information that could be gathered at that time about the church in England. But, not only is the work as authentic as it was possible to write at that time, but also it is one of the most beautiful of historical works. Here the author shows the artist's instinct for proportion and a keen sensitivity for the picturesque and the pathetic. His style is limpid and unaffected and charms the modern reader as it did those of his own day.

During his long and active life, Bede wrote many books on scientific matters, historical movements, and theological questions. His commentaries are based largely on the works of the great Latin fathers, but were written in the language of the English people and served to bring religion closer to those who knew no classical language. Indeed, Bede virtually summed up all the learning of his times in his writings and handed it on to the readers of his own beloved land.

Of him, his pupil and devoted disciple Cuthbert writes: "He lived joyfully, giving thanks to God day and night— yea at all hours—until the Feast of the Ascension. Every day he gave lessons to us, his pupils, and the rest of the time he occupied himself in chanting psalms." As his strength began to fail, "he was awake almost the whole night and spent it in joy and thanksgiving. And when he awoke from his short sleep, immediately he raised his hands on high, and began again to give thanks.

"On Tuesday before Ascension Day his sickness increased, his breathing became difficult, and his feet began to swell. Yet he passed the whole day joyfully dictating. At times he would say, 'Make haste to learn, for I do not know how long I shall remain with you, whether my Creator will not soon take me to Himself.'

"The following night he spent in prayers and thanksgiving; and when Wednesday dawned he desired us diligently to continue writing what we had begun. When this was finished we carried the relics in procession, as is customary on that day. One of us then said to him, 'Dearest master, we have yet one chapter to translate. Will it be grievous to thee if we ask thee any further?'

"He answered, 'It is quite easy, take the pen and write quickly.'

"At three o'clock he said to me, 'Run quickly and call the priests of this convent to me that I may impart to them the gifts which God has given to me. The rich of this world seek to give gold and silver and other costly things; but with great love and joy will I give to my brethren what God has given me.'

"Then he said, 'It is time that I go to my Creator. I have lived long enough. The time of my departure is at hand; for I long to depart and be with Christ.'

"Thus did he live till evening. Then I said to him, 'Dearest master, there is only one thing left to write.'

"He answered, 'Write quickly.'

"Soon I replied, 'Now this thought also is written.'

"He answered, 'Thou hast well said. It is finished. Raise my head in thy hand, for it will do me good to sit opposite my sanctuary, where I was wont to kneel and pray, that sitting thus I may call upon my Father.' So he seated himself on the ground in his cell and sang, 'Glory to Thee, O God, Father, Son, and Holy Ghost'; and when he had named the Holy Ghost he breathed his last breath."

Saint Edward the Confessor

IN ANCIENT TIMES the River Thames, flowing downward from Chelsea and Battersea, washed one shore of a small island known as Thorney. Here, in the days of Roman occupancy, stood a temple to Apollo which was destroyed by an earthquake during the reign of Antoninus Pius.

King Lucius founded a church on this isle in 170, but the Saxons, invading the country, destroyed everything on the small island, even the church, and the place remained desolate until Sebert, king of the East Saxons, restored the church "to the honor of God and Saint Peter." There is a legend that Saint Peter appeared at the dedication to give his blessing to the new edifice.

But the little church fell prey to idolatry once more with the Danish conquest and was not restored until King Edgar came to the English throne in the tenth century. This edifice, built by the Christian king of early England, cast a light all its own across the river and through the town "without shadow or darkness," illumined by the angels.

This holy place was particularly dear to King Edward. He was the son of Æthelred II and Emma, daughter of Richard, Duke of Normandy. His father had been forced to take refuge in Normandy when Sweyn was recognized as king in 1013. Here the boy was reared in the Norman court, a wild and gay place filled with temptations. But he resisted all temptation and developed a deep religious nature. He vowed to Saint Peter that, if he ever returned to his father's kingdom, he would make a pilgrimage to his tomb and church at Rome. In 1041 he was recalled to England and, upon the death of Hardicanute, became king.

As the rightful king restored to his throne, Edward spent much time in the little chapel on the isle of Thorney. It was the custom for great crowds to gather along the way from the palace to the chapel to beg from the king as he passed. One day a crippled Irishman called out to the king as he passed, "Four pilgrimages have I made to Rome for a cure, but in vain. Saint Peter has told me that if the king will carry me on his back to the chapel, I will recover."

Edward heard him and, amid the scoffs and jeers of his attendants and some of the people, took the poor man on his shoulders and bore him to the high altar. Instantly, the man stood on his feet and walked away cured.

At another time, as the king was at mass in the little chapel, his eyes were opened and he saw on the same high altar the Divine Child, pure and bright like a spirit, smiling at him.

Edward remembered his vow to Saint Peter and informed Parliament of his intent to fulfill it. But the members of this august body dissuaded him with many arguments. They pointed out the need of the country for his presence, the perils of the road to Rome both by sea and by the mountains, the danger of ambuscades at bridges and fords, and told him of "the false Romans, who covet the red gold and the white silver as a leech covets blood."

Although persuaded not to take the trip, Edward was unhappy until there appeared before him a hermit from Worcester. "Sir King," he said, "the Lord has come to me in a dream to tell how you may fulfill your vow though not traveling the dangerous road to Rome."

Edward was overjoyed and begged him to tell the nature of his dream.

"To the east," he replied, "stands the great and beautiful Saint Paul's, a minister to all who are there. But the West has no minister, save the little chapel on Thorney Isle. In my dream I saw rising by your hand on this island a monastery for the monks of Saint Benedict and a great church to Saint Peter to be the West Minister of London as Saint Paul's is the East."

In the sixteenth year of his reign Edward began the construction of his abbey. The kingdom of his fathers was falling apart, but the beautiful abbey was rising stone on stone. For the next fifteen years he devoted himself to building the abbey, the chase, and dispensing charity, caring little for the responsibilities of the throne and leaving the duties of his office largely to others. But, "at the cost of a tenth of the property of his realm," he built a monument to himself and to England which has lived in the hearts of all Englishmen, though few remember the king who built it.

Carved on the walls of his chapel at Westminster Abbey is a replica of Edward resting after the fatigue of the day upon a couch. Nearby is a money chest left open by his steward Hogulin. A scullion, thinking the king to be asleep, has crept in and is helping himself to the royal wealth. But the king is awake, and warns the thief to fly before Hogulin returns, or "he will not leave you a halfpenny." Afterwards Edward pleaded for the delinquent, saying, "He hath more need of it than we. Enough treasure hath King Edward."

Because of a generosity such as this, Hogulin would not entrust Edward with money, a condition which often embarrassed the king. On one occasion a beggar asked for alms, but the king found that he had no gold or silver about him. So, after a moment, he withdrew his royal ring from his finger and gave it to the man, who vanished.

Shortly after this, two English pilgrims found themselves in difficulty in Syria when suddenly their pathway was lighted up and an old man, "tarrying till his Lord should come," preceded by two torches, accosted them. They told him of their country and their saintly king, on which the old man "joyously, like a clerk," guided them to an inn where he revealed that he was John the Evangelist. Then he gave them the king's ring to return to him along with the message that in six months he would be in Paradise.

On Christmas day Edward fell ill and rapidly grew worse as the Festival of the Innocents approached. He was able to rouse himself to sign the charter of Westminster Abbey but could not attend the consecration of the relics. On the evening of the day of consecration he sank into a stupor from which he rallied only for a few moments to comfort his weeping queen with, "Weep not. I shall not die, but live. I am going from the land of death to the land of the living."

And "Saint Peter, his friend, opened the gate of Paradise, and Saint John, his own dear one, led him before the Divine Majesty." Edward was buried in his own abbey, in his royal robes and with the crucifix and the pilgrim's ring, the first of England's great to rest in the abbey.

Peter the Hermit

THE VILLAGERS of eleventh-century France knew him well, that strange hermit who came riding among them on an ass and preaching with such wild eloquence that they followed him scarcely knowing why or where.

He was called Peter the Hermit. Some say that years before he had started on a pilgrimage to Jerusalem but was turned back by the infidel Turk who held the city and all its holy places. Angered by this rebuff, he could not forget that the place where Christ was born and the hill on which he died were trod on by unholy feet. The more he remembered, the more he burned with righteous zeal to drive the heathen out and restore the land to the church.

One day he found himself in Clermont in a great crowd, all listening to the golden-voiced Pope Urban II. This beloved leader of the church was saying what had burned deeply in the wild Peter's soul but which he could not find words to utter. Pope Urban II begged for "the truce of God" in Europe while the Christianity of the West bent every effort to winning Jerusalem and the Holy Land from the barbarous Turk. Then he offered full and complete penance to any and all who would join in this holy Crusade.

Peter was fired with great enthusiasm. Mounting his ass, he rode away from Clermont and through the villages of France and along the Rhine, preaching to the poor of the countryside with an eloquence that was irresistible. Almost immediately he became an object of reverence among these simple people. Even his ass was worshipped, and villagers flocked to hear him and threw themselves at his feet when he had finished preaching.

Very soon Peter had gathered a great army of the poor yearning to set out upon the holy mission against the Turk. It was three or four months before the time set by Pope Urban II for the start of the first Crusade, but Peter's nondescript army of "paupers," the poor of the land, was gathered and could not be restrained. Thus, he divided them into five divisions, placed them under the leadership of men of their kind, and the tragic march of the Paupers' Crusade, the opening act of the first Crusade, began.

Three divisions, under Fulcher of Orleans, Gottschalk, and William the Carpenter, never reached Constantinople, the place designated for them to assemble before the march on Jerusalem. The two, led by Fulcher and Gottschalk, while roaming almost wild through Hungary, committed many crimes and excesses and could not be controlled by their appointed leaders. In revenge, they were set upon by the Hungarians and destroyed almost to a man. The third, led by William, joined in a wild "Judenhetze" or attack against the Jews in the towns of the valley of the Rhine, during which some 10,000 Jews perished, and it was scattered to the winds during the fighting that ensued.

The other two divisions, one under Walter the Penniless and the other led by Peter, although suffering greatly on the way, were under better control and arrived at Constantinople fairly intact in the early summer. Here they united and crossed the Bosporus in August. Peter remained in Constantinople.

By the end of October, these ragged and poorly-armed fanatics had met the Seljuk Turks and been wiped out. A heap of whitened bones was all that remained to tell the later crusaders the story of the Paupers' Crusade when they passed there the following spring.

Peter waited in Constantinople, a broken and disheartened man. When the main body of the first crusaders, the princes, arrived in May, 1097, he, with a small band of fanatics he had been able to collect, joined them and together they moved through Asia Minor to Jerusalem where Peter, now little more than a "fallen star," played a very minor role in future events related to the Crusades.

At the end of 1099 he went to Laodicea and sailed from there back to the West. Here he disappeared and was never heard of again. Albert of Aix records that he did become prior of a church of the Holy Sepulchre which had been founded in France and that he died in 1151.

Saint Bernard of Clairvaux

THE MONASTERY at Citeaux was dying for lack of novices. The older monks were devoted to Saint Benedict and followed his rule to the letter; but no youths came to join with them, and the old men would not live forever.

In 1098 Saint Robert, a restless soul who had been a Benedictine monk and then abbot of certain hermits living in the vicinity of Chatillon, had settled with twenty monks in a swampy place called Citeaux. Here Count Odo of Burgundy had built them a monastery and they had begun to live according to the strictest letter of the Benedictine rule.

Stephen Harding, an Englishman who was later canonized, became abbot in 1109 and faced the prospect of having to close the monastery because no new recruits could be found. In the midst of his deepest despair, when the end of the monastery seemed only weeks away, a band of thirty young men appeared at the gate asking to be admitted. At the head of the group was Bernard, and many members of the group were his relations and close friends. Bernard was a native of the area, a son of Tecelin who, as a knight, had perished in the first Crusade, and of Aleth, daughter of the noble house of Mon-Bar. But both parents had died while Bernard was a mere boy. Nor was Bernard fitted by constitution or disposition to follow in his father's footsteps. He chose the church and desired to enter a monastery. Despite the opposition of his relatives and the lure of ecclesiastical preferment, he had presented himself with a band of his relatives and friends at the gate of Citeaux and begged admission.

Others followed the example of Bernard and his band and the monastery began to grow rapidly. Very soon, it was able to send off daughter branches. In three years, four new monasteries had been established, all under the authority of the abbot of Citeaux and all known as Cistercian. By 1134 there were thirty houses of the order in Europe and new ones were being established.

One of the first branches of Citeaux was the monastery of Clairvaux, founded in 1115. Bernard was appointed abbot of this new monastery. Then began a career second to none in the history of the church.

Bernard was a great preacher, one of that small company of silver-tongued servants of God who, by the power of preaching, have been able to turn the tides of history and influence men in high places.

Clairvaux soon became the chief monastery of the order, due largely to Bernard's influence. Stories of his miracles spread throughout the area and the sick and afflicted came from afar to feel the healing power of his touch. The lame were seen to walk and the blind went away seeing. The lame and blind of heart listened to preaching, and went away healed. Now Bernard believed he had found his work and his happiness and he was content to serve his Lord as the abbot of Clairvaux.

But the Planner of men's lives would not have it so. Gradually Bernard was drawn into the affairs of the church and of the world. When, in 1124, Pope Honorius II was elevated to the chair of Saint Peter, Bernard was recognized as one of the great French churchmen of the age. Papal legates came for his counsel to the crude monastery of Clairvaux. Bernard was instrumental in obtaining recognition of the order of Knights Templars at the Synod of Troyes and figured in many other momentous happenings of the day.

But, with the death of Honorius, Bernard rose into a prominence in Europe which has given him the title of "Pope Maker." Two men laid claim to the papacy and a violent battle ensued. Bernard threw his support behind Innocent II and sought to prove that the claim of Anacletus II was unfounded. Rome was on the side of Anacletus II. But France, England, Spain, and Germany, through Bernard's influence in part, backed Innocent II.

The battle was long and bitter. Innocent II traveled throughout Europe with the powerful abbot of Clairvaux at his side, stayed at Clairvaux, and went with Bernard to parley with kings and princes. Wherever Bernard went, the power of his eloquence won over strong support for Innocent II. He was able to have Anacletus II excommunicated by the council of Pisa.

On the 25th of January, 1138, Anacletus II died and Cardinal Gregory was chosen as his successor, assuming the name of Victor. Bernard threw himself unreservedly into an attempt to unseat Victor, whom he characterized as the "antipope." His greatest triumph was the abdication of his enemy, an act which made possible the healing of the schism.

Now, Bernard believed he could return to Clairvaux and the quiet and peace of monastic life. But he had been too long a power in the Christian world and he could not hide from the affairs of the church. His eloquence was thrown against Abélard and resulted in the condemnation of this great schoolman at Rome.

Bernard's most illustrious work and his greatest disappointment were hinged on the second Crusade. In obedience to the command of the pope, he began preaching a Crusade. So powerful was his eloquence that at Vezlay, following one of his sermons, King Louis VII of France and his queen took the cross, and so many people followed that the supply of crosses was soon exhausted. Everywhere people flocked to hear him and were persuaded to join the march to the Holy Land.

The lamentable failure of this Crusade broke the power of Bernard. Although he consented to lead a third Crusade and was preparing to set out on the mission, the Cistercian abbots realized that he was physically and constitutionally unfit for the task and forbade him to undertake it.

Bernard was broken in health because of his austerities and the sadness over the loss of many friends and the failure of his Crusade. Although he continued in intellectual vigor and remained in touch with ecclesiastical affairs, the old power was gone. Age was taking its toll and life was slowly slipping away. On the twentieth of August, 1153, he passed to his reward, leaving a memory within the church that cannot be erased. Wherever the grey or white monks of the Cistercians work, the mission of Bernard goes on and the present unity of the church owes much to his genius and eloquence.

Saint Dominic

WHEN Saint Dominic was born at Calaroga in Old Castile, in 1170, heresy was rampant throughout the Christian world and the church was straining every nerve to combat it. The evil was growing worse as Dominic became a young theological student at Palencia and then a canon of the cathedral chapter of Osma, his native diocese.

His bishop induced him to become a canon regular under the Rule of Saint Augustine. So devoted and talented did he prove himself, that he was soon made prior or provost of the cathedral community.

After serving with his bishop on an embassy in behalf of the King of Castile, Dominic repaired to Rome where Innocent III ordered him to enter the fight against heresy by preaching among the Albigenses in Languedoc.

This was a most difficult but important charge. The Albigenses were especially dangerous heretics and their doctrines threatened the very life of Christianity. Theirs was an extreme form of Manichaeism which taught the existence of two gods. They believed that the good God had Christ for a son while the Evil One had given life to the devil. Matter, they held, was created by the evil spirit and was therefore essentially evil. Sexual intercourse, even in marriage, was considered evil as was the possession of material goods and the eating of flesh. Some so thoroughly abhorred matter that they thought it pious to commit suicide by starvation and to starve their children to death.

These doctrines had spread rapidly and threatened to engulf all Christianity. Frederick II tried to suppress the sect in Italy. In 1208, after the murder of a papal legate, Innocent III called on Christian princes to suppress the Albigensian heresy by force of arms. For seven years following this decree, the south of France was devastated by one of the most bloodthirsty wars in history. Albigenses were slaughtered by thousands and their property confiscated wholesale.

It was into this difficult situation that Dominic was sent. He saw the difficulty and believed that preaching and argument would show the Albigenses the evil of their position and turn them back to true Christianity. He traveled about the country on foot and barefooted, in extreme poverty, simplicity, and austerity, preaching and instructing in highways and villages and towns, and in the castles of the nobility. Often he organized formal disputations with leading Albigenses, lasting several days. Many times plots were laid against his life, but he was always fortunate and escaped.

This work brought many converts, but he considered his ten years of preaching and teaching a failure and left the work with great bitterness. In his last sermon at Languedoc he said, "For many years I have exhorted you in vain, with gentleness, preaching, praying, and weeping. But according to the proverb of my country, 'where blessing can accomplish nothing, blows may avail.' We shall rouse against you princes and prelates who, alas, will arm nations and kingdoms against this land . . . and thus blows will avail where blessings and gentleness have been powerless."

This threat was never carried out and Dominic returned to his native land to do a far greater work.

While working among the Albigenses, he had gathered about himself a little band of pious men who wanted to devote themselves to preaching and missionary work among the heretics wherever they might be found. At first, Innocent III refused to permit them to establish a separate order, but commanded that they affiliate with one of the established orders. Thus, for a period they served under the Augustinian Rule.

In 1216 Honorius recognized the group by commending them to the church with special mission to preach. Then, in 1218 an encyclical bull was issued, establishing them as "the Order of Friars Preachers." The order spread rapidly, so that by 1221, when Dominic died, there were more than 500 friars and 60 friaries, divided into eight provinces embracing the whole of western Europe.

Although failing at a task too great for any one man, Dominic succeeded in establishing an order of preachers and missionaries, the great Dominican Order, which spread throughout the world and has done much to combat heresy and teach the true gospel.

Saint Francis of Assisi

FRANCESCO BERNARDONE was born at Assisi, one of the independent municipal towns of Umbria, in 1181, son of a prosperous local merchant. His youth was all but unpromising. He had little education, even for those days. He was the leader of wild revels among the young men and youthful irregularities were part of his daily life. He was, however, conspicuous for his charities to the poor.

When his city and Perugia fell to battling over the return of the nobles who had been expelled from Assisi, Francesco took part in the battle and was made a prisoner. After a year in prison in Perugia, he was returned to his native town and to the old life of debauchery.

Soon he fell ill and was forced to remain in bed for some time. During this period he became dissatisfied with his former life. Then another illness brought back the conflict within himself but did not settle it. One day he gave an elaborate banquet for his friends. After they had finished eating and drinking and had sallied forth with torches and wild singing and shouting, they marched through the streets with Francesco crowned king of the revellers.

After a time the young men missed their king and, retracing their steps, found him in a trance. When he awoke, he was a changed man, devoting himself to solitude, prayer, and service to the poor. As soon as possible, he made a pilgrimage to Rome where he exchanged his clothing with one of the beggars sitting before Saint Peter's and spent the day begging with the others.

Soon after his return to Assisi, he was riding along one of the streets of the town when he saw a leper begging for alms. Francis, as he was now called, had an especial horror for lepers and rode on. But, realizing immediately his sin, he turned back, gave the leper all the money he had, and kissed his hand. From that day forward, he devoted himself to the service of the lepers and the hospitals.

Francis' father and brothers were worried about the strange actions of their beloved son and brother. He was fast dissipating his estate by giving lavishly to the poor and making huge donations for the restoration of the Church of Saint Damian. Also, he walked about the city in rags so that his companions of former days pelted him with mud.

Believing that Francis was unbalanced, they had him brought before the Bishop of Assisi and asked that he be legally disinherited. But, without waiting for the proper documents, Francis took off all his clothes and handed them to his father, a token that he renounced all claim to his inheritance. The bishop gave him a cloak and he went out into the woods of Mount Subasio, a devotee, for the remainder of his days, of "Lady Poverty."

During the next three years Francis lived in the vicinity of Assisi in abject poverty and want, ministering to the lepers and the outcasts of society. Often he visited the ruins of the little chapel of Saint Mary of the Angels to spend long hours in prayer. During one of these visits a vision came to him and he heard the words of the Gospel: "Everywhere on your road preach and say—The Kingdom of God is at hand. Cure the sick, raise the dead, cleanse the leper, drive out devils. Freely have you received, freely give. Carry neither gold nor silver nor money in your girdle, nor bag, nor two coats, nor sandals, nor staff, for the workman is worthy of his hire."

The next day Francis, then only a layman, went to Assisi and began to preach to the poor. Disciples joined him in this work of mercy. When the number had reached twelve, Francis told them, "Let us go to our Mother, the holy Roman Church, and tell the Pope what the Lord has begun to do through us, and carry it out with his sanction." Pope Innocent III heard their story and gave them his blessing. They returned to Assisi and devoted themselves to preaching and work among the poor.

Francis was chosen the superior and the little group was organized as the "Penitents of Assisi." Later, Francis chose the title of Friars Minor. They obtained from the Benedictine monastery on Mount Subasio use of the chapel of Saint Mary of the Angels and built themselves rude huts of branches and twigs about the chapel. But the friars had no settled abode and no possessions. They traveled everywhere, begging or working for their food and a place to rest, and ministered to the poor, the lepers, and the outcasts of society. Under guidance from Francis, they sought in every way possible to follow to the letter the instructions of Jesus and to imitate his way of life.

The work prospered, and Franciscans were recruited from many lands and places. New centers were established from which these friars penetrated into the poorest sections of Europe, carrying their work and their preaching.

Francis felt a close relationship to nature and was accustomed to call all of nature's manifestations "brother" or "sister." He preached one of his most beautiful sermons to the birds. He referred to "brother Wind," "sister Moon," and, when in his last illness he was cauterized, he addressed "brother Fire" with a plea to treat him kindly.

As the work of the Franciscans grew, two new orders were established by the founder, Francis. One, "The Second Order," was for nuns. The other, "The Third Order," was a confraternity of men and women who tried to apply the fundamental principles of the order without withdrawing from the world.

Francis did not devote himself wholly to the administration of the order, but traveled as did the other friars, preaching and ministering to the poor. During one of his trips, he was captured and taken before the Sultan of Turkey. No sooner had he entered the audience chamber than he began to preach the Gospel to these heathens. The Sultan was so impressed that he had Francis returned to the Christian camp.

During his absence, the order fell into difficulties which convinced Francis that he could no longer serve as its head. Consequently he resigned as minister-general, turning the duties of this office over to others, and devoted himself to the revision and final publication of the "rule" of the order and to preaching and service.

Two years before his death Francis traveled with several disciples to Mount Alverno, high in the Apennines, where he spent forty days in fasting and prayer. On the morning of the fourteenth of September, 1224, "he had a vision: in the warm rays of the rising sun he discerned suddenly a strange figure. A seraph, with wings extended, flew towards him from the horizon and inundated him with pleasure unutterable. At the center of the vision appeared a cross, and the seraph was nailed to it. When the vision disappeared, Francis felt sharp pains mingling with the delight of the first moment. Disturbed to the center of his being, he anxiously sought the meaning of it all, and then he saw on his body the Stigmata of the Crucified."

Those who were close to Francis at the time say that the stigmata were not a bleeding from wounds, but were "fleshy excrescences resembling in form and color the nails, the head on the palm of the hand, and on the back as it were a nail hammered down."

Francis was exhausted by his experiences on Mount Alverno and had to be carried back to Assisi. For the next few months, in great bodily weakness and suffering, he worked with his accustomed cheerfulness and joy. Then, on the third of October, 1226, he breathed his last, at the age of forty-five, worn out by service to the poor, the lepers, and the outcast of society, the most humble of the humble.

Meister Eckhart

MEISTER ECKHART, as he is affectionately called by many, was actually Johannes Eckhart, born at Strassburg in the thirteenth century, who died in a prison of the Dominican order, to which he had pledged himself as a young scholar and devout teacher.

Between Strassburg of about 1260 and the Dominican prison of 1327 stretches a life restless beyond that of ordinary men. There were years of intense study and brilliant preaching, years of striving to understand what God is and how men may become one with him, years of struggle with forces which could not or would not understand, and moments when he cried, as did his Master centuries before, "O Jerusalem, Jerusalem, that killeth the prophets and stoneth them that are sent unto her! How oft would I have gathered thy children together, even as a hen gathereth her chickens under her wings, and ye would not!"

Eckhart was a mystic—one who desired more than anything else to lose himself in God. He knew those great moments when self was absorbed and became one with the Divine. But he was not content to enjoy this alone. He thought about it and told others what it meant. He preached persuasively to those desiring the same loss of self in God, and often to those who laughed at his confession and those who hated all mystics.

Then he found the Brethren of the Free Spirit. These men traced their spiritual ancestry to Lambert le Bègue, a priest of Liège in the twelfth century, who founded the hospital and church of Saint Christopher and established an order of women devoted to the life of religion. Later, tradition says, he added to his order a group of men pledged to wait on the sick and minister to the poor. By Eckhart's time this group had acquired the name of "Beghards" and was in disrepute, since many of its members were wandering mendicants who made religion a cloak for living off charity.

But Eckhart saw in them something fine and noble and sought to interpret them to the members of the order and to the world in which they worked. They were to him not "Beghards" but brethren of the free spirit. It was this free spirit which he loved. Through it, through freedom from form and ritual, he believed men could find their oneness with God.

But the church, and especially the old established orders, did not see eye to eye with him. The Dominicans called Eckhart a heretic and sought to destroy his work. They cut sentences and paragraphs from his works, seeking to prove him guilty of teaching pantheism—the belief that all nature is God and God is nature, and man is one with nature and God.

When Eckhart came to trial, he was bitterly and unjustly

accused. He labored to convince his accusers of his true faith. "I am not as you say," he cried. "All nature, all the world, and all the worlds that are or ever shall be dwell in God even as the great works of our artists dwell in the minds of those who paint them. We see many things, but in God they are all one."

"Listen! He speaks as the accursed heretics! We will have none of him!" his accusers cried against him.

He pleaded with them. He preached as only he knew how. Many were near to believing, but those in authority would hear no more. He was condemned and ordered to prison by the Inquisition at Cologne. Here he made a conditional recantation. "Whatever I have written that is wrong, I would have as unwritten," he said.

The charges and the condemnation remained, and Eckhart lay in prison with the anathema of the church upon him. In a last attempt to clear himself, he appealed personally to Pope John XXII. In 1329 the pope issued a bull condemning certain propositions extracted from Eckhart's works. But by this time he was dead, and could not enjoy the partial clearing of his name by the church which he loved and to which he believed he had faithfully devoted his entire life.

Saint Joan of Arc

THE YEAR 1422 was black for loyal Frenchmen everywhere and the cries of those in bondage to foreign rule filled the land. Philip of Burgundy marched beside the hated English as they subdued all of France north of the Loire and put their king, the infant Henry VI, on the French throne. Charles, the uncrowned dauphin, was betrayed into the hands of his enemies by his mother, Isabella, and was powerless to stop the slow dismemberment of his kingdom. Marie d'Avignon was declaring that since France had been ruined by a woman it would be restored by an armed virgin from the marches of Lorraine.

In the meantime the small village of Domremy, partly in Champagne and partly in Lorraine, was the home of Jacques d'Arc, his wife Isabeau, and their daughter Jeanneton. Strange child, this Jeanneton. She never learned to read or write, although her parents were in easy circumstances. Deeply religious, she had received all her knowledge of church and tradition from her mother, who taught her to recite the Pater Noster, Ave Maria, and Credo.

Much of Jeanneton's time was spent with her father's flocks or in plying the needle, an art in which she was even more skilled than any of the women of Rouen. The advances of young men she repelled diligently, spending more and more of her time in prayer as she became a young woman. A favorite of the village and a maiden famous for her treatment of her parents, her kindness, and her consideration for others, Jeanneton hid within her heart a growing conviction that her destined work was far beyond the little village of Domremy and its people.

There were voices, clear and forceful voices,—the voices of Saint Michael, and Saint Catherine, and Saint Margaret, —urging her on. They would not let her rest or be content. They told her to see the dauphin and place him on the throne of France.

Naturally, when this peasant girl from Domremy sought audience with Charles, the uncrowned king of France, she was rebuffed. But the voices would not be silent, and she tried again and again until the English beseiged Orleans and the cause of the dauphin seemed hopeless. Then the plan of this girl to relieve Orleans and crown the dauphin at Reims was at least a last straw; and Robert de Boudricourt, governor of Vaucouleurs, made it possible for her to see the dauphin.

Charles was skeptical until the young girl convinced him of the divine nature of her mission by discovering him, though he was disguised in a crowd of his courtiers, and by reassuring him regarding his secret doubts as to his legitimacy. The last ray of skepticism died when Jeanneton told him a secret prayer which only he and God knew. So, after doctors and matrons had passed on the girl's religion and her chastity, Charles placed her at the head of between 4,000 and 5,000 men commissioned to relieve Orleans.

It was a strange sight, this march on Orleans. At the head of the army of soldiers rode a girl clothed in a coat of mail and carrying an ancient sword said to be that with which Charles Martel had vanquished the Saracens. The hiding place of the sword under the altar of the parish church of the village of Saint Catherine de Fierbois was revealed to Jeanneton by the voices. In her hand she carried a white standard of her own design embroidered with lilies. On one side was the image of God seated on the clouds and holding the world in his hand, and on the other a picture of the Annunciation.

Success crowned her efforts. Orleans was freed and the English were driven beyond the Loire. Hesitant and still very skeptical of the whole affair, Charles was persuaded to set out for Reims with an army of 12,000 men. His skepticism turned to wonder and then to worship as Troyes fell and he marched into Reims and to the great cathedral where, on the 17th of July, 1429, he was crowned king as Jeanneton, holding the sacred banner, stood beside him.

This was the zenith of Jeanneton's career. Her success at Orleans brought her the title of "Maid of Orleans" and her fame resulted in the change of her name to Jeanne d'Arc, —Joan of Arc. Afterward court intrigue played her false and led eventually to her capture during the campaign in defence of Compiègne. She could have been ransomed, but Charles was so little appreciative of her part in his own success and so hemmed in by court intrigues that he made no effort to effect her freedom and never again showed interest in her fate.

The University of Paris and the Inquisition, assisted by the renegade priest Pierre Cauchon, negotiated the sale of Joan to the English and finally effected her trial before the Inquisition. Accused as a heretic and a witch, Joan was condemned to death, but made her submission at the foot of the scaffold and was pardoned.

The English, however, did not accept this decision and, having been induced by those who had her in charge to resume her male attire, she was accused of relapsing and was sentenced to death. On the 30th of May, 1431, she was burned at the stake in the center of Rouen. Though the sentence was eventually revoked by the Pope in 1456, and she was raised to sainthood by Pope Leo XIII in 1894, the memory of the Maid of Orleans will always raise questions in the minds of many and pain in the hearts of those who love justice and fair dealing.

Saint Ignatius of Loyola

ANYONE knowing Iñigo Lopez de Recalde during the first twenty-six years of his life would possibly despise and at the same time admire the young man. Free in his relations with women, a gambler, and one quick to fight, he was capable of high courage, constancy, and prudence, and evidenced much skill in handling men. Certainly no one would charge him with religious zeal or imagine him wearing a pilgrim's cowl and begging along the highways.

When Charles V, ignoring the treaty of Noyon, decided to hold Pampeluna, the capital of Navarre, he placed a strong garrison there to resist the attack of the French.

One of his officers was Iñigo, fighting merely for the love of battle.

When the French succeeded in a last all-out attempt to take the city, a cannon ball shattered one of Iñigo's legs and badly wounded the other. The French took care of him for a while and then sent him back to his castle of Loyola, where medical care was able to save his life but was unable to avoid leaving him lame for the remainder of his days.

During his recovery, which was lengthened by complications, death was very near and Iñigo was given the last rites of the church. One night, however, he began to mend and was out of danger in a few days. While he was convalescing, two books came to his attention, books that were to influence his life in revolutionary ways. These were *The Life of Christ* by Ludolphus of Saxony and *Flowers of the Saints*, a series of pious biographies.

Reading these books and thinking on religious themes seriously for the first time in his life, this wounded soldier began a mental conflict which tore him between the lusts of his youth and the yearning to do great deeds for God. At last God won and Iñigo vowed to devote himself to him at all cost.

Lying awake one night, he saw the likeness of the Blessed Virgin with her Son. A great loathing for all that he had been seized him, so that never again did he desire the things of the flesh and the devil. This was the first of many visions which appeared to him in the years ahead, visions that were to direct his life and shape his character decidedly.

At this time Martin Luther was voicing protest against the evils within the church and was calling upon all true Christians to rise up against the abuses of men who called themselves true followers of Christ but were betrayers of the Crucified One. Loyola worked within the church to restore its purity and to recall to it those who had turned away in disgust or had lost faith.

Seven young men, with Loyola as their leader, had come

together in Paris, vowing to live in poverty and chastity and to travel to the Holy Land as missionaries and ministers to the sick and suffering. This was the beginning of the Society of Jesus, one of the most influential teaching and preaching orders of the church. Its troubles were many. Leaders of the church feared it as heretical, and its leaders were constantly in trouble with the Inquisition. Charges were lodged against Loyola time and again, but at each examination they were found to be baseless.

Ignatius, for that was what he was now called, carried his military experience into the order and established an organization with a general at its head and other officers resembling those of the armed forces. The government of all members was strictly military. An order came from above and had to be obeyed at all cost. For most of his life, Loyola was head of the order and his genius went into the writing of its constitution and rules. In addition to these documents, there was the *Spiritual Exercises,* a book of devotional directions that has never been equaled in all the literature of religion.

From a life of evil and of lust Ignatius had turned with absolute certainty to the most austere life of devotion to God. He tortured his body and came near to destroying himself in his zeal. Often Christ and his angels appeared to him in visions and directed his activity. Tempted to set about his missionary work unprepared, he was forced to study many years before the church would give him the authority he craved.

At last that authority came. He was made a priest and his order was accepted by Pope Paul III after much hesitation. From then until his death, nothing entered his mind but service to his Society of Jesus. He gave himself without stint to it and its problems. At times it seemed that he would fail and the order disappear. But such times seemed to bring out the genius of the man and he succeeded where others would have failed.

In 1556 Ignatius was too ill to continue as head of the society. He saw weaknesses in the order which he was unable to correct and became convinced that another, younger and stronger than himself, should be at the helm. Three fathers,—Polanco, Madrid, and Natal,—were placed in charge. Then the old leader lay down to die. Fever soon burned at his vitals and, on the 31st of July, without asking for or receiving the rites of the church, he passed to his reward. In 1609 he was beatified by Paul V and in 1628 Gregory XV made him a saint.

Today the Society of Jesus has come through many vicissitudes and is spread throughout the world. Its members teach and preach and render other services to the church and to those in need. The body of their first general lies under the altar in the north transept of the Gesù in Rome.

Saint Francis Xavier

THE PEOPLE of Goa, a Portuguese territory in India, one day saw a strange little man walking through the streets ringing a bell and calling upon all to come and send their children and servants to the church of the section for Christian instruction. His bright blue-grey eyes shone through heavy blonde lashes which matched his long saintly beard. His step was quick and his voice strong and clear. It is no wonder that many gathered at the church to see what this unique performance meant.

It meant that Francis Xavier was bent upon his beloved mission of gathering converts to Christ. And he went not where life was easy and men were friendly to the Christ, but to India and Japan and among the many little known islands of the Malay Archipelago where disease lurked at every turn of the road and fever stretched out its burning hands to tear at his all-too-frail body. For Francis was a Jesuit and a good soldier in that army of Christ called the Society of Jesus.

Back in Paris, where he had gone to study at the university, he had met another Spanish priest from his own Basque country called Ignatius of Loyola. This fellow countryman had won him and five others to an ideal. These seven had taken vows to devote themselves to the service of the church wherever it might need them, and under Ignatius as general, founded the Jesuit order.

Their first plan was a mission to Palestine to convert the Moslems there. Indeed, they set out on this venture and traveled by stages to Rome. On the way, Francis stopped at Venice and spent some months working in a hospital for incurables in that city. At Rome, Pope Paul III sanctioned their mission, but the war between Venice and Turkey put an end to the Palestine mission and forced the little group to spend the next year working in Italian cities, ministering to the sick and preaching the Christian message.

Then, after Francis had served three years as secretary of the Society of Jesus in Rome, a call came from the King of Portugal, John III, for two missionaries to work among his Indian dominions. Those first chosen by Ignatius were either needed more at home or fell too ill to make the trip. Francis was next in line and was ordered by his general to undertake the mission. He waited only for the pope's benediction before setting sail for this strange and fascinating land of challenge and promise.

During the next eleven years, Francis traveled among the cities of Portuguese India and the islands of the southern oceans preaching and ministering, giving freely of himself without stint. Often he was attacked by fever and lay sick for days. But, even in sickness he worked, refusing the advice of friends to leave this inhospitable land and return to his native Spain with its sunny hills and warm valleys.

As papal nuncio in the Indies, he taught all those who would listen. Wherever he found what to him was sin, he fought valiantly to destroy it. When the Judaism of Goa seemed too much for him, he appealed to the pope to set up the Inquisition to suppress it. When the Achinese fleet, under the Rajah of Pedir in Sumatra, attacked Goa, Francis roused the governor to action and saved the city.

When in Malacca, he met a Japanese exile by the name of Yajiro who fired him with zeal for the conversion of Japan. Accompanied by Yajiro, whom he called Paul of the Holy Faith because he had come to Francis as Paul had come to the early Christians crying, "Come over and help us," he set sail for Japan. There he worked with marked success and conceived the plan for a mission to China.

This mission was most daring, since China was closed to the western world and only the most careful planning made the scheme at all possible. But Francis succeeded again. He got as far as Chang-chuen-shan, off the coast of Kwangtung. While waiting here for his interpreter, he fell ill of a fever and lay near death for some time. Suffering intense pain and knowing not whether he would live or die, Francis arranged for a Chinese junk to carry him to Canton.

All was in readiness and the junk was provisioned and waiting to sail when the fever returned, this time to take what was left of his frail strength. In the depths of winter, just before the New Year, Francis of Xavier died and was buried close to the cabin in which he was waiting for passage into China.

Later his small body, one which could be put in a casket only five feet and one inch long, was taken to Malacca and thence to Goa and placed in a magnificent shrine where it is preserved to this day.

But the shine is not the most loved memorial to Francis Xavier. Francis would have loved more the Christian communities which he left scattered from Hormuz in Persia to Japan and the Malay Archipelago. He established and controlled the Society of Jesus in India and was so great an organizer and leader of men that Ignatius had chosen him as his successor at the head of the Society of Jesus. Indeed, only a few weeks before Francis' death, Ignatius had sent letters calling him back to Europe to prepare himself to take over the governing of the order.

This would have been a high honor, and Francis, being a good Jesuit, would have obeyed the summons of his general. But he was happier living and dying as the "Apostle of the Indies."

Saint Teresa of Avila

WHEN Teresa de Cepeda left her home at Avila in Old Castile to become a resident of the Carmelite Convent of the Incarnation, she was astonished at the lack of discipline and at the worldly life of the sisters. As a child, she had read many stories of the martyrs and pictured all religious people as holy and suffering saints. Although she adapted herself to life in the convent, she was most unhappy.

After more than 20 years in this environment of which she heartily disapproved, she suffered the loss of her father. This bereavement led her to much contemplation and prayer. One day, as she was entering the oratory, she came upon an image of the wounded Christ placed there for an approaching festival. This sight affected her so that she fell to the floor at the feet of the statue and wept bitterly. At this moment every worldly emotion died within her and she arose a changed person.

Teresa's sister nuns were angry with her. They said that she was trying to be better than they and taunted her with her peculiarities. Being an humble woman, Teresa went to her confessor, who advised her to take her problem to the provincial-general of the Jesuits. This official put her under a severe course of discipline.

After some time, as she was faithfully following the discipline given her, she heard a voice saying, "Thou shalt have no more converse with men, but with angels." After this she felt that Christ was close to her always and had a particular concern for her work. Indeed, she adopted the name of Teresa de Jesus to signify her closeness to the heavenly Bridegroom.

There followed many occasions when Teresa fell into a trance and saw Jesus "exactly as he was painted rising from the sepulchre." Although her confessor advised her to drive away the figure, and although she tried to obey his command, the vision grew more and more vivid.

Once the cross of her rosary was mysteriously snatched from her hand. When it was as suddenly returned, it was made of jewels more brilliant than diamonds. This miracle was visible only to her eyes.

At times Teresa experienced acute pain in her side. This she attributed to an angel who, she said, came to her with a lance tipped with fire, which he struck into her heart. At another time she was shown hell with all its horrors. The devil was sitting on her breviary, beating her and filling her cell with imps. These experiences continued for years and caused her much wonder and confusion.

Meantime the Reformation was gaining strength. Teresa, with many others, came to believe that the Reformation stemmed from the lack of discipline in the church and in holy places. This led her to decide upon founding a convent in which all the rules of the Carmelites would be observed with strictness. The leaders of the order and the sisters of the Incarnation opposed this idea bitterly, but Teresa persisted, taking her cause eventually to the pope. When permission was given by the pope, she made a small house in Avila ready and immediately installed in it four poor women.

This was to be an order of Descalzos or Barefoots, in

opposition to the laxness of the parent organization, the Calzados. Actually the sisters of her order were to wear sandals of rope, sleep on straw, eat no meat, live only in the cloister from which they were not to depart, and exist only on alms.

When the work was discovered, the Carmelites and townspeople were furious. To avoid violence, the matter was referred to the council of state in Madrid and eventually to the pope, who issued a new order permitting Teresa to devote her full time to the new sisterhood. Quickly the number in the infant order was increased to thirteen and no more were admitted.

So successful was this work that Teresa was permitted to found other houses. Her enthusiasm and devotion attracted Saint John of the Cross, another famous Spanish mystic who had proved his ardor by persecution of his body and his sanctity by repeated visions and mystical experiences. He felt that the laxity among the clergy should be stopped, and found in Teresa a kindred mind. With his aid, and that of other men of the period, she was able to found a number of convents for friars, who lived and worked very much as did the women in her houses.

The next few years Teresa spent in traveling, founding and organizing new houses, and encouraging the residents in their discipline and faith. Teresa's visions continued and she persisted in persecuting herself unmercifully. At all times she wore a particularly painful hair garment next to her skin.

XThe austerity of her life soon took its toll and Teresa died at Alva on September 29, 1582. After she had been buried, an odor of violets and a fragrant oil were said to be distilled from her tomb. When the tomb was opened nine months later, her body was perfectly preserved and the flesh was just as though she were sleeping.

One of Teresa's hands, cut off by a particularly fervent brother, performed many miracles. When, five years later, it was resolved to move her body to Avila, the sisters at Alva were permitted to keep the hand. Later, the body was returned to Alva and placed in a magnificent tomb. But this was not the end. Some years following this, her body was disentombed to be placed in a more splendid and beautiful tomb, but relic-seekers made unseemly havoc of her bones, so that little was left to place in the final resting-place.

Teresa's devotion was unsurpassed, and her ability to attract devout people to her cause and to organize them into houses was unexcelled anywhere. Her patience and good sense made her reforms work where with others they had failed. She did much to purify the order to which she devoted her life.

Martin Luther

LATE in the fifteenth century a son was born to the wife of a German coal miner named Luther. His parents called him Martin.

His origin and early training were not promising. Poverty was his early lot. The people around him during his early years were very poor and largely unlettered. They suffered constantly from lack of proper food and housing, and in their religious life they were lax.

But something in young Martin drove him to seek a better life. Defying the poverty of his surroundings, he attended the elementary school at Mansfeld and then went to the higher school at Magdeburg and later to one at Eisenach. To feed and clothe himself during these years, he sang and begged in the streets. But he was successful in educating himself.

At eighteen he entered the University of Erfurt and four years later became an Augustinian monk, in the face of opposition by his parents who wanted him to work in the mines.

From this time forward, Martin Luther rose in prominence and influence. In 1502 the emperor founded the University of Wittenberg, and six years later Luther was made a professor in that institution. Although Luther had attained a high education and sat in the chair of a professor, his overpowering interest was religion. He loved the church and the order in which he held ordination. This love made him suffer much when he saw how other men were abusing the sacred practices of this church. When he heard John Tetzel preaching indulgences and making this sacred practice a mere means for raising money, his anger flared up against those who would drag the church into the mire.

For a long time, Luther had been studying his church and its practices, and he had become convinced that many of the clergy of his day had gone far from the true religion. So convinced did he become that he posted ninety-five theses on the door of the University of Wittenberg, proclaiming that he would meet anyone in debate upon any of these issues.

In this challenge Luther expressed the thinking of many devout men who wished to see the church return to its original purity and splendor. As a result of the posting of the theses, a mass uprising against the church began.

Luther did not wish to injure the church. He had made a pilgrimage to Rome and climbed "the Stairs" on his knees. When he was less than half way up, it dawned upon him that man should live by faith and not by works. This became the core of his life. He read this idea in the Bible and found it in the sermons of the fathers. It was, he believed, the message that should be preached everywhere. Accordingly, he began to preach it.

But the church was not ready to hear him. Luther found himself persecuted and hounded throughout the land. Many who were not interested in the religious problems involved, but who wanted to gain control of the wealth of the church and destroy its political power, sided with Luther, using his movement for their own ends. Likewise, the poor flocked to him in great numbers, seeing in him a leader who could help raise them from their poverty.

Luther was tried for his heresy by the Diet of Worms and condemned, but escaped to the castle of a friend. There he wrote much, including a now-famous translation of the Bible into German.

When Luther saw how his cause, conceived in loyalty to a church which he believed was being sold into captivity by many in high position, was being used by the rich and powerful to make them richer and more powerful, and how the poor and ignorant used his crusade for non-religious aims, he was very unhappy and reached the end of his life a bitter and disappointed man.

Luther had fought for what he believed to be just and right. Even to the end he continued to fight. But the frailties of men made him doubt, and the lack of understanding within the church of his efforts sickened him at heart. Death came on the 18th of February, 1546, to relieve his suffering and close the book upon which he had written with pen of gold.

John Calvin

JOHN CALVIN was born in 1509 in Noyon, France, of parents in high esteem and comfortable circumstances. Young Calvin did not take seriously the early desires of his father that he devote himself to an ecclesiastical career. His interests were scholarly and the law fascinated him. The church was a "living," a source of income by means of which he could devote himself to study.

Unconsciously, no doubt, he planned to remain in the

service of the church, accepting ordination when the time came and holding his appointments as "livings" only. Until 1531 his chief interest was in classical scholarship.

But currents of dissatisfaction were running through the church of his day and time. Martin Luther was challenging the practices of many who boasted that they represented the true Catholic Church. The Protestant revolt was growing and shooting its roots far from the campus of Wittenberg and the German churches. A mind as virile and alive as that of Calvin could not remain untouched.

Calvin's "sudden conversion" came in the latter months of 1533 when he turned from the church of his childhood and youth and aligned himself with the Protestants. From this time forward, he regarded all other studies with indifference and gave his complete devotion to "piety." At twenty-five he broke all relations with the Catholic Church, resigned his "living," and gave himself whole-heartedly to work for the new cause.

This move laid him open to attack by the ecclesiastical powers of France and he had to live in moderate seclusion lest he be lodged in prison or come under official sentence and perhaps be restrained from further work. During the next two years he studied Hebrew and theology, wrote the first draft of his most famous work, *Institutes of the Christian Religion,* in Latin, and traveled about seeking quiet and peace for the pursuit of his studies.

It was in the early summer of 1536 that he determined to settle at Strassburg or Basel and devote himself to study. But Francis I and Charles V were at war, and Calvin could not travel directly to Strassburg. Consequently, he made a detour through Geneva. Here lived Guillaume Farel, a devoted Protestant who had suffered much in his attempts to plant the evangelical doctrine in this great city. He appealed to Calvin to abandon his plans and to remain to give aid to the infant cause. Calvin declined and prepared to move on to his planned destination. Then, as he tells us, "God had stretched forth His hand upon me from on high to arrest me." God's plan was different from his, and God prevailed. Calvin remained, and at twenty-eight began his career as a great religious leader.

Many people with different ideas opposed Calvin in Geneva. There were constant controversies. Amidst these Calvin rose to a position of unquestioned authority in the church of Geneva and in the lives of its citizens. Driven from the city by his enemies once, he returned stronger than before and imposed his beliefs and his policies upon the people with such force that his enemies were gradually eliminated.

Geneva prospered and grew under his leadership. Its religious and educational life was purified and strengthened. A number of highly trained and skilled men went out from Geneva to carry Calvin's principles and teachings throughout Europe and influence the growth of the Protestant movement everywhere.

When the occasion demanded, Calvin could be a hard and stern opponent. One day in 1553 he saw Michael Servetus in a Geneva church. This scholar and preacher was a particular enemy of Calvin and, by stopping at Geneva on his way to Naples, exposed himself to the mercies of his enemy. In his writings he had shown leanings toward what Calvin believed to be blasphemy and pantheism. Servetus was immediately arrested and later brought to trial. The case was taken by both Calvin and his foes as a test of the strength of each group and was vigorously championed by Philbert Berthelier and other foes of Calvin while it was prosecuted by Calvin and his friends. The result was complete conviction of Servetus and a verdict of death by burning.

Calvin regarded this kind of death as an "atrocity" and sought to have the sentence changed to beheading but was not successful. Servetus was burned the next day. The friends of Calvin have sought to clear him of any personal animosity, but the stain still remains on his memory.

Other controversies followed. Fighting hard and sometimes ruthlessly for his cause, Calvin wore himself out. Disease that had plagued him for most of his life, incessant work beyond his strength, and a conscientiousness above that of most men took their toll and eventually broke the none-too-rugged body. Death came on the 27th of May, 1564.

John Knox

DURING THOSE YEARS when Scotland was wavering between Catholicism and Protestantism, and powerful reform forces battled against equally powerful forces representing the Catholic Church, John Knox lived to advance the ideals of the Reformation and establish on Scottish soil the great Presbyterian Church.

Knox was not born to this role nor did he accept it without much hesitation and searching of heart. Son of William Knox, a prosperous Lothian peasant, and a pupil of John Major, whose alarm over the revolt of Luther was so great that he ceased to argue against the supremacy of the pope, Knox appeared in 1543 as "minister of the sacred altar" under the Archbishop of Saint Andrews. A career within the Church of Rome lay open to him and he appeared well content in it at that time.

But Knox began to feel the strain of the issues which were coming to the fore in Scotland. During the second quarter of the sixteenth century, Scotland was moving slowly in the direction of freedom in religious profession and toward friendship with Protestant England rather than with Catholic France. Bitter feelings flared into actual combat from time to time and men were burned for criticizing the church or suggesting rebellion against its authority. Knox found himself leaning toward freedom of religious conscience, but was drawn back toward the church by his early training and his priestly vows. His friends, who had watched him for some time, became convinced that once he made the decision to align himself with the Reformation forces he would become their leader, and set about to bring him to a decision.

By design, an appeal for a declaration of faith was made to Knox from the pulpit after he had refused the pleadings of his friends on the ground that he would not "run where God had not called him." At the close of the appeal, the speaker asked, "Was not this your charge to me? And do ye not approve this vocation?" The congregation answered as one man, "It was, and we approve it." So great was the appeal that Knox, "abashed, burst forth in most abundant tears and withdrew himself to his chamber." For days he remained in seclusion and in "heaviness." Then he came forth resolved and prepared. This was the turning point of his life.

Within a short time George Wishart, a close friend of Knox, was burned by order of the regent, Arran. This act was followed by the burning of John Rough, another friend. The fight was growing more bitter and Knox was becoming more the leader of the Protestant side. He preached so brilliantly and with such force that some of his hearers exclaimed, "Others sned [snipped] the branches; this man striked at the root."

When the castle of Saint Andrews, where Knox had taken refuge, fell to the French fleet in 1547, he was taken prisoner and thrown into the galleys on the river Loire, to remain in irons and under the lash for nineteen months. The years that followed saw Knox as a preacher in England, then royal chaplain, and one high in the respect of the young English King, Edward VI. When Mary Tudor succeeded her brother, Knox was forced to flee from England, first to Frankfort and then to Geneva.

At Geneva he met John Calvin and studied carefully his religious structure and discipline in that town. From this experience Knox developed much of his thinking and, in a sense, his future work in Scotland was a continuation of Calvin's work at Geneva.

Traveling to Scotland when he thought the time ripe, Knox quickly developed into a leader of the reform forces in that land. But, beginning as a movement for religious freedom, the forces led by Knox gradually developed an intolerance equal to that of their opposition. Freedom of conscience was soon put aside and in its place developed a Protestant intolerance more rigid than that of Geneva. Many began to wonder if the mere transfer of intolerance from Catholic to Protestant hands had been as wise at it had at first seemed.

Meantime Knox had taken up the fight against Mary, Queen of Scots, a Catholic whom many feared would return Catholicism to dominance in Scotland, and appeared before the queen to argue the Protestant cause with great keenness of mind. In the published accounts of this discussion are ideas of freedom, both of religion and of government, which were basic to the liberal trends of the times. When Mary asked, "Think ye that subjects, having power, may resist their princes?" Knox replied, "If their princes exceed their bounds, Madam, they may be resisted and even deposed."

From this point on, matters in the realm began to deteriorate rapidly. Mary married her cousin, Henry Darnley, a Catholic, in 1565 and the Protestant lords were swept into exile. This so depressed Knox that he wrote, "Lord Jesus, put an end to this my miserable life, for justice and truth are not to be found among the sons of men!" By the next year Mary had become infatuated with the Earl of Bothwell. Then Darnley was murdered and the queen was forced to abdicate and flee.

Knox took the leadership of the Assembly and was instrumental in having Moray, a Protestant sympathizer, made regent. This was a great victory for Knox and for the forces which he represented. And it came none too soon.

Weakened by his experiences in the galleys and his years of hard and unceasing work, he was failing fast. A stroke of paralysis was followed by a steady decline until the 24th of November, 1572, when, surrounded by "lords, ladies, and burghers," he died.

Thus ended a career which, despite its failures and shortcomings, led Scotland in the cause of religious freedom and helped establish that way of religious life known today throughout the world as Presbyterianism.

Saint Vincent de Paul

SLAVERY was a common practice in the sixteenth and seventeenth centuries throughout many sections of the world, and those who purchased slaves did not often ask how or why their chattels became men of bondage. So, when some Barbary pirates offered for sale a young man of French descent wearing the garments of a priest, the buyers in the slave market of Tunis asked no embarrassing questions.

This young man was Vincent de Paul, born on the twenty-fourth of April, 1576, at Pouy, in Gascogne, and educated by the Franciscans at Dax and at Toulouse. In 1600 he had been ordained priest. But, while traveling from Toulouse to Narbonne, he was captured by the Barbary pirates and taken to Tunis where he was sold as a slave.

Even in slavery so undeserved, Vincent did not forget that he was a priest, a servant of God. He continued to preach the Gospel when possible, and was successful in the conversion of his third master, with whom he escaped to Aigues-Mortes near Marseilles.

It was not long before the unusual abilities of Vincent were discovered by the church. Impressed by this young man, one de Berulle, later to be Cardinal, recommended him to become curate of Clichy, near Paris. This was the beginning of a rapid, but well-deserved, advancement in the church. Vincent exhibited especial talent in dealing with the problems of peasants and working with the poor and the sick.

In 1617 he received from the Countess of Joigny the means with which to establish his first organization devoted to charity, the *confrérie de charité*. This consisted of women who devoted themselves wholly to ministering to the poor and the sick.

So successful had he been in his work with the poor that, in 1619, Louis XIII appointed him royal almoner of the galleys. In addition to charity work among the galley slaves, Vincent established a hospital for them at Marseilles, two homes for foundlings at Paris, and in addition organized the *Filles de la Charité*. This last venture employed married women with domestic duties who devoted as much time as possible to supplementing the work of the *confréries*.

Among the many "missions" of Vincent to the poor and the sick was one established on the estates of the Gondi family. Here five priests helped Vincent in special work with the common people of the estate. Out of this grew the Congregation of Priests of the Mission, or "Lazarites" as they are often called. In 1624 the little company obtained a permanent settlement in the Collège des Bons Enfants in Paris, and in 1632 it was constituted a congregation with Vincent at its head, receiving from the canons regular of Saint Victor the priory of Saint Lazarus in Paris.

Vincent died on the twenty-seventh of September, 1660, at Paris and was buried in the church of Saint Lazare. But, although the body of this "prince among the poor" was committed to the dust, Vincent lived on in the organizations he had been instrumental in founding and in the work which he had begun.

Many years later, in 1833, some free-thinking individuals

made the charge that the church no longer had the spiritual strength to inaugurate a practical enterprise, that all its organizing power and glory lay in the dead past. In answer to this challenge, Frédéric Ozanam and others founded a society for social service and dedicated it to Vincent. They called their group the Society of Saint Vincent de Paul. This has been a layman's organization which has fought clerical authority. Indeed, its general council was suspended because it refused to accept a cardinal as its official head. Thus, it now works through local "conferences" or branches only.

John Wesley

YOUNG John Wesley was descended from a long line of English divines, many of whom attained high distinction in their chosen profession even though there was in each a streak of the rebel. Bartholomew Westley, an ancestor, was ejected from the rectories of Catherston and Charmouth in Dorset for his radical views in 1660. John Westley, another forebear, was sent to prison in 1661 for refusing to use the Book of Common Prayer and was expelled from the Church of England in 1662, after which he became a non-conformist pastor. Samuel Wesley, John's father, trained as a nonconformist, was loyal to the Established Church but married Susanna, daughter of Dr. Samuel Annesley, who was honored as "the Saint Paul of the non-conformists."

It was Susanna who wove the tradition of the nonconformists into the life of her son John, the founder of Methodism.

A child of the rectory, young John showed promise at an early age and was given the advantages of study at

Charterhouse and at Christ Church, Oxford. Though poor of health and a strict believer in method in the conduct of his life, he soon impressed his fellows as "a young man of the finest classical taste and the most liberal and manly sentiments." They also believed him to be "gay and sprightly, with a turn for wit and humor."

At twenty-two, Wesley describes himself as one with no notion of inward holiness, but "habitually and for the most part very contentedly in some or other known sin, indeed with some intermission and short struggles especially before and after Holy Communion." He was ordained in 1725 and spent the next few years preaching and teaching in and around Oxford, where he held the position of Greek lecturer and "moderator of the classes."

Gradually his taste for the company of worldly people waned and he spent more and more of his time with those who were especially attracted to religion. With his brother Charles he formed the Holy Club, a group of young men meeting evenings in some member's room and studying the Greek New Testament and the classics. They were ridiculed for living their lives by rule and were thus named "Methodists." Preaching, work with poor unfortunates in prison and out, and other services occupied these young men. But Wesley was not happy. He tells us that he preached much but saw no fruits of his labors. Then he adds, "Indeed it could not be that I should; for I neither laid the foundation of repentance nor of preaching the gospel, taking it for granted that all to whom I preached were believers and that many of them needed no religion . . . I did not preach faith in the blood of the covenant."

At the invitation of James Oglethorpe, founder of Georgia, Wesley set out for the new colony in 1735 to be its pastor. On the trip from England he was impressed by the calm faith of his Moravian fellow-passengers during a storm. While he was very much afraid, these men and women exhibited implicit faith in God's protection. This convinced him that he did not as yet have "the faith that casteth out fear."

Although in Georgia Wesley gathered a few faithful and earnest followers around him and did much to initiate the movement with which he was later to become wholly identified, he recognized that he lacked that which was most essential. He was extreme in his insistence upon proper observances and decorum. At the same time, he antagonized the authorities by refusing communion to a pious German because he had not been baptized by a minister with the proper ordination and by introducing "into the church and service at the altar compositions of psalms and hymns not inspected or authorized by any proper judicature."

Although the Georgia sojourn was considered by Wesley to be largely a failure, the fact was most significant that here was organized in 1736 a small band of serious members of his congregation to serve as a society for religious conversation and prayer. This was, according to Wesley, "the second rise of Methodism," the first having taken place at Oxford with the organization of the Holy Club.

Returning to London in 1738, Wesley made the acquaintance of Peter Böhler, a German Moravian who had been ordained for his work in Carolina. With this newfound friend he attended a meeting of the Moravian Society in Aldersgate Street. This was on Wednesday evening, May 24, 1738. The leader was reading to the congregation Martin Luther's *Preface to the Epistle to the Romans*. As Wesley tells the story: "About a quarter before nine, while he was describing the change which God works in the heart through faith in Christ, I felt my heart strangely warmed. I felt I did trust in Christ, Christ alone, for salvation; and an assurance was given me that he had taken away *my* sins, even *mine*, and saved *me* from the law of sin and death."

No one, not even Wesley, realized at that time just what this experience signified. It was the end of a struggle for Wesley. He had sought earnestly to serve God but always felt that he was not ready. He had seen others exhibiting a faith which he knew he did not have. His preaching and his teaching had lacked success and he knew that it was because he was not ready. Then came the experience in Aldersgate Street. From this moment Wesley knew that he was ready, and from this moment all the talents and skill of John Wesley began to flower. He had that power for which he had been searching so long.

The next few years saw the beginnings of that evangelistic work which resulted in Methodism. In February, 1739, Wesley heard the great Whitefield preach in an open field because the churches were closed to him. This irregularity at first shocked him, but, when he saw the effectiveness of this method of reaching souls, he was convinced and soon adopted the method himself.

During the remainder of Wesley's life, he had only one mission and to this he devoted himself completely. This mission was organizing and supervising the Methodist movement in England and Ireland. In the course of his evangelistic work he preached 40,000 sermons and traveled 250,000 miles. Eventually the work spread to America and Wesley's followers were sent there to carry it forward. Often mobs sought to attack Wesley or destroy his meetings, but his courage and keen wit always saved him and often turned enmity into fellowship.

Methodism grew and prospered everywhere under the skillful leadership of Wesley. Societies sprang up in towns and villages throughout Europe and America. Ministers were ordained and other clerical offices established and filled. The poor and the oppressed flocked to Methodist meetings by the thousands, so that no places were found large enough to hold the congregations. Outdoor meetings were held, great factory buildings were thrown open to the preachers, and wherever they went these men of God were importuned to preach by vast multitudes that assembled in a moment.

Then, on March 2, 1791, in his 88th year, John Wesley

laid down the burden and passed to his reward. The rebel and non-conformist had carried to its culmination the long tradition of his ancestors. Today Methodist churches throughout the world stand as living memorials to his genius and his devotion.

Father Damien

JOSEPH DE VEUSTER was born at Tremeloo, near Louvain in Belgium, on January 3, 1840, and educated for a business career in his native town. By the time he was eighteen, the enthusiasm for trade and commerce which motivated his first efforts had dimmed and in its place had grown a passion for religion so strong that he entered the Society of the Sacred Heart of Jesus and Mary, took the name of Damien, and consecrated himself unreservedly to missionary work.

When his brother, who was scheduled to go to the Pacific Islands as a missionary, was taken ill so that he was unable to carry out his assignment, young Damien, still in minor orders, volunteered to take his place. He was accepted, though the authorities had some fear lest he would not be able to meet the rigid requirements of religious life in these areas. The young man had not as yet been tried sufficiently and his spiritual mettle tested.

Arriving in Honolulu in March of 1864, Damien was ordained priest in Whitsuntide of that year and set about immediately to the task which had been assigned him. His devotion and unceasing work convinced his superiors that he was truly a priest at heart and one worthy of the mission to which he had been assigned.

While in Honolulu Father Damien became interested in the government's treatment of lepers. These poor unfortunates were shipped to the island of Molokai and left in a state of spiritual and physical destitution. Conditions on the island were unbelievably bad. Sanitation was almost unknown, food was scarce save that which grew wild, and the diseased persons were given no spiritual guidance. Theirs was a life of despair beyond imagination.

After studying the conditions at Molokai and becoming convinced of the great need existing there, Father Damien volunteered to take spiritual charge of the colony. Both his superiors in the church and those in the Hawaiian government gave him permission, and he set out for the island in 1873.

For the next sixteen years, Father Damien devoted himself wholly to relieving conditions on the island. He persuaded the Hawaiian government to assist him in his work of making physical improvements there. New and pure sources of water were discovered. He secured material for building better dwellings and worked with his own hands, showing the lepers how to construct homes that would be more comfortable and secure. He established farms and showed the lepers how, even in their affliction, they could raise food and prepare it wholesomely. The government helped by sending supplies and other necessary materials.

Father Damien mixed spiritual and physical help and guidance and brought a sense of spiritual well-being to the people which they had not known before. He gave to many the consolation that God cared for them even in their distress. He took from the colony the sense of spiritual doom which had rested over it and made the lepers better able to endure their physical affliction by holding out to them the hope of a joyful spiritual life in the beyond.

Working closely with the lepers and sparing himself not at all, Father Damien was stricken with leprosy in 1885. But he continued to work, sometimes alone and at other times with the help of other resident priests. As his health became poorer and the disease spread, he was forced to limit his work. Then, on April 15, 1889, he succumbed to the disease, leaving behind him a work that carried on not only in the lives of the lepers of Molokai but in the memory of all the world.

But Father Damien had known those who failed to understand him or his devotion. One of them, a Presbyterian minister, made some remarks which cast a shadow upon the work and motives of the priest. This so angered the author Robert Louis Stevenson, who had spent some time at Molokai and knew personally of Father Damien's work, that he wrote in a blaze of righteous indignation his *Father Damien, an Open Letter to the Reverend Dr. Hyde of Honolulu*. In this we have the true story of Father Damien and of his devotion, even unto death, to his church and his ideal.

Saint Thérèse of Lisieux

ON THE REGISTRY of the little town of Alençon in France she appears as Thérèse Martin. The official roll of sisters of the convent at Lisieux records her as Sister Teresa of the Child Jesus. But those who knew her best and loved her most called her the Little Flower of Jesus.

Behind this record and this love are a holy home and saintly parents, Louis and Zélie Martin. Both had wished in their youth to consecrate themselves to God and retire to the cloister, but had been denied. The vocation denied them was given to their children. One entered the Visitation Order while four others consecrated themselves in the Carmelite Convent at Lisieux.

Thérèse was their ninth child. Reared in an atmosphere of faith and devotion, the little girl turned naturally to things religious. The Benedictines, who educated her, continued the holy work started by her parents. When she was but fifteen, she applied for permission to enter the Carmelite Convent where two of her sisters had preceded her.

This was a thing unheard of in the order. A girl of but fifteen years was too young to realize all that such a move meant, and the superior refused the application, kindly but firmly.

This failure was not discouraging either to Thérèse or her father, who wanted her to enter the convent as eagerly as did she. So, both father and daughter set out to Rome to plead for her before the Holy Father, Leo XIII. This was the year of the pope's jubilee and all Rome was celebrating the occasion with the rest of the Catholic world.

The pope heard Thérèse's plea and considered it for some time. Then he handed down a decision. He would leave the matter in the hands of the superior of the convent. Back to Lisieux went the father and daughter to beg permission again from the superior. This time they were successful and Thérèse was admitted to the convent on April 9, 1888, at the unusual age of fifteen.

There for nine years Thérèse served God so beautifully and devotedly that she became known to all as The Little Flower, a child so sweet and tender that everyone loved her and marveled at her sincerity and understanding. Many miracles were performed through her intercession and untold numbers of people were helped by her prayers and work.

All too soon, on the 30th of September in 1897, she passed on, having proved even to the Holy Father that the devotion and sincerity of a child of fifteen can be deep and abiding. So great was the fame of her sanctity that she was canonized only seventeen years after her death on June 10, 1914.

☆

Mother Cabrini

WHEN, during the latter years of the nineteenth century the tide of Italian immigration to the United States and South American countries swelled to gigantic proportions, Pope Leo XIII became concerned about the spiritual and intellectual care of these immigrants. He called into his counsel a woman who had shown great devotion and considerable ability in caring for the Italian poor throughout Italy. This woman was Mother Frances Xavier Cabrini.

Born at Sant' Angelo, Italy, on July 16, 1850, of parents who ranked high in the Lombard nobility, Mother Cabrini had given evidence even in her early girlhood of exceptional piety and religious zeal. Impressed by the poor facilities available for the education of great masses of Italian peasantry, she organized a small community for the instruction of poor children and the training of teachers.

With only four sisters, she opened a house of instruction at Codogno in 1880 and found almost immediately that interest in this work was nation-wide. While demands for other houses were coming in from many places throughout Italy, Pope Leo XIII invited her to Rome and asked her to open a house there.

Here Mother Cabrini's genius was soon recognized to the extent that the pope asked her to go to the Americas to continue her work among the Italian immigrants there.

Mother Cabrini came immediately to New York and took charge of a school for the children of immigrants in Saint Joachim's Parish. Under her direction, the school prospered and the work grew beyond even her fairest hopes.

But Mother Cabrini saw that teaching was not the only need of her people. They needed adequate hospital care in illnesses. This vision led her to open Columbia Hospital in

New York in 1892. This venture also grew and prospered and its influence was widespread.

Within a few years another Columbia Hospital was opened in Chicago under her inspiration. Very soon, missionary sisters of the Sacred Heart of Jesus, for that was the name given her organization, were to be found throughout the United States teaching and caring for the physical needs and health of the poor, especially those of Italian extraction.

It was Mother Cabrini's practice to tackle a situation wherever she found it and trust to Divine assistance to see her through. Wherever she found the immigrant, the sick, or the ignorant, she began her work, establishing centers for their care and believing sincerely that she would not be left alone by the Divine. And her faith was always rewarded abundantly.

Mother Cabrini personally expanded her work far beyond the borders of the United States. She traveled to Peru, Chile, Argentina, Brazil, and Nicaragua, establishing houses of her Sisterhood. Twenty-five times she crossed the Atlantic on missions for the Sisters. These visits helped to establish centers in France, England, and in Spain.

When Italy entered the First World War, Mother Cabrini placed her houses in that country at the service of the Italian Government and three large military hospitals were confided to them.

When, on December 22, 1917, Mother Cabrini passed away, she left seventy houses scattered throughout Europe and the Americas, with more than three thousand devoted Missionary Sisters of the Sacred Heart of Jesus working to alleviate the ignorance and suffering of the poor. And among these poor her name is a memory which can never die.